Ancient Indian Coinage

Reconstructing Indian History & Culture
(ISSN 0971-3824)

1. Society in Ancient India; by Sures Chandra Banerji
2. Political Thought in Ancient India; by G.P. Singh
3. Early Indian Historical Tradition and Archaeology; by G.P. Singh
4. Vasantotsava: The Spring Festivals of India; by Leona M. Anderson
5. Ecological Readings in the Veda; by M. Vannucci
6. Vṛndāvana in Vaiṣṇava Literature; by Maura Corcoran
7. Social History of the Tamils (1707-1947); by P. Subramanian
9. Buddhism and Socio-Economic Life of Eastern India; by Bimal Chandra Mohapatra
10. Chandragupta Maurya; by P.L. Bhargava
11. Mṛtyu: Concept of Death in Indian Traditions; by Gian Giuseppe Filippi
12. Yama: The Glorious Lord of the Other World; by Kusum P. Merh
13. Sacred Complex of Ujjain; by D.K. Samanta
14. Vedic View of the Earth; by S.R.N. Murthy
15. Society in the Atharvaveda; by B.S. Kharade
16. Orissan History, Culture and Archaeology; by S. Pradhan
17. Education in Ancient India; by Mitali Chatterjee
18. Surā: The Liquor and the Vedic Sacrifice; by M.B. Kolhatkar
19. Human Ecology in the Vedas; by Marta Vannucci
20. Governance in Ancient India; by Anupa Chandra Pandey
21. The Cultural Glory of Ancient India: A Literary Overview; by Sures Chandra Banerji
22. KauṭilyaPs Arthaśāstra in the Light of Modern Science & Technology; by Sunil Sen Sarma
23. History of Jainism : With Special Reference to Mathurā; by V.K. Sharma
24. Cultural Tourism in India: Museums, Monuments & Arts : Theory and Practice; by S.P. Gupta; Krishna Lal; Mahua Bhattacharya
25. Ancient Indian Historiography : Sources and Interpretations; by G.P. Singh
26. Republics, Kingdoms, Towns and Cities in Ancient India; by G.P. Singh
27. Facets of Ancient Indian History and Culture : New Perception; by G.P. Singh
28. Kamakhya : A Socio-cultural Study; by Nihar Ranjan Mishra
29. History and Culture of Tamil Nadu as Gleaned from the Sanskrit Inscriptions Vol. 1 (up to *c*. AD 1310); by Chithra Madhavan
30. Lifestyle of the Vedic People; by Pranati Ghosal
31. History and Culture of Tamil Nadu as Gleaned from the Sanskrit Inscriptions Vol. 2 (up to *c*. AD 1310 - *c*. AD 1885); by Chithra Madhavan
32. Matrimonial Alliances and Ancient Indian Polity (*c*. 600 BCE to *c*. 650); by Preeti Prabhat
33. Artisans and Craftsmen of Northern India; by Kuldeep Singh Thind
34. The Evolution of Historiographical Tradition in Ancient and Medieval India; by G.P. Singh
35. Warfare in Ancient India: In Historical outline; by Soma Basu
36. Sanskrit Education and Literature in Ancient India; by Chitra Madhavan
37. Rājadharma in Mahābhārata; by Priyanka Pandey
38. Interstate Relations in Northern India: Circa 800–1200 CE; by Shiva Gopal Bajpai

Reconstructing Indian History & Culture no. 8

Ancient Indian Coinage

A Systematic Study of Money Economy from Janapada Period to Early Medieval Period (600 BC to AD 1200)

Rekha Jain

DK®
PRINTWORLD
Publishers of Indian Traditions

Cataloging in Publication Data – DK

[Courtesy: D.K. Agencies (P) Ltd. <docinfo@dkagencies.com>]

Jain, Rekha, author.

Ancient Indian coinage : a systematic study of money economy from Janapada period to early medieval period (600 BC to AD 1200) / Rekha Jain.

pages cm. – (Reconstructing Indian history & culture ; no. 8)

Reprint. Originally published: 1995.
Includes bibliographical references and index.
ISBN 9788124600511 (HB)
ISBN 9788124600528 (PB)

1. Coins, Indic – History. 2. Coinage – India – History. 3. Money – India – History. 4. India – History – 324 B.C.-1000 A.D. I. Title. II. Series: Reconstructing Indian history & culture ; no. 8.

LCC CJ3536.J35 2025 | DDC 737.4934 23

ISBN: 978-81-246-0051-1 (Hb)
ISBN: 978-81-246-0052-8 (Pb)
First published in India in 1995
Reprinted in 2017, 2025

Author: Rekha Jain (b.1962)

Printed and published by:
D.K. Printworld (P) Ltd.
Regd. office: "Vedaśrī", F-395, Sudarshan Park
(Metro Station: ESI Hospital), New Delhi - 110015
Phones: (011) 4172 2626, 98713 94815
e-mail: indology@dkprintworld.com
Website: www.dkprintworld.com

Dedicated to

my mother
Chandra Kala Jain

Preface

THE present work "Ancient Indian Coinage : A Systematic Study of Money Economy from *Janapada* Period to Early Medieval Period" deals with the gradual development of money in the form of coins from the sixth century BC to the twelfth century AD. Scientific study of ancient coinage of India started from the nineteenth century AD onwards. Initially, these coins were collected as curious objects for the sake of pleasure, but later on, attempts were made to decipher their legends. Scholars tried to classify them, and various catalogues were prepared which have been utilised to reconstruct the ancient history of India. Attempts were also made to study the content of the coin by chemical analysis. D.D. Kosambi tried to study the ancient coins from money economic point of view but not extensively.

For this study, catalogues of coins prepared by A. Cunningham, J. Allan, P. Gardener, Whitehead, A.S. Altekar, V.V. Mirashi and P.L. Gupta have been studied. Useful articles published in the *Journal of the Numismatic Society of India* have been utilised for the study. Besides these, there are scattered references to the coins in A. Cunningham's *Archaeological Survey Reports of India* and *Annual Reports of Archaeological Survey of India*. These catalogues, Reports and Journals give information about the coin types of the concerned rulers with their weights and the metallic contents. In writing such a work, it is essential to discuss briefly about the types of coins, their legends, description of the ruling authorities in order to understand the background of money economy in ancient India.

The material regarding money economy in ancient India is scanty. We have to depend on ancient coins. It is very difficult to get the detailed information from the study of ancient Indian coins. Besides, there are stray references of ancient coins in ancient inscriptions, literary works, and in the writings of foreigners. In this study, an attempt has been made to collect all these scattered sources at one place in order to examine them thoroughly and to draw new conclusions regarding money economy in different periods of ancient India.

I want to express my profound respect to Dr. M.L. Kothari, Director, Department of Business Management, Vikram University, Ujjain for the guidance and valuable suggestions. Besides, I owe an immense debt to Dr. S.S. Nigam, Reader, Department of Ancient Indian History and Archaeology, Vikram University, Ujjain who took great pains for going through the manuscript and gave useful guidance for improvement. Further, I want to express my hearty thanks to my Professors in Sydenham College of Commerce, Bombay for guiding me in the monetary aspect of the topic, whenever I approached them.

I am also indebted to Dr. A.M. Shastri and Dr. A.V. Narsimha Murthy for their invaluable suggestions.

Rekha Jain

Contents

Abbreviations

ABORI	:	*Annals of the Bhandarkar Oriental Research Institute,* Poona.
ARRMA	:	*Annual Report Rajputana Museum,* Ajmer.
ASIAR	:	*Archaeological Survey of India Annual Reports.*
BMCAI	:	*British Museum Catalogue of Ancient India,* London.
BMCGSK	:	*A Catalogue of Indian Coins in the British Museum. The Greek and Scythic Kings of Bactria and India.*
CCIM	:	*Coins of Catalogue of Indian Museum.*
CGD	:	*Catalogue of the Coins of the Gupta Dynasties and of Śaśāṅka, King of Gauḍa.*
CII	:	*Corpus Inscriptionum Indicarum,* London and Ootacamund.
EI	:	*Epigraphia Indica,* Mysore.
IA	:	*Indian Antiquary,* Calcutta.
IAR	:	*Indian Archaeology,* Delhi.
IHQ	:	*Indian Historical Quarterly,* Calcutta.
JA	:	*Journal Asiatique,* Paris.

JASB	:	*Journal of the Asiatic Society of Bengal,* Calcutta.
Jāt.	:	*Jātaka.*
JBORS	:	*Journal of Bihar and Orissa Research Society,* Patna.
JIH	:	*Journal of Indian History.*
JNSI	:	*Journal of the Numismatic Society of India,* Varanasi.
JRAS	:	*Journal of the Royal Asiatic Society of Great Britain and Ireland,* London.
MASI	:	*Memoirs of The Archaeological Survey of India.*
NC	:	*Numismatic Chronicle.*
NIA	:	*New Indian Antiquary.*
NNM	:	*Numismatic Notes and Monographs,* New York.
PRASWC	:	*Progress Report of the Archaeological Survey of Western Circle.*
ṚV	:	*Ṛgveda.*
Sel. Ins.	:	*Select Inscriptions bearing on Indian History and Civilization,* Calcutta.

Table of Transliteration

अ a	आ ā	इ i	ई ī	उ u
ऊ ū	ए e	ऐ ai	ओ o	औ au
	अं ṁ	अः ḥ	ऋ ṛ	
क ka	ख kha	ग ga	घ gha	ङ ṅa
च ca	छ cha	ज ja	झ jha	ञ ña
ट ṭa	ठ ṭha	ड ḍa	ढ ḍha	ण ṇa
त ta	थ tha	द da	ध dha	न na
प pa	फ pha	ब ba	भ bha	म ma
	य ya	र ra	ल la	व va
	श śa	ष ṣa	स sa	ह ha
	क्ष kṣa	त्र tra	ज्ञ jña	

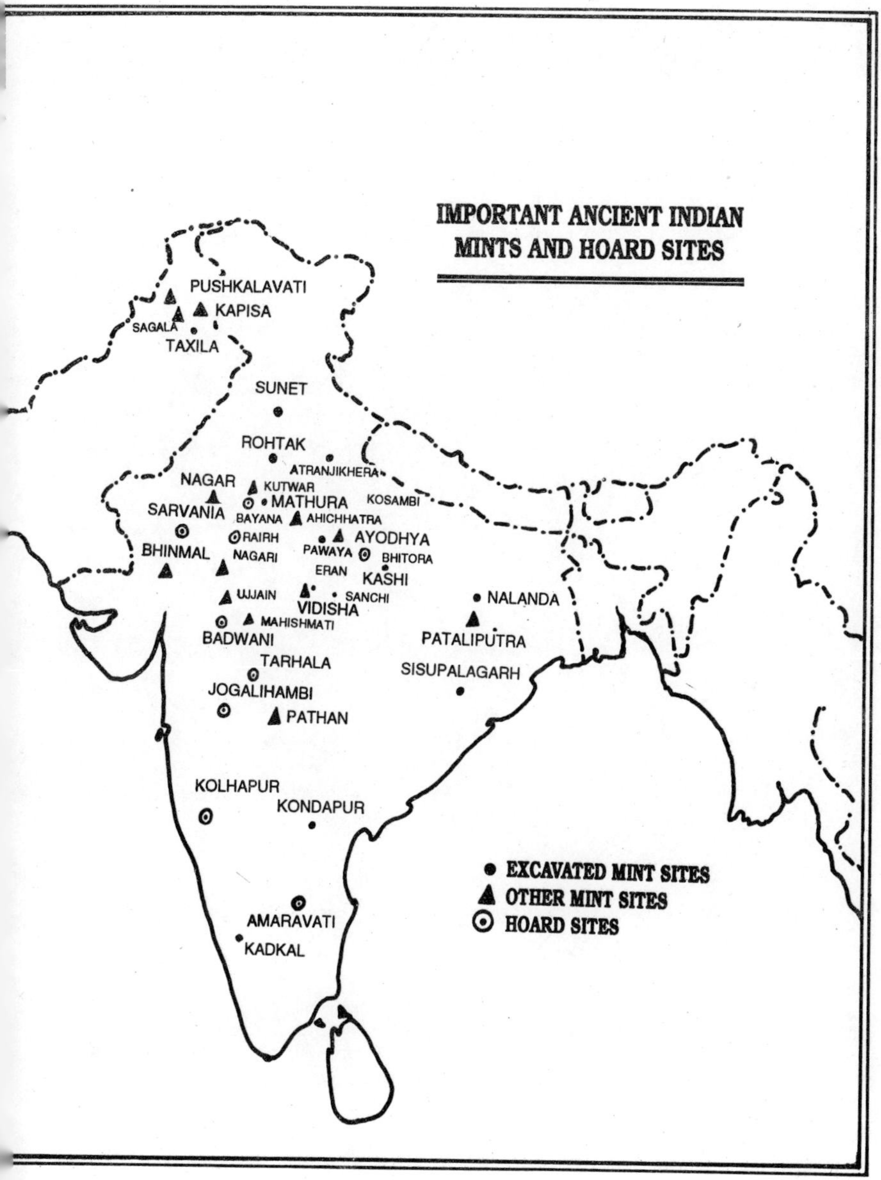

IMPORTANT ANCIENT INDIAN MINTS AND HOARD SITES

1

Meaning and Evolution of Money Economy in Ancient India

Every branch of knowledge has its fundamental discovery. In mechanics it is the wheel; in science, fire; in politics, the vote. Similarly, in economics, in the whole commercial side of man's social existence, money is the essential invention on which all the rest is based.[1] **GEOFFREY CROWTHER**

In order to understand the meaning of money economy in ancient India, it is essential to define money. Scholars have defined it taking into different considerations.

According to Geoffrey Crowther,[2] money can be difined as "anything that is generally acceptable as means of exchange (i.e., as a means of settling debts) and that at the same time acts as a measure and store of value". As such, to be a money, a thing must be generally acceptable. Many things are acceptable for particular purposes but are not generally acceptable in payment for anything. Accordingly, they are not money. Secondly, it should be legally recognised and not anything that is generally acceptable.

According to Walker[3] "Money is what money does". This definition is too wide. According to it, we can include all those things in money which perform the function of money. Thus, money does not comprise metallic coins and currency notes only. It also includes cheques, *huṇḍīs*, bills of exchange, etc. because they also perform the function of money. But as our subject of study is restricted only to ancient period, metallic coins alone deserve to be called as money.

A.G. Hart[4] defines money as follows — money is property with which the owner can pay off a definite amount of debt with certainty and without delay.

Robertson[5] is of the view that money is a commodity which denotes anything which is widely accepted in payment for goods or in discharge of other business obligations. This view seems to be reasonable because it refers to metallic money as that alone is generally acceptable by people left to themselves.

The above meaning of money as propounded by Robertson is supported even by dictionary definition of money.[6] Accordingly, money means pieces of gold, silver, copper, etc. stamped by government authority and used as medium of exchange. This definition also suits the meaning of money in ancient period as metallic money generally served the purpose of exchange. Paper money and bank money, which are current now, were conspicuous by their absence in the ancient period.

Barter Economy

In early period, before the advent of metallic coins, many commodities served the purpose of exchange or were treated as money. Thus, there was barter system and it involved several difficulties, such as, absence of common measure of value, necessity of double co-incidence of wants, difficulty in division of certain goods, settlement of debts, absence of good store of wealth and value, lack of standard weights and measures and ignorance of quality etc.

Emergence of Coins

It was to overcome these difficulties that money came into

prominence in the form of metallic coins. But barter system is prevalent even in modern times and has not completely disappeared as payments to farm workers, and village artisans are still made in kind in interior rural and tribal areas.

During the Harappan period, inscribed seals discovered with pictographic script were perhaps used for monetary transaction. As the script has not been deciphered, its nature cannot be ascertained. In the Vedic literature, golden pieces such as *niśkas*, *suvarṇas*, *śatamānas*, *pādas* and *kṛṣṇalas* have been mentioned in connection with gifts. These cannot be called coins because they were not guaranteed by any recognised authority and they were not used for ordinary transactions. The earliest coins of India are the punch-marked coins which started in the seventh or the sixth century BC. The early punch-marked coins were local with their respective characteristics. The later ones have five symbols punched one after another. Most of these coins are of silver and they are of thirty-two *rattīs*. These silver punch-marked coins known as *kārṣāpaṇa* were of uniform type and they were in circulation throughout the country. *Kārṣāpaṇa* was the standard coin with several denominations. There was state control over monetary system during the Mauryan period (319 -185 BC) because officers used to regulate the currency for medium of exchange. State officers and others were paid in cash. Later on, the state had to issue the debased coins because of the deficiency of silver.

After the fall of Mauryas, coins came to be divided into two classes — uninscribed and inscribed. Most of the uninscribed coins are found of the cast and die-struck technique, but some are of the punch-marked technique. Most of these coins are in copper and rarely they are in silver. These uninscribed coins reveal the importance of local money economy.

The inscribed coins are of two kinds — foreign and indigenous. After the conquest of territories of North-West India, the Indo-Bactrians issued coins, which remained Hellenistic in features but underwent appreciable change in fabric and appearances as well as in their weights, sizes and in shapes. First, they issued the coins of Attic standard of the

Seleucids. Gold coins were known as *staters*. The standard unit of silver coin known as *drachm* was of 66 grains. *Hemidrachm* was of 33 grains, *obol* of 11 grains and *tetradrachm* was equal to 4 *drachms*. There was change in metrology during the reign of Indo-Bactrian ruler Eucratides because of economic and commercial reasons. The *tetradrachm* and *drachm* were struck to the lighter weight of 80 and 20 *rattīs*. Some call it by the name of Indian standard while others by the name of Persian standard. Generally, most of the rulers issued coins in silver but some in copper. Nickel was issued by three kings namely Euthydemos, Pantaleon and Agathocles and lead by Strabo.

On these coins, there is bust or head of the king on the obverse with Greek legend. On the reverse, there are deities concerned with Greek mythology and legends in Prākṛt and Kharoṣṭhī. We find monograms on these coins, but thier precise meaning is unknown. These were meant either for the mint masters or names of money-lenders. The coins of the Scytho-Pārthian kings resembled those of the Indo-Greek rulers to a large extent. They adhered to the standard of the Indo-Greek coins.

The Kuṣāṇa ruler Kadphises imitated the diademed head of the emperor Augustus (31 BC to AD 14) on Roman coins. This imitation of coinage of Augustus by Kujula Kadphises indicates some trade relation of India with Rome during this period. Wima Kadphises and his successors Kaniṣka, Huviṣka and Vasudeva adopted the Roman standard for gold coins because it assumed international recognition for the purpose of trade and commerce. Gold coinage was the standard coin for Kuṣāṇa empire. There was overflow of gold to India from Rome. Copper coins were issued in large number by Kuṣāṇa rulers with variation in their weights. The later Kuṣāṇas, Sassānians and Kidāra-Kuṣāṇa continued to issue gold and copper coins in North-West India but they were inferior in comparison with the coins of early Kuṣāṇas.

The Purī-Kuṣāṇa coins issued by some local ruler or rulers who had hold over a small territory were confined only to Orissa and adjoining territories in Bihar and Andhra Pradesh. These Kuṣāṇa coins came there only through trade and travel as this region must have been a great trading centre during this period. The traders might have minted these coins for meeting their local needs.

The Roman coins are found in large number in south and a few in north. Gold coin was known by the term *aureus* and silver by *dīnāris*. These coins were brought into India by Roman traders for purchase of Indian commodities, such as, precious stones, pearls, scents, spices, perfumes, silk, muslin, etc.

The western Kṣatrapa rulers issued coins mostly in silver and some in copper and potin. The average weight of silver coin was about 35 grains. The weight and module of these coins appeared to have been based on either the Indo-Greek or Roman silver money. These silver coins seem to have been issued for trade with the Western world.

After the Mauryas, the inscribed coins were abundantly issued and widely in circulation. According to some scholars, the Indians learnt the fashion of putting the name of the issuing authority or legends in Brāhmī and portraits of kings on coins from foreigners. City coins, such as, of Vārāṇasī, Kauśāmbī, Vidiśā, Ujjayinī, Māhiṣmatī and Tripurā seem to be the earliest inscribed coins of India, and they were issued in the third and second century BC. The guilds of Taxila and the guilds of *gandhikas* (perfume dealers) of the city of Kauśāmbī also issued copper coins. These coins are of purely indigenous feature and character. These are round and square. These coins prove that after the Mauryas, trade was localised within limited areas in North India. These coins also indicate the prosperity and autonomy of cities.

The tribal coins began their appearance after the disintegration of the Maurya empire. Most of the tribes such as Yaudheyas, Kṣudrakas, Kunindas, Auḍumbaras and Kulutas were located in the Punjab. They issued die-struck coins. Another important new feature is the introduction of the coin legends, their names and place in Brāhmī script. Copper was the prime issue of all these republics, but it is difficult to generalise about the weight of these coins. A few tribes such as Auḍumbaras, Kulutas, Vatsa and Kośala issued silver coins which were based on the *hemidrachms* of the later Greek and Śaka kings. It was due to the influence of the foreign powers and, they might have had some trade relations with them. The copper coins found in large number were meant for ordinary transactions. The monarchial states such as Sūrasena, Pañcāla, Vatsa and Kośala also issued a large number of copper coins.

The credit for inaugurating of minting coins in lead goes to the *mahārathis*. They might have preferred this metal because it was easily available to them in the neighbourhood. It remained the prime metal of Southern Indian coinage for a considerable time.

The Sātavāhanas ruled for a considerable time and over a wide territory. They minted coins in potin, lead, copper and silver. Silver coins are not prolific. These Sātavāhana coins are the richest in the Deccan both in variety and quantity. The money economy of Sātavāhanas was regional in character. It is indigenous and it played dominant role in the development of coinage in south India.

The Gupta (*c.* AD 319-500) coins closely resemble those of the later Kuṣāṇas to whose imperial position they succeeded in the north-west. On these coins, the Gupta king is seen wearing the Kuṣāṇa overcoat and trousers, and on the reverse Ārdokṣo is seated on a high backed throne. The Guptas issued gold coins of the Roman standard because of their trade with Byzantine empire. Gradually, there was an attempt towards Indianization of Gupta coins in style, metrology and fabric. Samudragupta was the first ruler to have the metrical legends on coins. Some of the Gupta coins such as *vīṇā aśvamedha* and Tiger-slayer types are the artistic pieces. The gold coins of Candragupta II are found in larger number. The size, weight and fabric of Gupta silver coins are similar to those of the Kṣatrapa silver coins of Gujarat and Mālwā. Candragupta II issued the copper coins in the territory conquered from the Kuṣāṇas. The punch-marked coins and the Roman coins continued in circulation in the south during this period.

The Hūna invasion of India must have influenced the money economy of the Guptas by reducing the coin types and issuing the debased gold coins. The scarcity of Gupta coins as medium of exchange in comparison with the Indo-Greek, Kuṣāṇa and Sātavāhana coins suggest that money economy became weaker during this period.

Gold coins were rare, silver were few and copper not many in number, during the post-Gupta period (*c.* AD 500-800). Most of the coin types were issued in imitation of the Gupta coins. A few rulers of Bengal could have retained sufficient wealth in their treasures to imitate golden coins of the Guptas. In Uttar Pradesh, extremely rare golden coins were issued. The Hūṇas borrowed the Sassānian type from Afghanistan, the Gupta type from India and the Later Kuṣāṇa type from Kashmir. The silver coins of the Gupta dynasty were adopted by the Puśyabhūtis of Thāneśwar, the Maukherīs of Kānyakubja and the Maitrakas of Vallabhī. The Indo-Sassānian or Gadahiyā base silver or copper coins with rude imitation of Sassānian bust on the obverse and Sassānian fire altar with or without attendants on reverse were issued.

The coins of Kashmir followed the conventional Kidār type, and have seated Ārdokṣo and the standing king. In the south, the Kadambas are known as the originators of the *padmaṭaṅka* and the Cālukyas of Bādāmī of boar coins. The most striking feature of the south Indian coins was the revival of the punch-marked technique. There was the paucity of coins during this period. Money economy considerably declined.

There was revival of money economy on a wide scale in the early medieval period which can be linked with the revival of trade and commerce. Gadahiyā coins were issued in large number in Rājasthān, Gujarāt, Mālwā and Uttar Pradesh. Several varieties and denominations of these coins are found. The Śāhi rulers of Kābul issued the coins of their own devices, weight and fabric both in silver and copper in the ninth century AD. During the twelfth and thirteenth centuries AD, a number of Rājpūt dynasties and rulers adopted the Horseman and Bull type in silver and copper (of 51-52 grains). Generally the coins of Kashmir were of standing king on the obverse and the seated Goddess on the reverse in copper. Gāṅgeyadeva, the Kālacūrī ruler of Tripurī, issued coins of seated Goddess Lakṣmī in gold, silver and copper.

Most of the Rājpūt dynasties adopted the device of the seated Goddess type. The Kālacūris of Ratnāpura and the Candellās of Jejākabhukti issued coins in gold, silver and copper. The Paramāras of Mālwā issued in gold and the Kacchapaghāṭa rulers in gold and silver. Govindacandra of Gahadavāla dynasty issued coins in gold, silver and copper. Siddharāja Jayasiṁha and Kumārapāla issued coins in gold and some Yādava rulers of Bayana also issued coins in this metal. These coins seem to have been issued in ancient *dramma* standard of 66 grains. From the inscriptions and literary works, we come across several names and denominations associated with *cowries* which prove that they were widely used in various transactions by the people.

Silver *pala* or *satamāna* weighing 320 *rattis* was regarded as the standard of calculations in the monetary transactions in early medieval Orissa. Medieval Orissan inscriptions often speak of a coin called *māda* which was both of gold and silver. The coins current in south India during the medieval period were generally known as *padma-ṭaṅka* and *gadyāna*. From the inscriptions, we come across the names such as *drammas*, *gadyāna*, *paṇa*, *honu*, *hāga*, *kāgini*, *visa*, *gulika* and *bela*. Thus in the entire history of ancient period, metallic coins of gold, silver, copper, lead, nickel, etc. served as medium of exchange. Use of gold and silver was limited whereas copper, lead, etc. were used for ordinary transactions of small payments. It performed all the basic functions of money, that is, primary, secondary and contingent functions. Primary or original functions of money are medium of exchange and measure of value. Secondary functions are store of value and means of deferred payments. Contingent functions study money as basis of credit, basis of distribution of national dividend, helper in attaining maximum utilities to the consumers, helper in mobilising of capital and finally giver of a general form to capital.[7]

Origin and Antiquity of Coinage in India

The origin and antiquity of coinage in India is shrouded in considerable obscurity. The available evidence is scanty, dubious and capable of different interpretations. Scholars, therefore, came to divergent conclusions. There are certain stages and circumstances which led to the emergence of the coinage in India.

The Lydians in Asia Minor claim the honour of being the inventor of coins. This is clear from the statement of Herodotus who mentions that the Lydians were the first nation to introduce the use of gold and silver coins. The oldest coins of electrum, a natural alloy of gold and silver, are probably dated 700 BC.[8] Gradually, these coins were introduced in other regions. The question is whether coinage originated in India due to outside influence or indigenous and when was it introduced?

ORIGIN OF COINAGE

Greek Origin

H.H. Wilson[9] and James Prinsep[10] who were the pioneers in the field, held that the coinage became prevalent in Ancient India only after the advent of the Greeks on the Indian soil. H.H. Wilson asserted that it was likely that the currency of the country consisted chiefly, if not exclusively, of lumps of gold and silver not bearing any impression, until the Hindus had learnt the usefulness of money from their Bactrian neighbours and from their commerce, especially with Rome. James Prinsep had placed his main reliance on the obvious resemblance between the Indo-Bactrian coins on one side and those of the Auḍumbaras on the other, altogether ignoring the punch-marked coins. Later on, however, his further studies in the subject made him revise his opinion. He admitted that the Hindus had an indigenous currency of precious metals, even before the advent of Greeks, but maintained that the adoption of a die-device or of coined money, properly so-called, by the Hindus has to be placed subsequent to their coming into contact with the Greeks.

According to A.D.H. Bivar, ordinary punch-marked coins were evolved from some obscure counter marked pieces, originally comprising quite a few denominations of ancient Greek money discovered at Caman Hazuri locally of Kābul along with some other Greek coins, Persian *sigloi* and full-sized wheel-marked issues.

CRITICISM

This theory does not seem to be reasonable. There is no resemblance between the Greek coins on the one hand and the punch-marked coins on the other which represent the earliest coins of ancient India. Greek coins are always round and the punch-marked coins are rectangular, some square, some oblong, some oval and a few circular. Greek coins have regular inscriptions but punch-marked coins have none. Greek coins have usually a bust of the king on the obverse and the deity on the reverse, punch-marked coins never show these features. Devices on punch-marked coins are all Indian, nothing like them can be traced on any Greek coins. There is no similarity in the metrology of the Greeks and the punch-marked coins. The unit of the former *drachm* weights 67.2 grains while the unit of the latter *paṇa* weights about 56 grains.

Quintus Curtius, the historian of Alexander, tells us that among the presents given by the king of Taxila to Alexander the Great, were two hundred talents of Signati Angenti. This expression can only refer to coined silver money, and not to silver bullion. The statement of Curtius, is confirmed by archaeological discoveries. The larger Bhir Mound hoard of the punch-marked coins at Taxila found in the second stratum contained two coins of Alexander, the Great and one of Philip Aridaeus, which were in the mint condition, besides 1055 punch-marked coins of the usual type.[11] The stratification of the hoard and the mint condition of the coins of the two Greek rulers show that the hoard was buried not much later than 317 BC. Some of the punch-marked coins of this hoard were old, blurred and indistinct. These, therefore, must have been originally used at least about two centuries before the advent of the Greek into India.

A.N. Lahiri[12] does not endorse the Greek theory as

recently advocated by A.D.H. Bivar. It is his firm belief that ordinary punch-marked coins evolved from indigenous monetary issues. It becomes almost certain that the prototypes for the punch-marked silver coins of 32 *rattīs* and 5 symbols were provided by the same singularly archaic issues of the great *janapadas* of Kośala and Kāśī.

Iranian Origin

J.A. Decourdemanches[13] is of the view that punch-marked coins whether silver or copper, constitute simply an Indian variety of the Achaemenian coinage. Just as the Muslim rulers in later times issued some coins with Hindu symbols and inscriptions side by side with others with purely Arabic style and legends, the Achaemenian soverigns struck punch-marked coins with Indian symbols side by side with their own Persian *sigloi*. J. Allan[14] also thinks that it is very possible that the idea of a coinage came to India in the late fifth or early fourth century BC from Achaemenid territory, being suggested by the *sigloi*, although its character is entirely Indian. It is not impossible that the tradition of the great wealth of the Nandas owes its origin to their having been the first to issue coins on a large scale. The earliest finds at Paila. Set Mahet and Golakhpur in Gangetic Valley region indicate the region in which punch-marked coins originated.

CRITICISM

There is not much force in the arguments. Muslims issued the coins of Hindu type because they were already current in the country. Why should Achaemenian rulers issue coins with Hindu symbols, when none such existed in the country before their advent? How could they think of a shape for their Indian currency totally dissimilar from their own *sigloi*? Some *sigloi* punched on the reverse with counter marks similar to those on the punch-marked coins have been found. These counter marks put later on the *sigloi* would show that the punch-marked coins from which they have been borrowed were already current in India when the *sigloi* were introduced by the Achaemenian rulers. The shape, size and the symbols of the Persian *sigloi* are so totally different from those of the punch-marked coins that they can never be regarded as the prototypes of the latter. The *sigloi* have nothing like a group of four or five punch-marked symbols, the punch-marked coins have nothing like the king as an archer half kneeling to the right. The earliest punch-marked coins most probably originated in Madhyadeśa (Modern U.P.) and the Achaemenian influence had never penetrated to that region in the sixth or fifth century BC when the punch-marked coins had become quite common in that province.The weight of a *sigloi* was about 86 grains, a normal punch-marked coin usually weighs only 56 grains, the two weight systems show no connection whatsoever.

Babylonian Origin

James Kennedy[15] thought that the punch-marked coins, which formed the most ancient currency of India, were copied from Babylonian originals after the opening of the maritime trade with Western Asia in the sixth century BC. He argued on the basis of the similarities between Indian punch-marked coins and Babylonian punched-coins called *shekels*. Both are punched and bear no inscriptions on bust of kings or divinities. Both are flat and similar in shape. Both had standard weights but no standard size. Both used a small copper alloy. The *jātakas* show how Indian merchants used to go to Babylon for trade, and it is almost certain that India imported her supply of silver from that quarter in the form of spread-out plates, which determined the size of punch-marked coins.

Vincent A. Smith's[16] view was more or less the same. The introduction into India of the use of coins, that is to say, pieces of definite weight authenticated as currency by marks recognised as a guarantee of value may be ascribed with much probability to the seventh century BC when foreign maritime trade seems to have begun. There is reason to believe that the necessities of commerce with foreign merchants were the immediate occasion for the adoption by the Indian people of a metallic currency as well as of alphabetic writing. Later on, however, he slightly modified his view, for in his *Catalogue of Coins in the Indian Museum*, he has suggested that the earliest punch-marked coins, viz., the bent-bar pieces, were not earlier than 500 or 600 BC.[17]

CRITICISM

The theory of Babylonian origin is untenable. The punched symbols on the Babylonian *shekels* are quite diffferent in nature and character from those of the punch-marked coins. The weight system of the two currencies is also different. The standard weight of the Babylonian *shekels* is 132 grains while that of the punch-marked coin is 56 grains. The punch-marked coins originated most probably in Madhyadeśa (U.P.). The Babylonian *shekels* were known only to a few merchants of western India who occasionally kept visiting Mesopotamia. Nor are Babylonian *shekels* found in India. The antiquity of the Babylonian *shekel* does not go back beyond 525 BC. On the other hand, the Indian punch-marked currency was quite well established during this time.

Indigenous Origin

There are, however, a number of numismatists even among the Europeans who did not subscribe to the theory of foreign or late origin of the ancient Indian coinage. E.J. Rapson[18] thought that the punch-marked coins developed independently of any foreign influence. The same was the view of Edward Thomas.[19] He observes, "Designs, treatment and die devices (of ancient Indian coins) evince independent thought. The Indian figures follow the ideal models of their own land and bear no trace of the conventionalities of Greek art". A. Cunningham[20] did not believe in any foreign influennce or origin. Among the Indian numismatists, S.K. Chakrabortty[21] is inclined to agree with the view of A. Cunningham that coinage in India was evolved in about 800 BC.

D.R. Bhandarkar[22] after considering both the literary and archaeological evidence comes to the conclusion that the coined money was current in the Vedic Period. He accepted the view of M. Winternitz[23] that the Vedic period in all probability extends from *c.* 2500 to 800 BC. Following arguments were advanced by D.R. Bhandarkar in support of his view.

(i) Since gold coins like *niśkas*, *suvarṇas*, *satamānas*, *kṛṣṇalas* and *pādas* are mentioned in the Vedic literature, the conclusion becomes irresistible that coinage was known to India when the Vedic Āryans composed the Vedic literature.

Niśka mentioned in the Vedic literature was both a coin as well as an ornament. In one place in the *Ṛgveda*,[24] the sage Kakśivat describes how he obtained from the king Bhavya ten horses and ten *niśkas*. In the *Atharvaveda*,[25] another poet describes how his generous royal patron gave him a hundred *niśkas*, ten necklaces, three hundred horses and ten thousand cows. *Niśka* was also used as a necklace. In one passage of the *Ṛgveda*,[26] Rudra is described as wearing a *niśka*, which has been described as *viśvarūpa* in form. Probably *niśka* had numerous (*viśva*) symbols (forms) or ornamental designs or variegated scrolls upon it and was, therefore, called *viśvarūpa*. *Niśka* was undoubtedly an artistic piece, for Uṣā disclosing the beautiful view of the morning, is figuratively described as fashioning a *niśka* or wearing a garland.[27] But how could the word *niśka* come to signify both a currency and a necklace? *Niśka* denoted a necklace because it consisted of *niśkas* — the coins. The custom of stringing the coins into a necklace was prevalent in ancient India. How should we interpret the word *viśvarūpa*? As these *niśka* coins bore various *rūpas* or figures on them, the necklace was naturally *viśvarūpa*. More than three hundred devices have been marked on punch-marked coins. No wonder if the necklace of Rudra, which was made of *niśka* coins, has been described as *viśvarūpa*, i.e., covered with manifold *rūpas*. This additional evidence shows that *niśkas* were coined money and not merely metallic currency.

(ii) According to D.R. Bhandarkar, as distinguished from the *niśkas* known as stamped currency, there were *hiraṇya-piṇḍas* called unstamped metallic currency. It seems to have been collected from the gold dust from the beds of the Punjab rivers. It was stored in small bags. The ten bags which king Divodāsa offered to his priest along with ten horses, ten garments and ten lumps of gold, were probably ten small bags of gold dust.[28] Gold in its original dust form was difficult to handle and therefore it was melted down and transformed into ingots which are referred to as *hiraṇya-piṇḍas*.[29] It was also used for preparing different ornaments used for personal adornment both by men and women. Thus, we find from the *Ṛgveda* that both *hiraṇya-piṇḍas niśkas*, i.e, unstamped and stamped money were current at one and the same time.

(iii) In a passage of the *Ṛgveda*, request is made to Indra to bestow upon the devotee *manas* of gold along with cows and horses.[30] It seems probable that the poet is referring to a golden coin or piece as we know that *mīnā* was used by the Babylonians to denote a lump on ingot of silver or gold of definite weight before regular currency was introduced among them. This passage would show that some of the Vedic Indians knew the golden *mīnās* of Babylonia for which they prayed Indra to bring with him.

(iv) In the *Śatapatha Brāhmaṇa*, another gold piece named *śatamāna* is frequently mentioned in connection with the honorarium to be paid to the priests. In the ceremony of

Rājasūya sacrifice at the time of the royal coronation, two *śatamānas* attached to the two wheels of the royal chariot which were offered as *dakṣiṇā* to the officiating priest.[31] In two other passages of the *Śatapatha Brāhmaṇa*, another class of coins named *suvarṇa* has also been mentioned. The *Bṛhadāraṇyaka Upaniṣad*[32] mentions *pāda* in the concern of *Bahudakṣiṇā* sacrifice performed by king Janaka. He organised a philosophical tournament offering a most tempting prize to the winner which consisted of a thousand cows, each having ten *pādas* attached to its horns. One passage in the *Taittirīya Brāhmaṇa* states that one *kṛṣṇala* was given to each participant in the chariot race at the time of the *Rājasūya* sacrifice as the reward for his services.

(v) As we find so many symbols of pre-historic origin occurring in the punch-marked coins, it is difficult to avoid the conclusion that *kārṣāpaṇa* coinage must have been handed down to us from the pre-historic times. The symbols of pre-historic age are *svastika*, Mountain, a star of eight points and Ujjayinī symbol.

(vi) If any further evidence is required, it is furnished by the fact first brought to our attention by Elliot that these punch-marked coins have been discovered among the ashes of men who introduced primitive tombs known as *Pāṇḍukulis* (*Megaliths*) in south India and are unearthed from the ruins of buried cities in excavating the heed waters of the Ganges Canal.[33] As these tombs were considered to be of the pre-historic period, the introduction of the *kārṣāpaṇa* coinage must be attributed to about the beginning of the second millennium before Christ.

CRITICISM

Though *niśkas*, *suvarṇas*, *śatamānas*, *kṛṣṇalas* and *pādas* have been mentioned in the Vedic literature, we can hardly be justified in stating that currency was in use in the Vedic period. These were of gold, and are mentioned only in connection with the description of fabulous gifts of generous kings. They have not been used in the ordinary transactions of sale or contract. Some of them might have become well-known pieces of recognised weight and value, but they cannot be described as coins. There is no evidence in the Vedic literature that they were issued under the authority of the state or guilds, and were stamped with symbols guaranteeing their content and value. It is wrong to presume that *niśka* was stamped money and *hiraṇya-piṇḍa* was unstamped money.

Mīnā, however, was in early times merely the name of a definite weight in Babylonia and not of a coin, and the solitary Vedic passage will only show that some of the Babylonian *mīnās* had reached India. *Manā* as a regular weight or coin was foreign to Vedic India, as is shown by the disappearance of the word in later times and literature.

Against the pre-historic symbols on the punch-marked coins, it may be pointed out that these are not found on the punch-marked coins of the Paila and Golakhpur hoards which are of very early times. Further, we may say that these pre-historic symbols are the general symbols. They may occur on both by mere chance.

Against the last argument, it may be pointed out that no scientific archaeological excavations were conducted of the Pāndukuli graves and buried cities. No proper and exact record about the stratification of the coins was kept, and it would be unsafe to attach any value to it. Punch-marked coins were found in solitary case but not in all Pāndukuli graves. Punch-marked coins seem to have been borrowed by the south from the north and it is extremely unlikely that they could ever have circulated these in pre-historic times. Further, Roman coins were also found in these graves along with the punch-marked coins. From this, it is not wise to conclude that they were prevalent along with the punch-marked coins during the Vedic age. Besides, these primitive tombs of the south are dated fifth or fourth century BC.

STAGES IN THE EVOLUTION OF MONEY

The stages in the evolution of money are as follows :

Commodity Money

This is the first stage in the evolution of money. Every commodity was treated as money. The commodity money was in use in the barter stage. Many commodities like rice and wheat and animals like cow and sheep were used as money. This type of money had all the inconveniences as were in case of barter exchange. In the later period of barter economy, superior type of commodity money was introduced. It was in the form of precious stones, skins, tiger teeth, salt, etc. These articles were generally accepted for exchange. This type of money is the most primitive and had various disadvantages. These are : (i) absence of storage facility, (ii) lack of divisibility, (iii) absence of effective control, and (iv) loss of value after a lapse of time. In order to remove these disadvantages, metallic money was introduced.

Metallic Money

In this stage, commodity money was discarded and was replaced by pieces of different metals. Small pieces of metals, like, silver, copper and iron were used for the purpose of exchange. This money was durable and it was possible to make large and small pieces of such metals easily. The storage of metallic money was also possible. Thus it was definitely superior to commodity money. However, metallic money was not uniform as regards weight, size, shape and fineness. In the early period, inferior metals were used for preparing money but later on, they were replaced by precious metals, like, gold and silver. Gold and silver were selected for metallic money because of their scarcity. In addition, other metals, like, copper, lead and bronze were used for lower denominations. The early metallic money had certain disadvantages like loss of weight in handling, difficulty of carrying large number of metal pieces, counting of metal pieces and so on. Trade and economic activities developed considerably during the metallic money period.

Metallic Coins

In this stage, coins of specific size and weight were introduced in place of uneven pieces of different metals. The coins had the stamp of the king or emperor on one side and the value on the other. Exchange was much facilitated by these standardised coins. Mostly gold and silver were used for higher denominations while brass, copper, lead and nickel were used for lower denominations. Coins were introduced first in Greece during the seventh century BC. The right of issuing coin was free in the beginning but then the monopoly of minting coins was taken by the government. This was necessary for bringing uniformity in the metallic coins and for creating public confidence.

Thus, this is how the money evolved in the ancient period. But, in the present world, there is addition of two more stages in the evolution of money. They are paper money and bank money. Paper money is in the form of currency notes and bank money is in the form of cheques, drafts, bills of exchange, promissory notes and letters of credit.

Harappan Period

The first urbanisation took place during the Harappan period and some urban centres came into existence. It was due to the surplus production of raw material and finished goods, that led to the barter system. The huge granaries found in the cities of Harappa and Mohenjo-daro were replenished by the system of state tribute, and they fulfilled the function of modern state bank or treasury in the state economy. We have large number of stone weights following the definite weight system, the unit of which was 13 grains. Several stone weights have been discovered, which are the multiples of 2, 4, 8, 10, etc. of this unit. A few metallic pieces have been discovered but were not following the regular weight system.[34]

Writing also started. Seals discovered with pictographic script might have served the purpose of money economy during this period.

Ṛgvedic Period

During the Ṛgvedic period, golden metallic pieces such as *niśkas*, *suvarṇas* and *hiraṇya-piṇḍas* have been mentioned in connection with gifts. As the metal was limited, Ṛgvedic people generally used cow as the medium of exchange in ordinary transactions. In a passage of the *Ṛgveda*, the price of an image of Indra, which was being offered for sale, is said to be ten cows.[35] In another passage, a sage is said to have refused to sell his image of Indra even for a hundred or a thousand or even ten thousand cows.[36] In a third passage, it is said that the Bharata army went out for war impelled by the desire to acquire cows.[37]

Later Vedic Literature

The later Vedic literature, viz., the *Brāhmaṇas* and the *Upaniṣads* which are placed in *c.* 800 BC refer to golden metallic pieces such as *niśka*,[38] *śatamāna*,[39] *pāda*[40] and *kṛṣṇala*.[41] They have been mentioned only in connection with the gifts. These seem to be the ingots of calculated weight. We find transition from this stage to that of coin proper of recognised weight guaranteed by stamp of authority. Silver is rarely referred to in the *Vedas*, the *Brāhmaṇas* and the *Upaniṣads*.

COMMENCEMENT OF COINAGE

There is no doubt that there was no coinage during the early Vedic period. Some scholars are of the view that coinage originated in the later Vedic period. According to A.S. Altekar[42], the *kārṣāpaṇa* silver currency may not be earlier than *c.* 800 BC but the cast copper round and square coins, which are fairly common all over the Gangetic plain, may be earlier. According to D.D. Kosambi,[43] coinage in India could be as old as the eighth century BC. P.L. Gupta[44] is of the view that coins most probably originated some time in the seventh century BC in India at least a century before Lydia or China thought of them. A.K. Narain and Lallanji Gopal[45] placed the punch-marked coins in the sixth century BC at the earliest.

The origin of coinage appears to be associated with the second urbanisation which took place in the region of Gangetic Valley during the sixth century BC. This period was epoch making in the economic history because important changes occurred in it. Organised states leading to the establishment of peace and order came into existence for the first time. As a result, this period witnessed an all round development of agriculture, industry and trade. Local and international trade necessitated its origin. Both trade and industry were organised into guilds. Merchants became very prosperous. The increased use of iron for different purposes resulted in the surplus of wealth and prosperity. Many new arts and crafts came into existence, and they became localised and hereditary. Population increased by leaps and bounds on account of better means of subsistence and living conditions. A number of urban centres came into existence. The knowledge of mathematics and allied subjects increased. All these factors led to the origin of currency in the sixth century BC as known from the following evidences.

Literary Evidence

We infer the existence of the coinage in the sixth century BC from the literary sources. The *Aṣṭādhyāyī* of Pāṇini[46] gives the names of a number of coins *śatamāna, śāṇa, karṣāpaṇa, ardhapaṇa* or *bhāga, pāda, dvimāṣapāda, viṁśatika* and *triṁśatika*. The Buddhist canons and the *Jātaka* stories which contain very early information about the society refer to coins — *kahāpaṇa,*[47] *ardha-kahāpaṇa,*[48] *pāda,*[49] *māṣaka,*[50] *addha-māṣaka*[51] and *kākini.*[52] The date of *Aṣṭādhyāyī* does not seem to be much earlier than 400 BC. The date of the *Jātakas* is again a matter of controversy, but it is generally agreed that the text of *Tripiṭakas* was settled at *c.* 450 BC. The *kārṣāpaṇas* are also referred to in some of the *Dharmasūtras*[53] and Jaina canonical[54] literature. From the literary texts, it is clear that currency became well established in about the fifth century BC in the form of standard weight and was available in different denominations.

Archaeological Evidences

The larger Bhir Mound hoard of punch-marked coins at Taxila[55] found in the second stratum contained two coins of Alexander, the Great and one of Philip Ariaudus which were in mint conditions, besides 1055 silver punch-marked coins. The stratification of this hoard and the mint condition of the coins of the two Greek rulers show that the hoard was buried not much later than 317 BC. As some of these punch-marked coins of this hoard were old blurred and indistinct, it may be assumed that they were used at least about two centuries earlier.

The Caman Hazūri hoard contains Greek coins which are datable anterior to *c.* 400 BC. Besides these Greek and Achaemenid coins, a number of punch-marked coins of the Gangetic Valley origin, have been discovered but none of them belong to *kārṣāpaṇa* series. This also proves the sixth century BC as the date of these punch-marked coins.

Northern Black Polished Ware

In archaeological excavations at some sites, punch-marked coins were found with the North Black Polished Ware (NBPW). The North Black Polished Ware is considered to be essentially pre-Alexandrian — sixth century BC.[56] Punch-marked coins are found in association with this ware. Rupar III, Purānā Qilā, Ujjain II, Mathurā II and Kauśāmbī contained both NBP Ware as well as punch-marked coins.[57] This also proves that the punch-marked coins originated in the sixth century BC along with this type of ceramic.

By Carbon-14 dating also scholars have tried to suggest sixth or fifth century BC as the date of the punch-marked coins.

Now the question is whether in the sixth century BC coinage originated owing to the outside influence or it was indigenous?

According to some scholars, the punch-marked coins for the first time began to be manufactured in the region of Gangetic Valley. These early punch-marked coins have been discovered along with the Persian coins, Greek coins and bent-bar coins at Caman Hazūri and Taxila. It indicates that there were trade relations between the regions of the Gangetic Valley and Western Asia.

The north-western India may be the place of the origin of the Indian coinage because some Persian coins are found counter-marked, with punch-marked coins. Bent-bar coins have been discovered here. These coins were issued during the sixth or fifth century BC when it was the part and parcel of the Iranian empire. These bent-bars are different in weight and fabric from the Iranian coins. It seems that the Indian coinage either in Gangetic Valley or in the north-western India originated because of the inspiration from Western Asia where it originated earlier. But in the fabric and weight these coins of India at both places are indigenous.

Metal of the Original Coinage

There is controversy among scholars regarding the metal of the original coinage. Among the precious metals, gold alone was well-known in the Vedic period. Gold metallic pieces of definite value have been referred to in early texts but only in connection with the hoards of money, munificent gifts, etc. Further golden coins are conspicuous by their non-discovery. Silver is rarely referred to except in later *Saṁhitās*. Copper was also available.

According to S.K. Chakraborty,[58] copper came earlier into use than silver in India. Silver was mainly imported from abroad and so its purity stood in the way of its use for the manufacture of coins. A.S. Altekar[59] thinks that *kārṣāpaṇa* silver currency may not be earlier than *c.* 800 BC but the cast copper round and square coins may be earlier. This view does not appear to be correct. Copper coins are not known to be of so much early period. Cast copper coins[60] probably originated in about the beginning of the fourth or at the end of the fifth century BC. Copper punch-marked coins were issued around the beginning of the third century BC. P.L. Gupta[61] also thinks that copper came into use for coins most likely at the time of the Mauryas.

On the other hand, silver coins appear to have originated earlier. The earliest coins found at Kāśī and Kośala in the Gangetic Valley and bent-bar coins of Gāndhāra region of sixth century BC are of silver. The silver was preferred for the manufacture of coins because it served better as the medium of exchange with other regions. Besides, it carried value when melted. As indigenous silver was not available in much quantity, there is possibility of it being imported from the west.

Issuing Authority

D.D. Kasambi's[62] contention is that the manufacture of coins continued to be the traders function for a long time after the Indus period. The small marks were put according to a system generally understood at the time by those who handled the coins most frequently. It follows that traders were accurate in their workmanship and gave great value. The traders were simultaneously financiers, bankers and dealers in precious metals, they would have had good reason to assure themselves that a given coin continued to adhere to a standard of weight. P.L. Gupta[63] suggests, "If the traders and merchants had a hand in the origin of the coins, it would have been only in the formative period or the primitive stage of coinage".

As Indian coinage seems to have originated in connection with trade and commerce with the Western Asia, it is likely that in the beginning, these coins might have been issued by the traders.

Notes

1. Crowther, Geoffrey, *An Outline of Money*, p.4, London, 1955.
2. *Ibid.*
3. Seth, M. L., *Monetary Economics*, Agra, 1978.
4. *Money, Debt and Economics Activity*, p.3, New York, 1958.
5. Seth, M. L., *Monetary Economics*, Agra, 1978.

6. *Webster's New World Dictionary*, p. 485.
7. Nigam, S.S., *Economics Organisation in Ancient India*, p. 241, Delhi, 1975.
8. Chakrabortty, S.K., *A Study of Ancient Indian Numismatics*, p. 12, Delhi, Second edn. 1973.
9. *Ariana Antiqua*, p. 404, London, 1841.
10. *JASB*, I, p. 394; *Prinsep's Essays*, pp. 53-54.
11. *MASI*, No. 59, pp. 1-2.
12. *INSI*, XXXV, pp. 1-39.
13. *JA*, 1912, pp. 117-32; Bhandarkar, D.R., *Ancient Indian Numismatics*, pp. 118-20, Calcutta, 1921.
14. *BMCAI*, Introduction, p. xxi, London, 1936.
15. *JRAS*, 1898, p. 279.
16. *Imperial Gazetteer*, II, p. 183.
17. *JMC*, I, p. 183.
18. *Indian Coins*, p. 2, Strassburg, 1897; *JRAS*, 1895, p. 869.
19. *Prinsep's Essays*, I, p. 211.
20. *Coins of Ancient India*, p. 43, London, 1891.
21. *A Study of Ancient Indian Numismatics*, p. 71, Delhi, 1973.
22. *Ancient Indian Numismatics*, p. 71, Calcutta, 1921.
23. *A History of Indian Literature*, Calcutta, 1927.
24. I.126.2.
25. XX.127.3.
26. II.33.10
27. *Atharvaveda*, XX.127.3.
28. *ṚV*, VI.47.23.
29. *Ibid.*, I.117.12.
30. VIII.78.2.
31. V.4.32.4, 26.
32. III.1.1-2.
33. Elliot, *Coins of Southern India*, p. 45, 1886; *JASB* III, p. 44; Bhandarkar, D.R., *Ancient Indian Numismatics*, pp. 109, 168, Calcutta, 1921.
34. *JNSI*, XV, p. 14.
35. *ṚV*, IV.24.10.
36. *Ibid.*, VIII.1.5.
37. *Ibid.*, III.33.11
38. *Śatapatha Brāhmaṇa*, XI.4.1, 1; XI. 4.1.8; XIII. 4.17; XXIII. 4.1.17, *Gopatha Brāhmaṇa* 1.3 b, 1.3.8, *Pañcaviṁsa* III.7.6.1, *Chāndogya Upaniṣad* IV.7.ff.
39. *Śatapatha Brāhmaṇa*, V.4.3.24; V. 4.3.26; 5.5.5.16; XII. 7.2.13; XII. 7.9.14; XIII.1.1.4; XIII.1.2.32; XIII.4.1.6; XIII.4.1.13; XIII.4.2.7; XIII.4.2.10; XIII.1.2.32; XIII.4.1.6; XIII.4.1.13; XIII.4.2.7; XIII. 4.2.10; XIII.4.2.13; XIV.3.1.32; *Taittirīya Brāhmaṇa*, 1.8.9.1; I.3.78. 1.7.82;

1.8.6.5; II. 6.4.5.

40. *Bṛhadāraṇyaka Upaniṣad*, III.1,1-2, etc.
41. *Taittirīya Brāhmaṇa*, 1.3.6.7.
42. *JNSI*, XV,p. 26.
43. *Indian Numismatics*, New Delhi, 1987.
44. *Coins*, New Delhi, 1969.
45. *The Chronology of Punch-marked Coins*, p. 5.
46. *India as Known to Pāṇini*, p. 475.
47. *Majjhima Nikāya* II,163, *Aṅguttara Nikāya*,1.250, II.83; *Vinaya Piṭaka*, II.294; III.288; IV.249; *Jāt*.I,112, 121, 195, 478, 483, II, 20, 112, 247, 289, 305, 424, III, 448, IV. 138, 378, 449, IV, 343, 404.
48. *Jāt*., I, 340, III, 448.
49. *Vinayapiṭaka*, III, 47, V. 77.
50. *Jāt*., II. 424, 425, III, 130; IV.326, 446, 449, VI.346.
51. *Dīgha Nikāya*, 1.166, *Aṅguttara Nikāya*, II.160.
52. *Jāt*., 1.120, VI. 346.
53. *Gautamadharma Sūtra*, XII. 6-8, 19, *Vasiṣṭhadharma Sūtra*.
54. *Uttarādhyayana*, 20.42.
55. *MASI*, No. 59, pp. 1-2.
56. Ray, S.C., *Stratigraphic Evidence of Coins in Indian Excavations and some Allied Issues*, p. 6, Varanasi, 1959.
57. *JNSI*, XXII, pp. 1 f.
58. *A Study of Ancient Indian Numismatics*, pp. 40-41, Delhi, 1973.
59. *JNSI*, XV, p. 26.
60. *Ibid*., XXXV, pp. 1-39.
61. *Coins*, p. 18, New Delhi, 1969.
62. *Indian Numismatics*, pp. 91, 153, New Delhi, 1981.
63. *Coins*, p.7, New Delhi, 1969.

2

Research Methodology

In ancient India, money was nothing but pieces of gold, silver, copper, etc. stamped by government authority and used as medium of exchange. The territories covered during the period were from Kashmir in the north to Kanyākumārī in the south and from Baluchistan in the west to Assam in the east. This study deals with the money economy of *janapada*, Maurya, post-Maurya, Gupta, post-Gupta and early medieval periods, and the impact of it on the socio-economic set up.

Objectives of the Study

In the studies so far made, only the situations have been studied but in the present study, cause-effect approach has been adopted in the historical perspective. Thus, the present study is carried out with the following objectives:

1. To trace the money economy during the *janapada* period, study local and universal standard coinage, symbols on them and their significance, source of the metal and its impact on trade and commerce;
2. To study the growth of money economy during the Mauryan period, the factors which gave rise to the increasing necessity of money, coin varieties of the period and its impact on the economy;
3. To examine the sound monetary system dur-

ing the post-Mauryan period which included the foreign coins of the Indo-Greeks, Indo-Scythians, Indo-Parthians, Indo-Kuṣāṇas, Roman and the Indigenous coins. Also to study the impact of these coins on the economy of the period;

4. To study the money economy during Gupta period and the gradual movement towards the Indianisation of coinage system;
5. To find out the causes of the decline of money economy during the post-Gupta period and its revival in the early medieval period.

To sum up, the objectives of the study are to compile, classify and correlate the available numismatic and allied data to study the money economy existing in ancient India and analyse the background, problems and situations closely associated with it.

Compilation of the Source Information

The information for the present study is drawn from both primary and secondary sources. Primary sources include the ancient literary works, inscriptions, coins and the accounts of the foreigners. The secondary sources of information include catalogues, journals, commemorative volumes, etc., a list of which is given in the Bibliography. However, a critical estimate of some of the sources will not be out of place here. The sources for reconstructing the history of money economy in Ancient India may be divided as follows: (i) Coins, (ii) Inscriptions, (iii) Literature and (iv) Writings of foreigners. These sources are scattered and limited. Therefore, an attempt has been made to utilise them after critical examination.

COINS

Ancient coins have been discovered on surface, in excavations and in hoards. A large number of ancient coins have been melted and many are still buried. The evidence of coins is partly internal and partly external. The internal evidence pertains to the physical body of the coin itself while the external evidence concerns with the outside association of coins.

Internal Evidence

Metallurgy : Ancient Indian coins are found in gold, silver, copper, potin, lead, etc. Market value was determined from the content of the coin. Gold and silver coins were meant for big transactions. Gold coins of the Kuṣāṇas and the Guptas were required for the Roman trade. Copper coins were used for ordinary transactions. The large number of copper coins during the post-Mauryan period (200 BC-AD 319) suggests that money economy penetrated deeply into the life of common people and it was very sound. The paucity of coins during the post-Gupta period reveals weakness of money economy but there was revival of money economy during the early medieval period which is proved by the abundance of coins. Debasement in silver coins of the Mauryas and gold coins of the Guptas indicate financial difficulties. Copper was not used as an auxiliary to silver and gold, but as an independent currency in the ancient region of Avantī.

Metrology : Coins were issued according to the calculated weight standards. The issue of the silver punch-marked coins known as *kārṣāpaṇa* to the standard of 32 *raṭtīs* throughout the country indicates centralised money economy. *Kārṣāpaṇa* was the unit and there were several denominations. The standard of the copper *kārṣāpaṇa* was 80 *rattīs*. The introduction of the silver coins by the Indo-Bactrians in the conquered territories on the north-west India of light standard of 36 grains from 66 grains was due to commercial reasons. The Indo-Scythians, and Indo-Parthians and western Kṣatrapas issued their coins of the light standard. The Kuṣāṇas and the Guptas issued gold coins of the Roman standard of 123 grains because it assumed international recognition. There was prevalence of ancient *śatamāna* or *pala* standard of 320 *rattīs* as the basis of circulation in monetary transactions as well as of the *mādha* coins (40 *rattis*) in the ancient Kaliṅga (Orissa) during early medieval period. There were also regional monetary standards prevalent. The variation in the weight of coins was due to the rise and fall in the prices of gold and silver. The ancient weight standard of Greek coin known as *drachm* was revived in the early medieval period.

Coin Types : It is possible that the traders and merchants had a hand in the origin as well as in the primitive stage of coins. In course of time, it was only the state whose authority was above challenge or suspicion that ultimately undertook the responsibility of minting coins. It became their prerogative or attribute of political independence or symbol of sovereignty. Ruling authorities of ancient India issued thier distinct types of coins inspired by commercial or other considerations in order to avoid confusion for identification. These coin types may help us to determine money economy in different periods.

Symbols and Monograms : Symbols and monograms indirectly throw light on the money economy of ancient India. The subject-matter in the symbols of the *kārṣāpaṇa* coins shows an agrarian society. The symbol of steelyard or balance on the punch-marked coins indicates that it must have been used in the process of coinage as well as in other trading activities. The minute reverse marks on the punch-marked coin might have been the marks of the money testers. The *svastika* symbol on the coins of Taxila and a cross and ball on Ujjayinī coins prove them as mint cities and trade centres. The ship symbol on some Sātavāhana coins may indicate the sea borne trade. The symbols on punch-marked coins could well disclose to the experienced shroff the particular village, town or city, mountain or riversite where it was manufactured as also the name of the mint master or the authority who had issued it. The monograms on the coins may indicate a mint city or mint master.

Legends : City name coins seem to be the earliest of the inscribed monetary coins of India. The coins with the names of cities belong to the third or second century BC. These coins seem to have been issued by the town corporations and prove the prosperity and autonomy of towns. The *negama* coins from Taxila of the third or second century BC with legends indicate that merchant guilds were authorised to issue coins. A coin with the legend *gandhikānām* of about the third-second centuries BC may prove that it was issued by the perfumers guild of Kauśāmbī. Inscriptions on the coins mention the name of the ruler, his title, date, denominations, etc. They tell not only the name of the issuing authority but also something about the authority itself.

External Evidence

Geographical Distribution of Coins: Coins were not confined to the dominions of the sovereign power but were far beyond their borders. It was not only due to political conquest and popularity of coin series but also due to commercial relations.

Coin Hoards : The coin hoards may give quantitative idea of money issued by an authority. They may also tell the qualitative value of a coin series. The large number of gold coins of Candragupta II proves that his reign was of great prosperity. The presence of the punch-marked coins of the Gangetic Valley in the Caman Hazūrī (Kābul) hoard and of punch-marked coins of Magadha in Taxila hoard prove commercial relations with north-west India. The circulation of the punch-marked coins continued up to the second or third century AD along with the Indo-Greeks, Indo-Scythians, Indo-Parthians and Indo-Kuṣāṇas and is borne out from a number of finds of these coins.

Overstriking : A coin when struck by the emblem or inscription (or both) of another authority, it is known as an 'overstrike'. An overstrike may be due to the conquest of the state in which the understrike circulates, but a king may overstrike a piece issued by a preceding authority in his own kingdom, with or without the implication of a violent succession to the throne. The Jogalthambi hoard of silver coins proves that Gautamīputra Sātakarṇi overstruck the silver coins of the western Mahākṣatrapa ruler Nahapāna. Candragupta II of the Gupta dynasty overstruck the silver coins of the western Kṣatrapas after the conquest of Gujarat and Mālwā. Besides political, there might be some economic motives in overstriking them.

There are some limitations for reconstructing the history of money economy on the basis of coins. There is much conservatism in regard to the types and fabrics of coins. The same type of coin continued even after the change of dynasty and transference of power from one people to another. This is specially noticed in Kashmir where standing king and Ārdokṣo type continued for one thousand years. Gadahiyā type of coins in early medieval India is a good example of imitation. Besides, the coins are of small size and there is not sufficient space.

INSCRIPTIONS

Inscriptions supply stray information regarding money economy. They mention the names current during their times in ancient India. From the Hāthīgumphā Jaina inscription[1] dated about first century BC, it is known how Khāravelā as a young *yuvarāja* is represented to have mastered *rūpa*, i.e., science of coinage. *Prati* as another name of *kārṣāpaṇa* (punch-marked) coin is mentioned in the Nasik cave inscription[2] dated about second century AD of Uṣavadāta. In the Nasik inscriptions[3], the coin denominations of the time of western Kṣatrapas such as *kārṣāpaṇa*, *suvarṇa*, and *kuṣāṇamūla* have been mentioned. From this inscription, it is known that 70,000 *kārṣāpaṇas* were equal in value to 2,000 *suvarṇas* and thus 35 *kārṣāpaṇas* would be equal to one *suvarṇa*. The Nānāghāṭa inscription[4] mentions the numerous *kārṣāpaṇas* given in charity in connection with sacrifices performed by Nāganikā, wife of Sātakarṇi. These *kārṣāpaṇas* served as the standard money during the second century AD. Public endowments were made and recorded in terms of the *purāṇa* or ancient *kārṣāpaṇa* of the punch-marked variety. In the pillar inscription of Huviṣka at Mathurā,[5] it has been mentioned that an endowment of 1,100 *purāṇa* coins was deposited with two guilds which undertook to make provisions of public benefaction in consideration of the interest accruing on the original sum. This inscription informs that *kārṣāpaṇa* was also known by the name of *purāṇa*.

The Sāñcī inscription[6] dated AD 412-13 of Candragupta II records that the grant of a sum of 25 *dīnāras* or gold coins to the Buddhist *Saṁgha* at the monastary of Sāñcī. Some Gupta inscriptions refer to coins. *Dīnāra* and *suvarṇa* are meant for gold coins and *rūpaka* for silver ones.

The Goṭha-Mangloda (Rajasthan) inscription of the time of Druhlana dated AD 608 refers to the *drammas*. Originally, *dramma* was a silver coin of Attic standard weighing 66 grains. From the several inscriptions of a period between AD 900 and 1100, *dramma* became a common stanadard money. Several varieties of *drammas* such as *Ādivarāha*, *Vigrahapālīya*, *Ajayadeva* and *Pārupatha* are known from inscriptions. Some inscriptions also refer to denominations of *dramma* such as *rūpaka*, *paṇa*, *pañcīyaka*, *vodri* and *viṁśopaka*. Among inscriptions, the Siyadoni inscription,[7] Somanātha temple inscription of Shergarh,[8] Ahar inscription[9] and the Kaman inscription[10] are important as they mention the varieties and denominations of *dramma*. The name *kārṣāpaṇa* of the silver coin was retained even in the tenth century AD as known from the Bījāpur (Rajasthan) inscription.[11]

From the several inscriptions, it is clear that silver *pala* or *śatamāna* weighing 320 *rattīs* was regarded as the standard of calculation in the monetary transactions in Medieval Orissa. Medieval Orissan inscriptions often speak of a coin called *māḍha* which was both of gold and silver.[12] There are references to coins, mints and denominations of coins in the contemporary inscriptions of the south. Among the coins mentioned in the inscriptions of the south, the following may be noted — *drammas*, *gadyāna*, *paṇa*, *honu*, *naga*, *kāgiṇi*, *visa*, *gulika* and *bela*.[13]

LITERATURE

As known from the *Mahāvagga*, there was a text of the *Rūpasutta* which mentions a set of rules concerning coins, the science of coinage. It was studied by the individual in order to become either *rūpadarśaka*, *lakṣṇādhyakṣa* and *sauvarṇika*.

Vedic Literature

The Vedic literature mentions *niśka, suvarṇa, śatamāna* and *kṛṣṇala* in connection with charities. D.R. Bhandarkar[14] regards them as coins. Actually, these were simply ingots of calculated value. These cannot be called coins because these have not been used in connection with trade as medium of exchange.

Aṣṭādhyāyī of Pāṇini

The *Arhiya* section of *Aṣṭādhyāyī*[15] (*Adhyāya* V, *Pada* 1, *Sūtras* 19-37) furnishes some important data in respect of the oldest coinage of India. This work gives the names of a number of coins *śatamāna, śana, kārṣāpaṇa, ardhapaṇa* or *bhāga, pāda, dvimāṣapāda, viṁśatika* and *triṁśatika*. Pāṇini also mentions *niśka* as a piece of gold equal to some standard weight. *Kārṣāpaṇa* was the standard money of the time of Pāṇini.

Buddhist Literature

The Buddhist canons and *Jātaka* stories contain very early information about the society. The *Jātaka* stories not only mention the names of coins but also the role played in the manifold transactions of the people of the early period. There were three types of gold pieces — *māṣaka, suvarṇa* and *niśka*. There is also mention of gold *kārṣāpaṇa*, used in connection with the hoards of money, munificent gifts and so forth. Silver *kārṣāpaṇa* was looked upon as the standard coin. Copper *kārṣāpaṇa* was also known. There were several denominations of *kārṣāpaṇa* meant for ordinary transactions as depicted in the *Jātaka* tales.

Buddhaghoṣa, author of the fifth century AD, possessed useful knowledge regarding science of coins. The passages from Buddhaghoṣa's *Kaṅkhāvitaraṇi, Sāmantapāsādikā* and *Viśuddhimagga* give valuable information about ancient Indian currency.[16] A passage from his commentary *Sāmantapāsādikā* on *Vinayapiṭaka* is as follows :

> At that time at Rājagṛha, one *kārṣāpaṇa* was equal to 20 *māṣakas*.

The passage from *Viśuddhimagga* informs about the local significance of coins. The Pāli commentaries such as *Sārathadipaṇi* mention *rudradāmaka* and *rudradāmakādi* coins. The *rudradāmaka* coins were minted by Rudradāman, the great Satrapa who ruled in AD 150. The coins called here *rudradāmakādi* were issued by others.

Arthaśāstra of Kauṭilya

The *Arthaśāstra* of Kauṭilya is useful work for the study of money economy in ancient India. In it, coinage and the mint are described only in one chapter (Book II, chapter XII). Here it is stated that superintendent of mint (*lakṣaṇādhyakṣa*) shall carry on the manufacture of silver coins (*rūpya-rūpa*) made of four parts (i.e., one-fourth) of copper and sixteenth (*māṣa*) of any one of the metals *tīkṣṇa, trapu, śīsa* and *añjana*. These shall be *paṇa, ardhapaṇa*, (half *paṇa*), *pādapaṇa* (quarter) and *aṣṭabhāga paṇa*. Copper coins (*tāmra-rūpa*) made up of four parts of alloy (*pādājīva*) shall be a *māṣa, ardhamāṣa, pādamāṣa* (*kākiṇi*) and *aṣṭabhāga māṣa* (*ardha-kākiṇi*). The copper *māṣaka* may be no other than the copper *paṇa* of 80 *rattīs* so-called because it was one-sixteenth of the standard silver coin in value. *Paṇa* has been used in the specification of salaries and fines. *Paṇa* was meant for silver in case of salaries and in fines it was meant for copper. Kauṭilya has also referred to the counterfeiters of coins. The examiner of coins regulated currency both as a medium of exchange and as legal tender.

Mahābhārata, Dharmaśāstra Writers and Patañjali

In the *Mahābhārata*,[17] there are coin names such as *niśka, suvarṇa, śatamāna, śaṇa* and *prati*. *Niśka* and *suvarṇa* are the names of the gold coins. The early *Dharmaśāstra* writers Manu, Viṣṇu and Yājñavalkya mention the copper coin *paṇa* in the sense of payment to be made as fines for offences. Manu refers to *purāṇa, śatamāna, kṛṣṇala, dharaṇa* and *pala*. Patañjali has used *rūpa* in the sense of coin, and the officer known as *rūpatarka* to examine coins is identical with *rūpadarśaka* of Kauṭilya.

Jain Canonical and other Jaina Literary Works

Some Jaina canonical works[18] refer to coins. A false (*kuda*) *kāhāvana* is referred to in the *Uttarādhyayana*. *Māṣa*, *adhamāṣa* and *ruvaga* are mentioned in the *Sūtrakṛtāṅga-Sūtra* and in the *Uttarādhyayana Sūtra*. *Kahāpaṇas* are also referred to by the author of *Vasudevahiṇḍi*.

The *Aṅgavijjā*, a text originally compiled during the Kuṣāṇa period, furnishes important data of money in circulations. The gold, silver and copper coins were current. The *kahāpaṇa* was used as a general term. *Dīnāra*, *suvarṇa* and *sateraka* (derived from Greek *stater*) were gold coins. The ancient silver punch-marked coins were known as *ādimūla* (*purāṇa*). *Khattapaka* coins were issued by the western Kṣatrapa rulers of Gujarat and Mālwā. Copper coins were called by the term *nāṇaka*. Sub-multiples of the standard of gold, silver and copper coins have been mentioned.

The *Bṛhatkalpa-Bhāṣya* composed in AD 600 or earlier and the *Āvaśyaka Cūrṇi* (*c*. AD 676) of Jinadāsa Mahattara throw interesting light on the current coins, and give exchange values of different coins. In the *Niśīthacūrṇi* written in AD 676, *Varmalāta-drammas* have been mentioned. From the *Āvaśyaka Ṭīkā* of Haribhadra Sūri, it is known that goldsmiths (*heraṇṇīya*) could detect false coins (*rāvaga*) in darkness. The *Purātana Prabandhasaṁgraha* mentions *bhūmapriya-drammas* and *pārupatha drammas*. *Ṭaṅkaśalās* (mints) were there for manufacture of coins. The *Kharatavagacchāvalī* refers to *dvaivalaka drammas* and *pārupatha drammas*. From the *Lekhapaddhati*, it is known that *pārupatha drammas* were minted at *Śrīmāla*, and *vīsalapriya drammas* were tested thrice.

Mathematical Works

There are certain mathematical works[19] which give the names of coins while citing numerical examples. The Baksli Manuscript (AD 200) refers to coin names *dramma*, *dīnāra*, *stater māṣaka*, etc. Bhāśkarācārya in the *Līlāvatī* mentions that 16 *drammas* are equal to one *niśka*. Mahāvirācārya of the ninth century AD in his work *Gaṇitasārasaṁgraha* gives references to coinage while devoting a special section entitled *Suvarṇa-Kuttikarah* in his treatise (VI. 168-225) to the intricate problem on gold.

The *Gaṇitasāra* of Śrīdhara and the medieval Gujarati commentary throw valuable light on contemporary denominations. They may also help us in reckoning the purchasing power of several denominations. A number of coin denominations associated with the *cowries* clearly prove that they were widely used in various transactions by the people. A number of types current are known from Ṭhākkura Pheru's work *Dravyaparīkṣā* written in *V.S.* 1375.

WRITINGS OF FOREIGNERS

Some stray references by foreigners in their writings are useful for the history of money economy in ancient India. Quintus Curtius, the historian of Alexander, tells us that among the presents given by the king of Taxila to Alexander the Great were two hundred talents of *Signati argenti* (coined silver money). The *Periplus* (AD 80) mentions that old *drachmai* bearing the Greek inscriptions of Apollodotus and Menander were current in Barygaza. The Chinese Pilgrim Fa-Hien seems to have been correct when he stated that *cowries* formed the common medium of exchange.

Classification of Coins

After completing the compilation of the information from various sources, the coins were classified as under:

In Chronological Sequence

This was done to study the origin of the money economy in ancient India and its evolution in the historical perspective. This classification also helped the researcher in tracing out the alien impact on the coins and in understanding the political and cultural significance of various symbols marked on them.

According to the Weight and Size

This classification was done to formulate an idea regarding the quantum and velocity of the money-economy in ancient India. The numismatic studies in India lack a scientific methodology to analyse these aspects, still the present study has been an humble attempt to utilise the experiences and conclusions of scholars who worked previously in this connection.

According to the Metal Used

A thorough study of the metal used for the manufacture of coins of various types and periods was done. Simultaneously the purity and debasement of the metal was also taken into consideration. As a result of such classifications, an attempt is made to analyse the standard and value of the money-economy of a period while taking into consideration the historical and political situations also.

According to the Dynastical Regimes

Coins were also classified according to the genealogical sequence of dynasties issuing these. Such classification enabled the scholar to locate and explain the regional and genealogical variations, legends associated with them and the extent of their circulation. The division between the local and standard coins was also done on the basis of this classification.

According to the Purpose of Issue

Such classification, no doubt, was a complex affair, still with the assistance of the academic contributions of the numismaticians, it was made possible and on its basis, the real nature of the issue was worked out.

According to the Technique of Manufacture

On the basis of this classification, the punch-marked, cast and minted coins and their various types were identified.

Such identification paved path for tracing and narrating the evolution of the system of coinage in ancient India. Further, the techniques of the manufacturing coins and the centres where these were minted were also known on the basis of this classification.

These classifications had thus been an important part of the present study. These classifications are summarily laid down in the tabular form in the Appendix.

Analysis

It had not been possible to give definite data and statistical diagrams in the present study. Still, the source-information was analysed through the following methods:

Macro and Micro Approaches

Several specific and representative coins or coin-types were studied and on this micro basis, the conclusions derived from the macro analysis were reinterpreted, verified or modified.

Inductive and Deductive Approaches

'From general to particular' and 'from particular to general' are the essential attributes of these approaches. For the purpose of present study also, many particular conclusions were arrived at on the basis of a number of commonly known observations, and on the basis of some specific coins of some specific periods, some new generalisations were made and fresh themes were laid down.

Historical and Dialectical Approaches

Historical analysis, on the basis of the elements of thesis, anti-thesis and synthesis, particualarly from the angle of Marxist dialactical philosophy has been adopted by scholars like D.D. Kosambi. The results of these approaches are very surprising and encouraging particularly in the light of the study of socio-political conditions during the transitional periods. Therefore, these approaches are also utilised for the present study.

Traditional Approach

Historians and scholars contributed a lot to various aspects of money-economy in ancient India. Their approach had mainly been to write or re-cast history on the basis of numismatic findings. Their writings are descriptive, informative and sometimes critical. As the present study is aimed at the systematic writing and critically describing the evolution of money economy in ancient India, the traditional approach had also been a part of the analysis and presentation.

However, the present study is a rational synthesis of all these mehtods on the basis of which the logical, critical and analytical thinking over the available and existing source-material was done and the re-estimated, modified or thoroughly re-written description was put forth and fresh conclusions were derived. The study is also supplemented with maps, photos and charts in order to make the subject-matter more comprehensive, interesting and understandable.

Hypothesis

Following hypothesis which formed the basis of our study in the beginning have proved to be true :

(i) Money-economy of very high order was prevalent in Ancient India,

(ii) Economic and commercial development in Ancient India was greatly influenced by money-economy prevalent at that time,

(iii) Money-economy and commerce influenced each other in their growth and led to modern monetary system,

(iv) Barter system remained in vogue throughout the period.

Limitations

There is no direct evidence available regarding money-economy in ancient India. We have to draw inferences mainly from coins which provide only limited information. Besides, the conclusions derived from it cannot be considered as absolute because they can change with the discovery of new coins.

Notes

1. Sircar, D.C., *Sel. Ins*, p. 214, Calcutta, 1965.
2. *Ibid.*, p. 165.
3. *Ibid.*, pp. 164-66.
4. *Ibid.*, pp. 194-95.
5. *Ibid.*, p. 152.
6. *Ibid.*, p. 281.
7. *EL. I*, pp. 169 ff.
8. *Ibid.*, XIII, pp. 133 f.
9. *Ibid.*, XIX, pp. 58 f.
10. *Ibid.*, XXIV, pp. 332 ff.
11. *Ibid.*, X, pp. 17 ff.
12. Sircar, D.C., *Studies in Indian Coins*, pp. 48-72, Delhi, 1968.
13. Murthy, A.V. Narasimha, *The Coins of Karnataka*, pp. 72-80, Mysore, 1975.
14. *Ancient Indian Numismatics*, p. 71, Calcutta, 1921.
15. *JNSI*, XV, pp. 27-41.
16. *Studies in Indian Coins*, pp. 91-107, Delhi, 1968.
17. *JNSI*, XVIII, pp. 143-56.
18. *JUPHS*, XVIII, pp. 67 ff.; XIV, pp. 107-10.
19. Satya Prakash and Rajender Singh, *Coinage in Ancient India*, pp. 299-324, New Delhi, 1968.

3

Money Economy During *Janapada* Period (*c.* 600-320 BC)

THE *Janapada* period (600-320 BC) was politically and economically important in Indian history. Politically, it marked the end of tribal stage of society while it also gave rise for the first time to the organised states. These states formed some definite territorial units. Among these states, Magadha gradually became very powerful by the policy of imperial expansion of its rulers at the cost of other states of northern India.

Political and Economic Importance

Bimbisāra,[1] who ruled from *c.* 540-492 BC increased his power by matrimonial alliances and he conquered Aṅga, Ajātaśatru, who reigned from *c.* 492-462 BC, annexed Kāśī, Kośala and Vaiśālī. Then four rulers Udai, Aniruddha, Muṇḍa and Darśaka ruled after one another in all probability for about twenty years. In about 440 BC, Śiśunāga succeeded to the Magadha throne and ruled for forty years, i.e., till 400 BC. During his reign, he destroyed the power of Avantī and added it to the growing kingdom of Magadha. The successors of Śiśunāga ruled up to *c.* 364 BC and then, the Nandas came into power. They ruled up to 321 BC. They uprooted Aikṣvākus, Pañcāla, Kāśī, Haihayas, Kaliṅga, Asmaka. Kuru, Mithilā, Sūrasena and Vītihotras. These organised states brought stability and led to increase in production. Trade and commerce developed, and they were organised into guilds. Towns and cities came into existence. The local and international trade with the west during this period necessitated the origin of money economy. Generally the coins of this period are made of silver and are divided into two categories with their respective characteristics.[2] The early coins issued by the respective states were local, but the later coins issued during the time of the powerful Magadha rulers were of uniform weight and fabric and they were prevalent throughout the country. They were of various denominations and hence served the purpose of ordinary transactions also.

LOCAL COINAGES

The earliest coins of India are known to be the silver punch-marked coins. They were so-called because they have a number of symbols punched upon them by different punches and one after another. These coins seem to have originated during the sixth century BC when *Janapadas* came into existence. The various states[3] of which the coins are known are Sūrasena (region round Mathurā), Uttara Pañcāla (Rohilkhaṇḍ region), Dakṣiṇa Pañcāla (Doāb, Gaṅgā to Cambal), Vatsa (south of Gaṅgā up to Avantī), Kuṇāla (probably, modern Goṇḍa-Bahrāica districts), Kośala, Kāśī (Vārāṇasī), Malla (District Deoriā and its surroundings), Magadha, Vaṅga (Bengal), Kaliṅga (Orissa), Āndhra (Godāvarī and Kṛṣṇa), Aśmaka (area south of Godāvarī in Maharashtra) Mūlaka (neighbouring state of Aśmaka including Hyderabad), Saurāṣṭra (Kāṭhiāwāḍ region) and Gāndhāra (north western region).

The coins of each of these states differ from the another in their execution, fabric, weight, quality of metal and symbols. The coins of these states were current prior to the fourth century BC and they gradually disappeared when the Magadha empire extended. There were local mints in these states. These coins were issued both by the recognised guilds as well as states.

The states of Sūrasena, Uttara Pañcāla, Dakṣiṇa Pañcāla, Kuṇāla, Saurāṣṭra and Aśmaka used only one symbol on their coins and their symbols differed in their form and execution. The coins of these states, excluding Aśmaka and Kuṇāla, are pieces cut from metal sheets and stamped subsequently. The coins of Aśmaka and Kuṇāla were produced by pouring out molten metal on a flat board and stamping them when the metal was still soft.

Aśmaka Coins

The Aśmaka coins are thick, circular or oval, slightly scyphate. Their symbol is in bold relief with a deep circular incuse. The thick round edge countenances a wax impression. The symbol is simple, appears like two small pulleys attached to a bigger pulley with two separate belts. They are known in three distinct weights—99 to 108 grains, 45 to 58 grains and 21 to 23 grains.

Kuṇāla Coins

Like Aśmaka coins, the Kuṇāla coins are also thick dumpy pieces, but in shape, they are irregular and linear. The symbol upon them is impressed in bold relief with a deep circular incuse. The major difference between the Aśmaka and the Kuṇāla coins lies in the fact that the latter coins have a few small symbols around the central one, which are mostly four. These small symbols appear to have been punched at the same time when the bold symbol was punched. The bold symbol on these coins appears like a lotus pattern or three semi-circles with rounded ends placed around a pellet. The coins weigh 105 and 50 grains.

Saurāṣṭra Coins

The coins of Saurāṣṭra are thin small pieces of about 15 grains in weight. Almost the full die appears on them, only the sides are slightly out of flan. The symbol represents a bull surrounded by several minute symbols.

Sūrasena and Pañcāla Coins

The coins of the other three states — Sūrasena and the two Pañcālas — are approximately of the weight standard of 25 grains. In execution and symbology, the coins of Sūrasena and Uttara Pañcāla are almost similar. They are tiny thick pieces with only a portion of the punch or die impressed. Fish, bull, elephant with or without a rider are the main symbols found on the Uttara Pañcāla coins. Sūrasena coins have a cat or a lion like animal placed over two inverted semi-circles and taurine, suggestive of a hill. Taurine, Triskelis, crescent, etc. are found in the field on the right. The reverse of the coins of both the states is found almost blank. The Dakṣiṇa Pañcāla coins are distinct from the coins of these states. Here the coins may be identified in about a hundred varities, according to the form of the symbol. The symbols are round, composed of dots, solid and hollow circles, pellets, lines, squares, taurines, etc. These components are arranged variously in a systematic way to form the symbols. But on no coin is the symbol seen in its full form, the punches being bigger than the flans. The reverse is found stamped with quite a large number of minute marks, punched with such a heavy striking that the relief of the obverse symbols is smashed between the blows of the hammer and the resistance of the anvil, so they appear very blurred.

Gāndhāra Coins

Gāndhāra that is north-west India issued coins of the peculiar shape of a concave long bar, about 1" to 1.75" in length averaging about 0.4" in width. The bars appear to be strips cut from oblong ingots. These coins are known as Bent-bar coins. But A.D.H. Bivar[4] has used the term 'wheel-marked, to denote them. The symbol is a circular design composed of six tridents and a pole radiating from a central circle. Sometimes on the obverse, i.e., on the concave side, some minute punches are also noticed, which were subsequently punched on them as test marks. These coins have been discovered from a number of ancient sites like Taxila and Carsada in north-western India and Mirzakah and Caman Hazūrī in nothern Afghanistan.

The date of these coins seems to be fifth century BC. These coins are generally found between 150 and 180 grains. These coins are found in the part of the country which was within the bounds of the Persian Empire from the end of the sixth to the middle of the fourth century BC. Some scholars like Allan[5] think that these coins were based on the weight standard of the Persian *sigloi* and represent double *sigloi*. On the other hand V.S. Agrawal[6] and A.N. Lahiri[7] are of the view that these coins were issued to the Vedic standard of 100 *rattīs*.[8] According to D.C. Sircar,[9] *śatamāna* was equal to 320 *rattīs* as evidenced from the *Mahābhārata* and early *Dharamaśāstra* writers. This type of *śatamāna* can only be metallic piece and not a coin.

Vaṅga Coins

The coins of Vaṅga are thin, rectangular pieces, about half an inch in size and 50-52 grains in weight. They bear three distinct symbols : (i) a single decked ship; (ii) a wheel; and (iii) a six-armed symbol consisting of six arrows placed around a double circle.

The coins of Vatsa, Kośala, Kāśī, Magadha, Kaliṅga and Āndhra are thin in fabric and those of Malla and Mūlaka are thick and dumpy. The four symbols on the coins of all these states are found in three distinct orientations — (1) Two symbols in two pairs constitute the four symbols. Symbol of each pair face inwards-towards themselves, (2) one pair of one symbol and two odd symbols, i.e., three symbols constitute the group of four symbols; four different symbols constitute the group. Magadha and Vatsa issued coins in all the three forms; Kāśī issued only in the first two forms; Mūlaka in the second form, Āndhra in the second and third forms, Kośala, Malla and Kaliṅga only in the third form. These arrangements of the symbols appear to have evolved from one into the other.

Vatsa Coins

The coins of Vatsa are broad, thin pieces about an inch in size and round in shape. The symbols on them are geometrical patterns, animals, whirls and a scorpion like objects associated with some other marks. The coins weigh about 50-54 grains.

Kośala Coins

Kośala coins may be distinguished in two distinct fabrics. The earlier coins are broad, thin round pieces and have a battered obverse due to the large number of minute punchings on the reverse. The later coins are of a medium thick fabric. They also bear minute marks on the reverse, but they do not disturb symbols on the obverse. The symbols on these coins are mostly geometrical patterns, elephant bull and horse, and some forms of trees are also seen. Kośala issued coins of the monetary unit of 24 *rattīs* (42 grains/standard known as *tripāda kārṣāpaṇa*). The Kośala coins of the large size which weigh about 79 or 80 grains are most probably *dvikārṣāpaṇa* pieces of the 12 *māṣaka* standard.

Kāśī Coins

The Kāśī coins are cup-shaped or saucer like due to the mode of punching the symbols. Here on these coins, one pair of symbols is smaller in size than the other. These are known as *adhyardha kārṣāpaṇas* or one and half *kārṣāpaṇas* of 48 *rattīs* each. This coinage had two other lower denominations namely *pāda-kārṣāpaṇas* (i.e., quarter *kārṣāpaṇas*) and *pādārdha kārṣāpaṇas* (1/8th *kārṣāpaṇas*) respectively weighing 8 and 4 *rattīs*. Here, on these coins, one pair of symbol is smaller in size than the other. The weight of the coins is approximately 75 grains.

Āndhra Coins

The Āndhra coins are small, thin pieces of irregular shape and bear neatly punched symbols. An elephant facing left or right is the most common symbol and is found almost on all coins. Another frequently seen symbol on these coins is a conventionalised form of tree. Other symbols are mostly geometrical patterns made by circles, taurines, dots, curved lines, etc. The bull is also occasionally found. The coins weigh about 20 grains. Kaliṅga coins are very similar to Āndhra coins in their fabric and weight. They also follow one of its varieties for their symbols. They seem to be related with Āndhra coins.

Mūlaka Coins

A Mūlaka coin is a small thick round piece of 65 grains. Of its four symbols, two are the repetition of the same symbol. The symbol in a pair is a simple one, made of semi-oval lines, the two odd symbols are (i) six knobbed rays around a circle, and (ii) a duck-like bird flying over a hill.

Malla Coins

The coins of the kingdom of Malla may be grouped into two distinct series. The coins of one series appear like dumpy ingots and weigh 65 grains. They bear two symbols, one bigger than the other and are composed of simple lines. The coins of the other series are of two denominations. The coins of the higher denomination weigh 48-50 grains and bear four symbols and those of the lower denomination weigh only 10-12 grains and have two symbols. Their symbols are simple geometrical patterns.

MAGADHA COINS

The coins of Magadha may well be distinguished as belonging to two periods: (i) those that were issued when it was merely a kingdom and they may be called 'local' and (ii) those that were issued during the period of its imperial expansion and are found all over the country. The local Magadha coins are known in three distinct series, probably belonging to three periods. The coins of the first series are of two denominations. The higher denominations are thin, weigh 125 grains. The coins of the lower denoimination weigh only about 3 grains and have only a small lotus symbol. The coins of the second series are found in four denominations. The weights of the two denominations are 92-97 grains and 46-49 grains respectively. The coins of the other two denominations in this series are quite different in their fabric from these coins. The coins of the two denominations weigh 13-16 grains and 7-8 grains respectively. The coins of all the four denominations, though made of two different fabrics, have the symbols of a common type which appear to be some kind of six-armed symbol.

The Magadhan coins of series III are thin, broad pieces, similar to the coins of Vatsa, Kośala and Kāśī. They weigh about 72 grains and bear four well-executed bold symbols (i) the Sun, (ii) a six-armed symbol, (iii) a standing bull and (iv) a lion standing. These three series of coins were issued by the rulers of Magadha when their capital was Girivrāja, i.e., Rājagṛha.

STANDARD COINS

It appears that the Magadha monarchs finally put a stop to various experimentations with standards of weight and evolved a single denomination full *kārṣāpaṇa* coin of 32 *rattīs*, i.e., 56 grains. The *kārṣāpaṇa* series itself follows on from here three and four mark coins which are known from a famous hoard found at Golakhpur, a *muhallā* of Patna. This hoard also contained five mark *kārṣāpaṇas* which set the style for the future. Among the five symbols, the sun and six-armed symbol became more or less permanent. There is controversy among scholars about the Magadhan ruler who issued the *kārṣāpaṇa* of 32 *rattīs* with five symbols including the sun and six-armed symbol as well as attribution of these coins to the respective Magadhan rulers.

The coins of Period I from Golakhpur hoard contained 82 per cent of silver, 15 per cent of copper and 3 per cent of other impurities. The coins of Period III & IV according to Durga Prasad contained 72 to 80 per cent of silver, varying in different coins.[10]

Chronology of the Standard Coins

A.N. Lahiri[11] has tried to place the punch-marked coins of the

Magadha rulers in the chronological order as follows. The link coins of Series A, which were evidently the earliest of the five symbols 32 *rattīs* full *kārṣāpaṇas* might well have been introduced by Magadhan monarch Bimbisāra who was well acquainted with the monetary issues of both Kośala and Kāśī. The solar and the six-armed symbols were made constant and it may be incidentally noted that they were invariably retained by all of Bimbisāra's Magadhan successors till the downfall of the Mauryas.

Next in age may be the broad-flan of SeriesB known from the Golakhpur (Patna) hoard. These coins might have been issued during the reign of Ajātaśatru who shifted the capital from Rājagṛha to Pāṭaliputra.

Similarly, the broad-flan coins which strikingly retain the form of the six-armed symbols of the Golakhpur coins and are known from the Bhābhuā (Shahabad District) area and also from Jaunpur and Aurihar may be placed at a later date and may be called the coins of Series C. They might have been issued during the reigns of Udayin or Śiśunāga.

Then probably followed the thin and worn (twice issued) coins of Series D, well-known from the specimens of the 1924 Taxila hoard. These coins were originally issued with the group of five symbols by an earlier authority like a Nanda monarch but were after a considerable circulation picked up by a later authority like a Maurya sovereign and reissued by representing fresh sets of five symbols or the original blank reverse.

P.L. Gupta[12] has also tried to fix up the chronology of the punch-marked coins. According to him, the coins issued during the time of Bimbisāra are those four symbol coins which have two of their symbols (i) Sun symbol and (ii) Six-armed symbols with three arrows and three ovals alternatively placed and are known from Bhābhuā. They weigh about 72 grains.

The punch-marked coins of the new permanent standard of 32 *rattīs* known as *kārṣāpaṇa* started with the imperial expansion of Magadha from the time of Ajātaśatru who shifted his capital from Rājagṛha to Pāṭaliputra and annexed

Kāśī, Kośala and Vaiśālī. During his earlier reign, he used the coins of heavier weight with three or four symbols with the sun or six-armed symbol as known from the Golakhpur hoard. This hoard also contained the five mark *kārṣāpaṇa* of 32 *rattīs* which set the style for the future. The coins of Period I may be attributed to him and to some of his successors.

After Ajātaśatru four rulers — Udai, Aniruddha, Muṇḍa and Darśaka have issued some of the later varieties of Period I and most of the varieties of Period II. The coins of Period III were probably issued by Śiśunāga and his successors. Many coins of class I of this period which are the earliest in the series, are restruck coins, i.e., they are struck over older coins of an earlier period. These double-obversed coins of class I suggest that they were issued after some political upheaval. The fifth ruler after Ajātaśatru was deposed by the people and his *amātya* Śiśunāga was placed on the throne. This abrupt change of the rule in all probability is reflected in these coins. They may be the coins of Śiśunāga.

During the time of the Nandas, the local coinage of the states, so exterminated, would have ceased and their place was taken by the coins of the Magadha empire. In this period, the coins of the Period IV were introduced in these territories. That the coins of Period IV were the issues of the Nandas is evident from Bhir mound hoard of 1924. The hoard contains bulk of the Series IV. According to D.D. Kosambi, Magadha influence in Gāndhāra region is clear from its coins found in Taxila. It was in favour of Taxila as indicated by presence of Magadhan coins in the community, coins that could only have come in payment for goods originating in or shipped through Taxila.[13] It is also possible to suggest that this transitional phase, 16 *māṣas* seems to be the ideal weight of the coin in the epoch of the Nanda kings who are credited with the standardisation of weight. It was most probably the Nandas who initiated the bold reform in the punch-marked currency in the matter of weight, symbols and fabric. Nandas are famous for their wealth. The Nandas extended their empire to most of the sub-continent north of the Vindhya hills except the north-west (present Pakistan). Besides the Nanda coins are found all over the continent.

That the *kārṣāpaṇa* coins were introduced by the Nandas is indirectly clear from the Caman Hazūri hoard. This hoard contains Greek coins which are datable to 400 BC. It also contains a number of punch-marked coins of the Gangetic origin but none of them belong to *kārṣāpaṇa* series. This suggests that the *kārṣāpaṇa* series were issued after 400 BC during the reign of the Nandas.

Import of Silver

The question is what was the source of the metal for the manufacture of these punch-marked coins. It is well-known that there was paucity of silver, and India had to depend upon the foreign countries for its supply. During sixth or fifth century BC Gāndhāra, Sindhu and some portion of Punjab became part and parcel of Persian empire. It seems that India had extensive trade relations with Iran and its neighbouring countries. The internal trade also prospered. There was Grand Trunk Road leading from Rājagṛha through Benāras, Sāketa, Śrāvastī towards Taxila and the frontiers linking India with central and Western Asia. Even Megasthenes testifies to the Royal Road leading from the North West Frontier up to Pāṭaliputra with a length of 10,000 stades (about 1,156 miles). Some Persian coins counter marked with the punch-marked coins indicate the mutual trade relations between India and Persia. Different *Janapadas* might have benefited by the trade with Western Asia. Perhaps they obtained silver for the manufacture of the coins from these foreign countries of Western Asia. The ratio between gold and silver in India was 1 : 8 while in Persia it was 1: 133. It is not improbable that India might have exported gold in order to obtain silver.

Symbols

There is difference of opinion among scholars as to whether the five symbols on the obverse were punched all at the same time by the issuing authority or by different people at different dates. V.A. Smith thought that the numerous obverse punches seem to have been impressed by the different moneyers through whose hands the pieces passed and the reverse marks may be regarded as the signs of approval by the controlling authority.[14] But the same grouping of the symbols, noticed on a large number of coins from a single hoard, as pointed out by other writers, proves that generally they were stamped on the coins at the same time by the issuing authority.[15]

It seems that in the beginning of the *Janapada* period, the reverse side of the coins was left blank at the time of minting, but some time later, individual minute marks of indefinite varieties were impressed upon them. These reverse marks are quite different from those found on the obverse. The reverse mark system was probably used by traders and not by kings. The symbols on the reverse of earlier coins of the *Janapada* period appear haphazardly and in large numbers. It is difficult to state which of these was more important? They appear to have been punched successively by different bankers or shroffs as the coins passed through their hands. It is believed that these minute marks might have been the marks of the money testers (*rūpatarkas* or *rūpadarśakas*). What was the actual system of putting these marks by these authorities and at what intervals? D.D. Kosambi suggests that the period of indication of these marks might have been the cycle of twelve years. The theory of D.D. Kosambi[16] is interesting but it still lacks proof. It has to be admitted that the reverse marks on the early coins appear much crowded and unsystematic to be the marks of checking authorities. Walsh[17] has suggested that the reverse marks were the mint or area marks. It has been noticed that as a general rule, the lighter or the more worn out a coin is, the more is the number of symbols on its reverse.

Significance of Symbols

Formerly, it was believed that these various symbols were punched in a haphazard manner on the coins by the persons who issued them. But sustained research by these scholars proved beyond doubt that these symbols have certain significance. This conclusion is further confirmed by a passage in the fourteenth section of *Viśuddhimagga* which points out that though the symbols on the *kārṣāpaṇas* or punch-marked coins may be unintelligible to a boy or rustic, they can disclose to the experienced shroff the particular village, town or city, mountain or river site where it was manufactured as also the name of the mint-master or the authority who had issued it. No less than 300 varieties of symbols may be identified on these coins. They were used with some definite weight system. They enable to isolate the coins of one area from those of another, of one state from those of another and of one period from those of another.

Theobold[18] divided the various punch-marked coins into six classes as follows :

1. Human figures such as *agni*,
2. Implements and works of man such as *stūpas*, bow and arrow,
3. Animals — bull, elephant, horse, goat, dog, etc.,
4. Trees, branches or fruits: with railings, supporting *chatra*, umbrella, etc.,
5. Symbols connected with solar panels or Śaivite worship, *liṅga*, *triśūla*, etc.
6. Miscellaneous and unknown symbols.

Thomas[19] divided them, however, into four categories as follows :

(i) Heavenly bodies such as Sun,

(ii) Man and Animals,

(iii) Home life such as plough, cups, vases and bows,

(iv) Imaginary devices such as *caitya* and tree.

According to P.L. Gupta,[20] the subject-matter used in the symbols shows an agrarian society depicting natural and man-made objects, religious and mystical symbols (some Buddhist), human figures (possibly deities) and abstract shapes. He is surrounded by the elements of nature such as animals, birds, fish, reptiles, insects, trees and plants of many kinds. The elephant is shown on one type with a rider, the dog as a popular subject and the horse, camel, buffalo, goat are all represented. One of the most beautiful representation of man is the former appears on a rare coin in series I where two bulls are shown yoked to a plough. Some of the more troublesome creatures of nature are also represented — the rhinoceros, snake, scorpion, crocodile as well as the cactus or thorn edge.

The man-made products of this society are profusely illustrated though identification of many them is difficult. Among the most interesting is the steelyard or balance which must have been used in the process of coinage as well as other trading activities. Various utensils can be recognised such as candleabrum, arrow tipped standard and elephant goad. The only weapons seem to be the bow and arrow and the spear which is seen in combination with many other, objects.

Religious, mystical and ritualistic symbols are common though once again it is difficult to know what they mean. The taurine "  " as an adjunct with other marks is a mark of auspicious meaning. In series IV appears tree in railing. It seems to represent the sacred tree. Buddha found enlightenment under a *pīpal* tree at Gayā. There are many wheels which cannot be identified as Buddhist.

The other aspects of Indian society which can be seen on the coins relate to the abstract phenomena which are expressed by geometric shapes and designs. Some of these appear to be celestial objects, indicating that observation of the skies was practised and that some importance was attached to it.

Durga Prasad's[21] view is that the earlier punch-marked coins have six time more numerous Indus Valley symbols than those on the later coins. There are 29 symbols on the punch-marked coins with similar marks on the seals found in Indus Valley. This view is untenable because the coins in the early hoards of Golakhpur and the Paila hoard have very few of the Indus Valley symbols. Among the common symbols, we have squares, rectangles, wheels, arrow-heads which being common objects, could have been selected by people widely separated from each other. It is held that the symbols on the Indus Valley seals have a syllabic value which is unlikely to be the case on the punch-marked coins. According to Durga Prasad,[22] a few of the symbols appear to correspond with the description of some of the *mudrās* in *Tantra* literature. But the works relied upon are of much later period than the punch-marked coins.

The most common and permanent symbols are the Sun and the six-armed symbol. Solar dynasties were ruling in Ancient India. It is, therefore, not improbable that the solar symbol was originally intended to denote the solar origin of the dynasty of the issuer and when once it had become popular, it may have been mechanically copied on the coinage of other dynasties as well. According to P.L. Gupta,[23] the Sun indicates the eternal authority of the state. The six-armed symbol is not personal but possibly connected with the mint.

On most of the punch-marked coins, there are five symbols on the obverse. Two of these symbols, the Sun and the six-armed symbol are constant. Durga Prasad[24] has suggested that the third symbol probably changed with the king, the fourth with the year and the fifth with the locality. D.D. Kosambi[25] is of the view that they may refer to the names of the ruler, his father and his grandfather. According to P.L. Gupta,[26] the third, fourth and fifth marks, which are termed as class, group and variety marks also vary. It is equally possible that one of the symbols may have stood for the Governor, the other for the mint-master and the third for the place or province of issue.

P.L. Gupta[27] has tried to determine the chronological sequence by the fabrics of the coins. The coins of the Periods I and II are manufactured from thin broad pieces which are not known in subsequent periods. A few coins of Period II are found to be made of medium fabric which is the exclusive fabric of Period III. This fabric is rarely seen in this series. The rare use of medium fabric in Period II and thin fabric in Period III indicates the transition from one fabric to the other. The coins of Period IV are also the medium fabric and show their continuation along with Period III but some of the coins of Period IV are found of thick fabric showing transition towards Period V.

Copper Currency

Copper currency was also prevalent during the *Janapada* period, but it was not so popular like the silver one. A. Cunningham[28] identifies the coins found in Pañcāla region with *viṁśatikas* and their lower denominations.

Early cast copper coins are uninscribed, and are divided into two broad sub-categories — (1) Local and (2) Universal. Universal types are found in both round and square shapes. They bear the devices of Elephant, *svastika*, triangle-headed standard and taurine and on the reverse crescent-topped three-peaked hill, hollow-cross, tree in railing and taurine. They come from almost all over northern India. The local issues bear on the obverse "Elephant, triangle-headed standard, *svastika* and a symbol consisting of a pellet with four crescents around and in the reverse 'taurine, hollow cross, elaborate tree in railing and crescent topped three-peaked hill". A.K. Lahiri[29] is of opinion that uninscribed cast copper pieces of the universal types were widely current during the Maurya rule, because they are often found along with silver punch-marked coins, majority of which are believed to be of the Maurya period. But rare uninscribed cast coins, which were evidently in use in restricted localities, probably originated in an earlier time, i.e., about the beginning of fourth or even at the end of the fifth century BC. It is possible that the local types of uninscribed cast issues were probably minted by local guilds in isolated regions. P.L. Gupta[30] attributed these coins to the third century BC. A.S. Altekar[31] thinks that it is quite possible that the motifs of these coins may be earlier than the punch-marked silver coins and were later adopted by the Mauryas.

That the Indians had been using cast coins even before the invasion of Alexander, the Great is proved by the statement of one of his companions, viz., Nearchus. According to him,

Indians used only cast bronze, but not hammered. Cast coins referred to by Nearchus were evidently uninscribed. This proves that even before the Mauryas, cast coins were current. It is possible to attribute the universal cast coins found in northern India to the Nandas who conquered this region.

Issuing Authority

There are various opinions regarding the issuing authority among the scholars. V.A. Smith[32] observed that the punch-marked coinage was a private coinage issued by guilds and silver-smith with the permission of the ruling authority. But after the systematic study of the coin hoards of definitely provenance, D.B. Spooner,[33] D.R. Bhandarkar [34] and E.H.C. Walsh[35] suggested that the punch-marked coins were issued by a central authority, i.e., the state. Among later writers commenting on Smith's views, J.N. Banerjee[36] says: 'There is little doubt that the marks were those of central authority that guaranteed the genuineness of the metal and the correctness of the weight. S.K. Chakrabortty[37] says that practically all or the majority of the coins examined by Smith are surely state issues, but at the same time, he also maintains that originally the punch-marked coins were being issued by private bankers whose symbols have not yet been recognised by scholars owing to insufficient study and to the fact that the private issues were mostly called back and given new impression when the state entered into the field.

According to D.C. Sircar,[38] there is some evidence to show that all punch-marked coins were not issued by the state, that some of them were certainly issued by guilds and silver-smiths as Smith suggested and that such coins were in circulation side by side with those issued by the states. The evidence is primarily supplied by a passage in Buddhaghoṣa's *Visuddhimagga* composed in fifth century AD.

This passage makes it abundantly clear that the symbols on the *kārṣāpaṇas* or punch-marked coins only indicated the place wherein a particular piece was made and the goldsmith who made it. Apparently, none of the symbols indicated the state in which it was made or by which it was issued. If there was any such symbol, that would have naturally been regarded as far more important than the others and Buddhaghoṣa could have hardly failed to mention it. Thus the manufacture of the *kārṣāpaṇa* referred to in the *Visuddhimagga* passage, was not directly associated with the state's permission as it is not known from it. The minting of coins in villages is also an interesting information supplied by the passage.

Money-Economy As known From Literary Sources

Some literary works give useful information regarding money-economy during *Janapada* period. The *Arhīya* Section of the *Aṣṭādhyāyī* (*Adhyāya* V, *Pāda* 1, *Sūtra*, 1937) furnishes some important data in respect of the oldest coinage of India.[39] The general sense governing these *sūtras* is that of *Tena Kṛtam* (V.I.37), 'purchased with that' and *Tad-arhati* (V.I.63) 'worth that'. An attempt has been made by scholars to bring together the available evidence from the *sūtras* and their commentaries and to discuss it with a view to identifying the denominations and value of those coins in the light of facts known from ancient Indian Numismatic history.

Gold Coins

Pāṇini mentions *niśka* in three *sūtras*. The first means 'purchased for' or 'worth' one *niśka*. The second refers to a transaction concluded for two or three *niśkas*. In the third, there appears to be the real title indicating the degree of opulence of the person so designated. Pāṇini does not name the *suvarṇa* coin but same is implied in *Sūtra Hiraṇya — parimāṇam dhane* (VI.2.55) which refers to a person's wealth in terms of coined gold e.g. *dvi-suvarṇa-dhanam*. In another *sūtra*, Pāṇini refers to pieces of gold equal to a standard weight. Whereas literary evidence supports the existence of gold currency. So far not a single specimen of a gold punch-marked coin of any denomination has been found in any hoard.

Silver Coinage

ŚATAMĀNA

Śatamāna is referred to in the *sūtra* V.I.27. An article purchased for one *śatamāna* was called *śatamānam*. The denominations of *śatamāna* are known as *ardha-śatamāna*, *śāna* and *ardha-śāna*. Pāṇini refers to a range of prices in terms of *śāna* coins (V.1.35; V.1.36). This shows *śāna* to have been quite a popular coin. This *śāna* as a real silver coin was one-eighth of one *śatamāna* as stated positively in the *Mahābhārata* (*Araṇyakaparva*, 134.14).

VIṀŚATIKA

Pāṇini knew a coin called *viṁśatika*. (V.1.27; V.I.32; V.1.24; V.1.63). D.C. Sircar takes it to be 2/5 of *śatamāna*, i.e., 40 *rattis* or 72 grains. V.S. Agrawal means it to be a punch-marked coin of 20 *māṣas*.

TRIṀŚATIKA

Besides *viṁśatika*, Pāṇini also mentions a specific coin named *triṁśatika* (V.1.24), a name which is found only in *Aṣṭādhyāyī* and not elsewhere. D.C. Sircar regards *triṁśatika* to be coin of 60 *rattīs* or 108 grains while V.S. Agrawal takes it to be of 30 *māṣas* or 60 *rattīs* of the *kārṣāpaṇa* series.

KĀRṢĀPAṆA

Kārṣāpaṇa was the standard money of the time of Pāṇini. When Pāṇini refers to big sums (V.1.27, 29, 34) without specifying the name of the coin, it is the silver *kārṣāpaṇa*. The word *rūpa* in Pāṇini's *Sūtra* (V.2.120) has been used in the sense of the symbols stamped on a *kārṣāpaṇa* coin. *Kārṣāpaṇa* had its sub-multiples of which Pāṇini mentions 1/2 as *ardha* (V.1.48) and *bhāga* (V.1.49), 1/4 as *pāda* (V.1.34) and 1/16 as *māṣa* (V.1.34). Besides Pāṇini uses both *kārṣāpaṇa* (V.I.29) and *paṇa* (V.1.34).

Copper Currency

The copper *māṣa* was a sub-multiple of the copper *kārṣāpaṇa* and weighted 5 *rattīs*, i.e., 1/16th of a *tāmrika paṇa* of 80 *rattīs*. The *kārṣāpaṇa* was the standard unit of copper currency also. Pāṇini refers to *adhyardha-māṣa* which shows his acquaintance with an actual coin called *ardha-māṣa*. This *ardha-māṣa* was a copper coin.

Pāṇini's *Aṣṭādhyāyī* merely mentions the denominations of coins, but the case is different in regard to the Buddhist *Jātakas*. They reveal what part the stamped metallic currency played in the manifold transactions of the people at the early period.

From the evidence of the *Jātakas*, it appears that some sort of gold coinage was prevalent. As gold is the most precious metal, it was used in connection with the hoards of money, munificent gifts and so forth. In the *Kuhaka Jātaka*,[40] there is a mention of specific class of coins — gold coins — namely *niśkas* for the valuation of rich farmer's hoarding. In the *Vasantara Jātaka*,[41] there is reference to a thousand *niśkas*. In a third *Jātaka*, we find two classes of coins specified, viz., the *kārṣāpaṇas* and *niśkas*.[42] The number of *kārṣāpaṇas* is one thousand while the number of *niśkas* is one hundred. The first evidently is the silver and the second is the gold money of the country of Kāśī.

Another class of gold coins known to *Jātaka* literature is *hiraṇya-suvarṇa*. In the *Bhūridatta Jātaka*, there is mention of the *hiraṇya*, *suvarṇa*, etc.[43] The phrase *hiraṇya-suvarṇa* occurs also in *Jātaka*.[44] *Suvarṇa* in this as in other places where it is associated with *hiraṇya* must stand not for gold but a type of gold coins. Gold coins of a still smaller denomination called *suvarṇa-māṣaka* have been used. In the *Udaya-Jātaka*, there is mention of *suvarṇa-māṣaka*.[45] Again in the *Saṅkhapāla Jātaka*, there is reference to *suvarṇa-māṣaka*.[46] *Māṣaka* denotes a coin of the *māṣa* weight. A *suvarṇa-māṣaka* is therefore a gold coin which is equal to one *māṣa* in weight according to the standard of gold coinage.

Thus, three types of gold coins were current. Of the lowest value was the *māṣaka*, of a higher denomination was the *suvarṇa* and of a still higher denomination, the *niśka*.[47]

Kārṣāpaṇa is frequently referred to in the *Jātaka* literature. It was of three varieties — gold, silver and copper. Gold *kārṣāpaṇa* however appears to be seldom referred to, the common types being either silver or copper. The *Bābu Jātaka* tells us of a merchant of Kāśī country who, when died, left behind a treasure of forty crores of gold pieces.[48] Here the treasure is stated to consist of forty crores of gold pieces which are afterwards referred to as *kārṣāpaṇas* by giving of which the hoard is said to have been exhausted.

Silver *kārṣāpaṇa* was looked upon as the standard coin. Its different divisions were *ardha-kārṣāpaṇa*, *pāda-kārṣāpaṇa*, *catur-māṣaka*, *tri-māṣaka*, *dvi-māṣaka*, *eka-māṣaka*, *ardha-māṣaka* and *kākaṇika*. There were wide circulation of this money in the society depicted by the *Jātaka* tales.

The *Gāmanī-canda Jātaka*[49] refers to the pair of oxen being twnenty-four and of the horse one thousand *kārṣāpaṇas*. Of course, there must be silver *kārṣāpaṇas*, as copper or gold *kārṣāpaṇas* would be too low or too high a price to pay for those animals. Another *Jātaka* gives us the story of a landed proprietor who loses his parcel of a thousand *kārṣāpaṇas* which falls into the river he is crossing. The parcel is, however, swallowed by a big fish which is caught by a fisherman, and is sold for seven *māṣakas* to the landed proprietor who is thrilled with joy to recover his money as his wife was dressing the fish.[50] These two must be silver *kārṣāpaṇas* as the seven *māṣakas* mentioned here as the price of the fish can be a copper token of silver money only.

A professional assessor is paid eight *kārṣāpaṇas* as his fee[51] and a rice plump dog is bought for one *kārṣāpaṇa*.[52] A decent ass is for eight *kārṣāpaṇas* and a fawn for one or two *kārṣāpaṇas* only.[53] A bundle of grass, again fetches one *māṣaka*[54] and for the same coin can be had a jar of liquor.[55] A *māṣaka* or *ardha-māṣaka* again is the daily wage of a coolie.[56] And a dead mouse is purchased for a single *kākaṇika*[57] almost the lowest money price of the day, to serve as food to the cat in a tavern, and so on. The fact that in the early Buddhist works when any big sum of money is specified, no name of the coin is adduced, that of *kārṣāpaṇa* being understood as is quite clear by its occasional metion.[58] *kārṣāpaṇa* has also been referred in the sense of copper. A carriage in Benāras has been taken by the hour costs eight *kārṣāpaṇas*. The same amount was considered to be a remuneration fit for a barber. Again, tailoring repairs if well done, in a suburb of Benāras, brought in money at a rate of 1000 pieces a day.[59] Similarly a fisherman is fixed eight *kārṣāpaṇas*.[60]

From the account of *Jātakas*, it is known that treasure troves were the property of the state and the mis appropriation and improper use of such hoards made one liable for punishments. In one *Jātaka*[61] the king says that masterless money comes to me. The same idea is repeated in such phrases as treasure trove is a royal prerogative.[62] Unclaimed treasure belongs to king.[63] This royal privilege is also referred in the *Dharmasūtra*.[64]

The commentary *Sāmanta-Pāsādikā* of Buddhaghoṣa on the *Vinaya Piṭaka* tells us that during the time of the king Bimbisāra in city Rājagṛha, a *kahāpaṇa* was equal to twenty *māṣakas*. Therefore one *pāda* equalled five *māṣakas*. This statement is confirmed by the *Saratthadīpanī* of Śāriputta Thera, a commentary on the *Sāmanta-pāsādika*.[65]

The *Kātyāyana Smṛti* preserves a tradition that *kārṣāpaṇa* equalled twenty and not sixteen *māṣakas*.[66]

The above coin standards and their denominations as known from literary sources are also actually known from the specimen during the *Janapada* period. The coins of the weight between 150-80 grains found in the Gāndhāra region may be identified with ancient *śatamāna*. Coins of the weights 90, 80, 43, 20 and 7 grains found here may be meant for the denominations of *śatamāna* as mentioned by Pāṇini.

Actual Specimen

Actual specimen of *viṁśatika* and *trimsatika* are also available. Durga Prasad obtained heavy *kārṣāpaṇa* of silver from

Rājagṛha. From their fabric and symbols, it can be said with certainty that they represent an earlier stage than the 32 *rattī kārṣāpaṇa*. The coins with the weight of 78 to 80 grains should be identified with *viṁśatika* and those weighing 104 grains and 105-07 grains or about 58 grains with *triṁśatika*.

The silver punch-marked coin of which numerous hoards have been found in various parts of India should be identified with *kārṣāpaṇa*. It was the standard medium of exchange from about sixth century BC. A few early copper punch-marked and cast coins discovered may be identified with the *Tāmrakārṣāpaṇas* of the literary sources.

Foreign Coins

During this period, foreign coins were prevalent in north-west India because of their rule and trade relations. This is clear from Caman Hazūrī Hoard, a locality of Kābul (1938) and the Bhīr Mound hoard of Taxila. The former hoard comprised few denominations of Greek, Money, Persian *sigloi* along with Indian coins known as full-sized wheel-marked coins or Bent-bar coins. The Bhīr Mound hoard of Taxila contains a large number of punch-marked coins, Bent-bar coins and two Greek coins of Philip and Alexander.

Some silver coins of the Cock and Caduceous type with the Greek legends having the Indian weight 56 grains are attributed to Sophytes, ruler of Punjab in the fourth century BC. According to Arrian and Strabo, Alexander during his invasion of India met this ruler with whom he came to an understanding. He should be identified with Pāṇini's *Saubhūti*. That the Greek Colony of the Yavanas continued during the Maurya period is confirmed by the inscriptions of Aśoka.

Notes

1. Gupta, P.L., *Silver Punch-marked Coins of the Magadhan Maurya Kārṣāpaṇa Series*, Bombay, 1985. *The Chronology of Bimbisāra and his Successors as fixed* by P.L. Gupta has been utilised.
2. Gupta, P.L., *Coins*, p. 10 f, New Delhi, 1985.
3. *Ibid.*
4. *NC*, 1954, p. 163.

5. Allan, J., *BMCAI*, London, 1936, Indian edn. 1975.
6. *JNSI*, XV, pt. I, pp. 27-41.
7. *Ibid.*, XXXV, pp. 1-39.
8. *Śatapatha Brāhmaṇa*, XIII. 2.3.2.
9. *Studies in Indian Coins*, pp. 48-72, Delhi, 1968.
10. Gupta, P.L., *The Amravati Hoard of Silver Punch-marked Coins*, p. 3, Hyderabad, 1963.
11. *JNSI*, XXXV, pp. 1-39.
12. *Coins*, Hyderabad, 1963, *Silver Punch-marked Coins of the Magadha-Maurya Kārṣāpaṇa, Series*, Bombay, 1985.
13. Bhandarkar, D.R., *Indian Numismatics*, p. 154, Calcutta, 1912.
14. Smith, V.A., *CCIM*, Oxford, 1906, Vol. I, p. 133.
15. Allan, J., *BMCAI*, London 1936, p. xix.
16. *Indian Numismatics*, p. 153, New Delhi, 1981.
17. *Punch-marked Coins from Taxila, MASI*, p. 59.
18. *JASB*, 1890, pp. 182-268.
19. *NC*, IV, p. 263.
20. *Silver Punch-marked Coins of the Magadha-Maurya Kārṣāpaṇa Series*, p. 188, London, 1985.
21. *NS*, XLVI.
22. *NS*, XLVII.
23. *Silver Punch-Marked Coins of the Magadha-Maurya Kārṣāpaṇa Series*, p. 25. Bombay, 1985.
24. *NS*, p. xlv and xlvii.
25. *Indian Numismatics*, p. 153, New Delhi, 1981.
26. *Silver Punch-marked Coins of the Magadha-Maurya Kārṣāpaṇa Series*, p. 1, Bombay, 1985.
27. *The Amravati Hoard of Silver Punch-marked Coins*, p. 148, Hyderabad, 1963.
28. *Coins of Ancient India*, London, 1891.
29. *JNSI*, XXXV, pp. 1-39.
30. *Coins*, p. 18, New Delhi, 1969.
31. *JNSI*, XV, p. 26.
32. *CCIM*, Oxford, 1906, Vol. I, p. 133.
33. *ASI, AR*, 1915-16, p. 153.
34. *Ancient Indian Numismatics*, pp. 98-99, Calcutta, 1921.
35. *MASI*, No. 19, *JRAS*, Suppl. Oct. 1924, p. 175.
36. *Comprehensive History of India*, Vol. II, Ed. by Sastri, K.A., Nilakanta, p. 777, Bombay, 1977.
37. *A Study of Ancient Indian Numismatics*, pp. 129-30, Delhi, 1973, Second edn.
38. *Studies in Indian Coins*, p. 103, Delhi, 1968.
39. *JNSI*, XV, pp. 27-41.

40. *Jāt.*, I, 375 & ff.
41. *Ibid.*, VI. 546. 28, 576.6.
42. *Ibid.*, IV. 458.6, 460.28, 461.7 & 10.
43. *Ibid.*, VI. 186-3.
44. *Ibid.*, VI. 69.18.
45. *Ibid.*, IV. 106.1, 107.17.
46. *Ibid.*, V. 164.15.6.
47. Bhandarkar, D.R., *Ancient Indian Numismatics*, p. 52, Calcutta, 1921.
48. *Jāt.*, I. 478.7 and 16.
49. *Ibid.*, II. 305-19. 306, 19.20.
50. *Ibid.*, II. 424.19-20.
51. *Ibid.*, IV. 138. 1.7, 16-20.
52. *Ibid.*, II.247.2.
53. *JRAS*, 1901, p. 883.
54. *Jāt.*, III.130.8.
55. *Ibid.*, I.350.11.
56. *Ibid.*, III.326.17
57. *Ibid.*, I.120-20.
58. *Ibid.*, IV.378. 13-15, VI. 97. 1-2 etc.
59. *JRAS*, 1901, pp. 88. 3-4.
60. *Jāt*, I.483.21. 3. IV.485.
61. *IV.*, 485.
62. *Jāt.*, I.398.
63. *Ibid.*, VI.348.
64. *Gautama Dharma Sūtra*, X.43.
65. *JNSI*, XV, pp. 27-41.
66. Bhandarkar, D.R., *Ancient Indian Numismatics*, p. 186, Calcutta, 1921.

4

Money Economy During Mauryan Period (*c.* 319 to 187 BC)

MONEY economy seems to have made considerable headway during the Mauryan period. This is known from the *Arthaśāstra* of Kauṭilya as well as from the findings of the silver punch-marked coins in different parts of the country. They are of uniform type, and they were in circulation throughout the country. Most of the coins are silver but some are also in copper. They are of definite weight with certain denominations. The issuing of coinage was the duty of the State, and it was the highly evolved system. Salaries were paid in cash and coins must have been used even in ordinary transactions. Gradually, the great debasement of coinage is noticed.

Increasing Necessity of Money

The Mauryan rulers brougnt about the unification of northern India by their conquest, and they ruled over vast empire. In order to defend the different parts of the far-flung empire, they maintained the strong army. Besides, they employed vast bureaucracy consisting of superintendents and subordinate officers. The Mauryan state was in necessity not only to pay a large standing army and a great number of civil servants, but also to facilitate the growth of trade. The pressure of rapidly increasing volume of trade in the new areas opened up in the south required large amount of money than the old trading system between India and Mesopotamia. The punch-marked coins of the Mauryan period are found in great quantity in the south. Most of them seem to have travelled from the north as they do not show any sign of having been minted there. This shows commercial relations between the north and south during the Mauryan period. Artisans were organised into guilds (*śreṇīs*) and thier products had to be paid in cash. Articles were to be traded at source. The trader was forced to add value to his product by further manufacture and for transportation. This undoubtedly helps to explain the remarkable homogeneity of coin types throughout the country; since the merchants would have been continuously carrying coin to and fro in the trading process. The circulation of money was not confined to the town as the farmer was allowed to trade his own food surplus and pay his taxes in cash.

Besides trade, money was needed to finance great buildings built by Maurya kings for instance, Candragupta Maurya is known to have built the great palace. Aśoka built several pillars and *stūpas*. This required huge amount of money. Aśoka is known to have spent large sum of money for the propagation of Buddhism. As there was scarcity of silver for the manufacture of coins, the Mauryas seem to have imported silver in large quantity from the Greek kingdoms of Western Asia and Egypt. India maintained not only diplomatic relations but also carried on a brisk commercial exchange with these countries. From the account of Megasthenes, it is clear that large number of foreigners used to reside in Pāṭalipūtra, capital of the Mauryas.

Metal and Coins

Kauṭilya does not speak of the minting of gold coins at all although reference is made eleswhere in the *Arthaśāstra* to the making of the *suvarṇa* by the goldsmith. Thus gold appears to have been outside ordinary use. As Kauṭilya's *suvarṇa* and *dharaṇa* are practically of the same weight standard, it may be inferred that 16 silver *dharaṇas* made one gold *suvarṇa*.

Paṇa and *māṣaka* mentioned in the *Arthaśāstra* are regarded as the standard coins respectively of silver and copper. None of the names such as *śatamāna, śaṇa, viṁśatika* and *triṁśatika* are found in the *Arthaśāstra*. On the other hand, the *Kātyāyana Śrauta-Sūtra* contains a reference to a coin called *śatamāṇa*. It shows that *śatamāna* was known till Mauryan period.[1] Kātyāyana on Pāṇini (V.1.25) records one more name, viz., *prati* which seems a new name for *kārṣāpaṇa*. In the *Arthaśāstra*, coinage and the mint are described only in one chapter (Book II, chapter XII). Here it is stated that the superintendent of the mint (*lakṣaṇādhyakṣa*) shall carry on the manufacture of silver coins (*rūpya-rūpa*) made up of four parts (i.e., one-fourth) of copper and one-sixteenth (*māṣa*) of any one of the metals *tīkṣṇa, trapu, śīsa* and *añjana*. There shall be *paṇa, ardha-paṇa* (half-*paṇa*), *pāda-paṇa* (quarter) and *aṣṭabhāga paṇa*. Copper coins (*tāmra-rūpa*) made up of four parts of alloy (*pādajīva*) shall be a *māṣa, ardha-māṣa* (half *māṣa*), *pāda-māṣa* (*ardha-kākaṇī*). The copper *māṣaka* may be no other than the copper *paṇa* of 80 *rattīs*. It is so-called because it was one-sixteenth of the standard silver coin in value.

In the *Arthaśāstra*, the word *rūpa* has been used in the sense of a coin. A coin was thus usually called a *rūpya* owing to a *rūpa* being imprinted on it by the stroke of a hammer. From the content of *Arthaśāstra*, it seems that another coin *ṣoḍaṣa bhāgika*[2] also existed.

It appears that a coin of 32 *rattīs* known as *kārṣāpaṇa* continued to be the standard until during the Mauryan period. Several punch-marked coins of the Mauryan period discovered at different places are based upon the *kārṣāpaṇa* of 32 *rattīs* and its denominations. *Dvikārṣāpaṇas* of this weight standard were found in the hoard of Sultānpur of the former Bombay Presidency. Their weight was 108 grains. The Lolapura hoard consisted of 1351 pieces which were all *ardha-kārṣāpaṇas*, each weighing about 26.5 grains. The *pāṇḍya* hoard of punch-marked coins seems to have consisted of *ardha-kārṣāpaṇas*. The weight of its coins is said to vary between 19 to 25 grains. Quarter *kārṣāpaṇas* are often known as *pādas*. The Koṅkaṇa find weighing between 12.9 and 14.7 grains are obviously 1/4 *kārṣāpaṇa* pieces of 32 *rattīs* standard. *Dvi-māṣakas* are found in Patna Museum. Silver *māṣaka* of 2 *rattīs* known as Minuscules bearing Mauryan symbols have also been found at Gāndhāra, Narmadā Valley, Nāsik and Mahānadī Valley.[3]

It appears that the local Bent-bar coinage of Taxila-Gāndhāra did not end until 312-03 BC when Taxila and Gāndhāra were incorporated within the Mauryan realm of Candragupta.[4] The specimen weighing about 43 grains are obviously intended to be *pāda-śatamāna* or *dvi-śāna* and small Bent-bar coins weighing about 19.5 grains are obviously intended to be *śāna*.[5]

The unit of old copper money known as *paṇa* or *kārṣāpaṇa* weighs 80 *rattīs* or 146 grains.[6] In ancient Avantī, Ayodhyā, Kośāmbī, Gāndhāra and Magadha, copper coins based on 80 *rattīs* and its sub-multiples have been found.[7]

Nature and Value of Kauṭilya's *Paṇa*

There is controversy among scholars about the nature and value of Kauṭilya's *paṇa* which is the standard coin very often mentioned or implied in the *Arthaśāstra* in the specification of salaries and fines. Kauṭilya[8] prescribes the various grades of salaries to be paid to the kings officials and dependants as 48,000, 24,000, 12,000, 8,000, 4,000, 2,000, 1,000, 500, 250, 120 and 60 of the standard coin, no doubt *paṇa*. The chief conductor of sacrifice, the teacher (of the princes), the Chief Minister, the Chief Priest, the Commander-in-Chief of the army, the crown prince, the queen mother and the chief queen were each to receive 48,000, while the artisans and craftsman (carpenters, etc.) were allotted 120 and servants doing miscellaneous work only 60.

Scholars do not agree as to the value of the coin (*paṇa*) intended and the period for which the salary was to be paid. K.P. Jayaswal[9] holds that the salaries were yearly and that the *paṇas* were coins of silver. V.R.R. Dikshitar[10] thinks that the salaries were to be paid monthly, while K.V. Rangaswami Aiyangar[11] believes that the salaries were paid monthly in golden *paṇas*, P.V. Kane[12] holds that the salaries were meant to be paid monthly in copper *paṇas* by Kautilya.

As to the question whether the salaries mentioned in the *Arthaśāstra* were intended to be monthly or annual, attention of scholars may be drawn to the following passage occurring in chapter 28 of the work. Shamasastry translates it as follows, "Three hundred and fifty-four days and nights is a working year. Such a work (actually, such a year, i.e., such annual work) shall be paid for more or less in proportion of its quantity at the end of the month of *Āṣāḍha*." This may suggest that the salaries of the royal officials as mentioned in the *Arthaśāstra*, were paid on an annual basis.

P.V. Kane[13] observes "Artisans and Craftsmen, were, according to Kauṭilya, to get 120 *paṇas* a month,* while according to Manu, even the lowest menial was to get a *paṇa* a day. Therefore 120 *paṇas* of copper were the monthly salary of an artisan (according to Kauṭilya)." It will, however, be seen that Kauṭilya specifically describes *paṇa* as a silver coin while he may have spoken of annual and not monthly salaries. If calculated on this basis, an artisan, according to *Arthaśāstra*, received 10 silver coins a month. We have seen how 16 copper coins were usually regarded as equivalent to one silver coin.

It is well-known that ancient Indian works of law often speak of the three fixed fines or amercements called *sāhasa*, viz., *prathama sāhasa* (first amercement), *madhyama-sāhasa* (middle amercement) and *uttama-sāhasa* (highest amercement) Manu[15] (VIII. 138) and Viṣṇu (IV. 10) state that the first, middling and highest amercements are respectively 250, 540 and 1080 *paṇas*. Nārada (*sāhasa* verses 7-8) says that the lowest limits of the three amercements are respectively 100, 500 and 1000 *paṇas*. There is absolutely no doubt Manu and Yājñavalkya mean by *paṇa* the copper coin of 80 *rattis*. In chapter 74 of the *Arthaśāstra*, Kauṭilya gives the following specification of the three fixed fines: (1) first amercement — between 48 and 96 *paṇas*, (2) Middle amercement — between 200 and 500 *paṇas* and (3) highest amercement — between 200 and 1000 *paṇas*. It will be seen that broadly speaking,

---

* If this were yearly, they would get only 10 *paṇas* a month.

there is not much disagreement amongst the authorities on the amounts of the amercements. Most authorities speak of *paṇa* as a copper coin. Kauṭilya alone regards it as a silver coin. If it is the same as his *dharaṇa*, which weighs nearly 80 *rattīs*. It was, therefore, suggested that by *paṇa* in these cases, Kauṭilya probably means the well-known copper coin of 80 *rattīs* and not the silver *paṇa* mentioned elsewhere in the *Arthaśāstra*.

It may be further pointed out that often the same amount of *paṇas* for particular offences are prescribed by Kauṭilya and, Yājñavalkya who undoubtedly uses the name *paṇa* for the copper coin. In chapters 89-90 of the *Arthaśāstra* Kauṭilya prescribes the following punishments :

(1) when one falsely accuses another of theft, while in reality the latter is guilty of adultery, the complainant shall be fined 500 *paṇas*; he who lets off an adulterer by receiving money shall pay a fine of eight times that amount,

(2) adultery with a nun shall be punished by a fine of 24 *paṇas*.

(3) a man forcing his connection with a harlot shall be fined 12 *paṇas* while many persons committing rape on a single such woman shall each of them pay a fine of 24 *paṇas*.

The above three regulations may be compared with Yājñavalkya II. 304, 296 and 294 respectively. It will be seen that the numbers of *paṇas* prescribed by Yājñavalkya for the offences in question are exactly the same as in the *Arthaśāstra*. The fact that the same amounts of *paṇas* for particular offences have been prescribed by both Kauṭilya and Yājñavalkya creates a difficulty in regarding Kauṭilya's *paṇa* as a silver coin when Yājñavalkya *paṇa* was certainly a copper coin. This no doubt suggest that Kauṭilya's *paṇa* in case of fines was really a copper coin (*māṣa*, 1/16th of the standard silver coin in value).

It seems that just as the name *kārṣāpaṇa* was applied to the coins and weight of gold, silver and copper although it was often exclusively used to indicate the silver coin, the name *paṇa* even if it was often regarded as the exclusive appellation of the copper coin, was similarly sometimes applied to coins of gold and silver as well.

The annual income of civil servants as mentioned by Kauṭilya in *paṇa* identified with silver coins is possible looking at the immense value of Mauryan coinage indicated by the abundance of modern funds — more even than that of the Nandas. The different interpretation of *paṇa* in the sense of copper coin in connection with the fines is due to traditions.

Technique of Manufacture

How the coins were manufactured in the early period is nowhere recorded in the extant literature. However, Kauṭilya, the Minister of Candragupta Maurya, has incidentally referred to the counterfeiters of coins (*kūṭa-rūpakāraka*) in his *Arthaśāstra*, the book on the state craft, which was compiled in the fourth century BC. Therein, he has given a list of objects that were used in the manufacture of coins. It shows that metal was first melted in crucibles (*māṣa*) and purified with alkalis (*kṣāra*); then the metal was beaten into sheets on an anvil (*adhikarṇi*) with a hammer (*muṣṭikā*) and then cut into pieces with clippers (*saṇḍānsa*) and finally, they were stamped with dies or punches having symbols (*bimbatarika*).

The actual coins of the period also show that they were cut and clipped to adjust them into proper weights. Unlike today, they have the shapes of all conceivable linear geometrical forms, round oval and elliptical. These ancient coins bear the stamps of one to five punches, i.e., unlike today more than one punch was used to stamp the coins. By reason of this manufacturing technique, these coins are known as punch-marked coins.

Symbols of the Coins

On the obverse of the Mauryan silver punch-marked coins, there are generally five symbols. The common symbols found on these coins are peacoak on the hill, crescented hill, steelyard, triangle headed standard, caduceous, bull, elephant, Taxila mark (i.e., *svastika*), etc. These coins were issued by the Mauryan rulers and symbols on them carry significance.

D.D. Kosambi[15] has suggested that the symbol on the hill may denote descent. The peacock on the hill would denote descent of the dynasty from peacock. Aśoka's edict shows that Aśoka was fond of peacock. The peacock on the hill became the dominant symbol of the Mauryas. The elephant on the hill would denote descent of the dynasty from the elephants or gods having elephants as their mounts. Walsh[16] has suggested that all the coins having elephant upon them may be taken to be the issues of the king because elephant is well-known in connection with royalty. The crescented hill occurs on several Mauryan objects including the Aśoka edict from Rampurwa. It is found to be impressed upon the pillar of Candragupta's palace at Pāṭaliputra trenches. This symbol is also engraved on the Sohagaura copper plate dated 320-300 BC. The standard symbol of the Mauryas occurs on a bead in the Allahabad Museum and on a disc from Pāṭaliputra. Caduceous is known to be the symbol of the Maurya King Aśoka.

The representation of human figures is noticed from the beginning of the Maurya period. According to P.L. Gupta[17] probably all are intended to represent deities rather than living individuals and one of them may be Viṣṇu or Kṛṣṇa. Another has been identified as Kārttikeya or Śiva. A female with small child suggests mother Goddess. These human figures sometimes took the place of the Sun and the six-armed figure.

D.R. Bhandarkar[18] has suggested that one set of symbols refers to seven *ratnas* or treasures, the possession of which was regarded as constituting paramount sovereignty. These seven symbols were (1) *cakra* or wheel, (2) *hastin* or elephant, (3) *aśva* or horse, (4) *maṇi* or gem, (5) *strī* or women, (6) *gṛhapati* or treasurer, (7) *parināyaka* or councellor.

Among these *ratnas*, there are only three human beings and it is indeed true that we never get more than three homo-signs on the punch-marked coins. There are several difficulties in accepting D.R. Bhandarkar's theory even with reference to the limited class of homo-sign punch-marked coins. Even three human figures have only two other symbols making their total number five. *Cakra* and *aśva* are conspicuous by their absence.

On the reverse, tiny marks of the traders disappeared very soon during the Maurya period and they were replaced by a single large reverse mark, such as 'Taxila mark' or some other characteristically Mauryan stamp.

Maurya's administration was highly centralised and well organised. Probably, the principal reverse marks on them were widely accepted and they were not, therefore, subjected to any further periodical checking. Walsh[19] has suggested that the reverse marks were the mint or the area marks. This may be so in few cases, but we have to remember that coin with some symbols like peacock on the hill or Taxila symbol has been found all over the country. It is very doubtful whether they did ever denote any mint or provincial or district area. It is also suggested that the fourth symbol on obverse shows some definite relation with its reverse symbols.[20]

The Mauryan coins show distinct features. These are thicker, with more copper and they are crudely minted, though the average weight is the same. The variation is more than that observed in the earlier coins. The superb accuracy of the weighing is lost.

Chronologically P.L. Gupta[21] has divided the punch-marked into six classes from the point of view of fabric and he has included the Mauryan coins into Series V and VI. The coins of Series V are known to be of a medium and thick fabric both mixed together. The coins of Series VI are exclusively of thick fabric.

Study of *Rūpa-Sutta*

It seems that *Rūpa-Sūtta* must have assumed the shape of science of coins during the Maurya period because of the manufacture of so many punch-marked coins. It is also confirmed by the evidence of the *Arthaśāstra*. In chapter XII of the *Adhyakṣa-Pracāra*, Kauṭilya speaks of *rūpya-rūpa* and *tāmra-rūpa* which cannot but signify silver and copper coins respectively. He also specifies an officer called *rūpadarśaka* whose duty was to examine the coins in actual circulation or received as revenue into the royal treasury. Buddhaghoṣa while commenting on a passage from the *Mahāvagga*, speaks of it as *Rūpa-sūtta* which can only mean a set of rules concerning coins, the science of coinage.[22] It was studied by an ordinary individual for pursuing a profession to enable him to turn either a *rūpadarśaka*, *lakṣṇādhyakṣa* or s*auvarṇika*. It was also a subject of serious study to a prince to make him fit for administration. *Rūpa* must therefore have been a science of coins which dealt with his subject, not only from the Minister's and assayer's but also from the economist's and administrators point of view.

Copper Coins

The use of the copper coins gradually increased during the reign of the Mauryas as Kauṭilya refers to them. The unit of the copper money was the *paṇa* weighing eighty *rattīs* or 144 grains. It seems that during the later years of Aśoka's reign, silver began to be replaced by copper coin. Punch-marked, cast and die-struck copper coins of this period are known. At some places, it was merely auxiliary to the silver currency, but in some regions like Avantī and Gāndhāra, copper standard developed as local currency.

The punch-marked copper coins were known as *paṇas*. These have been discovered in Madhya Pradesh, Rajasthan and Magadha. In Madhya Pradesh, the important places are Ujjain, Eran[23] and Vidiśā. They have five symbols. They are of square shape and large size. The reverse of some coins is blank but the common symbol on most of the coins is Ujjayīnī. These coins might have been issued in the third century BC.

A second most remarkable series of copper punch-marked coin is represented by the specimens of Madhipur (Bhāgalpur, Dist. Bihar) hoard.[24] The coins record a puzzling wide range of weights.

The punch-marked coins discovered from Nagari near Chittor in Rajasthan are interesting.[25] They are small round punch-marked coins which display symbols on both the sides. The coins fall into at least half a dozen group and are of an indeterminate standard with weights ranging from three to hundred grains. The number of symbols varies from one to four on the obverse and one to three on the reverse according to the availability of the space on coin flan. The symbols are mostly familiar ones and are commonly seen on five symbols of silver punch-marked coins. They include the Sun, the six-armed symbol, the human figure in three forms, a tree in railing, a bull, a peacock on hill, Ujjayinī symbol, a six-peaked hill and Caduceous.

The Ujjain symbol, which does not occur on the silver punch-marked coins, is quite common on the copper punch-marked coins from Nagari and Eran. These copper punch-marked coins were probably the local issues of the famous Mādhyamikā *Janapada*. The occurrence on them of the two symbols namely the solar and the six-armed ones evidently points to their connection with their ordinary five symbol punch-marked coins. They might have been issued in the third or second century BC.

Cast Coins

Uninscribed cast coins[26] which belong to this period are always in copper. They may be divided into two broad sub-categories (i) Coins of Universal type and (ii) Coins of local types. Coins of universal type are known both in round and square shape. Typical examples of round shapes are certain coins bearing the devices of elephant on the obverse and crescent topped three-arched hill on the reverse. They are found almost all over India. Uninscribed cast coins of universal type which of square shapes are represented by certain extensive issues which bear on the obverse the elephant, *svastika*, triangle headed standard and taurine and on the reverse crescent topped three-peaked hill, hollow cross, tree in railing and taurine. Universal type cast coins both round and square shapes are generally of simple designs and known to bear traditional symbols commonly seen on punch-marked coins.

Those of the universal type are often found along with silver punch-marked coins, majority of which are believed to be of the Maurya period. It thus appears that uninscribed cast copper pieces of the universal types were widely current during the Mauryan rule. We do not know who issued the universal types of uninscribed cast coins. They might have been minted by influential commercial guilds with the approval and according to the authorised specifications of the central authority.

The local issues bear on the obverse elephant, triangle headed standard, *svastika*, and a symbol consisting of a pellet with four crescents around and on the reverse taurine hollow cross, elaborate tree in railing and crescent topped three-peaked hill. Thus, the uninscribed cast coins of the reverse local types also bear like their universal counterpart traditional symbols.

From the evidence of the statement of Nearchus, companion of Alexander, the Great, it is clear that the Indians has been using the cast coins. Cast coins referred to by Nearchus were evidently uninscribed. Archaeological evidence also corroborates what Nearchus said about the contem-porary coins of India. Uninscribed cast coins came from the early strata in archaeological excavations. These rare uninscribed cast coins coming from early strata were evidently in use in restricted locality and they probably originated in earlier time, i.e., about the beginning of the fourth or even at the end of the fifth century BC. Of course, it is possible that these local types of uninscribed cast coins were minted by local guilds in isolated regions.

Both in Gāndhāra and Avantī regions, a large number of local copper coins were issued during the Maurya period. Taxila and Puṣkalavati were two great centres of these local copper coins in the Gāndhāra region.[28]

Coins of various denominations were issued. Their designs are numerous and varied. Many of the coin types are inter-related. Punch-marked coins, larger cast coins and uninscribed die-struck coins were issued in this region.

During the later years of Aśoka's reign, the minuscule silver coinage of the Mauryan empire was replaced by somewhat larger cast copper coins and they soon became the standard low denomination coinage. The low denomination coinage in copper initiated in little earlier by Aśoka became popular in this region. The denominations of coins confirm to the copper *kārsāpaṇa* standard which like most early Indian weight standards, was issued on average weight standard.

Besides, uninscribed die-struck coppr coins began to be issued in the Gāndhāra region because of the influence of the Greeks. These coins bear the devices on both the sides and are called double die-pieces. These coins might have been issued by the guilds, and these are also known as *negama* coins.

Similarly large number of copper coins of low denominations began to be issued from Ujjain during the Maurya period. These are punch-marked cast and die-struck coins. These are both round and square. These have also been discovered from the layer II (Maurya period) of the excavations conducted at Ujjain. Like the punch-marked coins, the coins of this area have five symbols but on the reverse, they have a single symbol a cross and ball known as Ujjayinī symbol. The Ujjain symbol seems to have represented a meeting of four cross roads which was applicable to Ujjainī as a Junction of trade routes. A. Cunningham has divided these coins into five different groups according to their weights (1) 17-18 grains group 1/8, (2) 30-36 grains 1/4, (3) 53-54 grains 3/8, (4) 71-72 grains 1/2 and (5) 107-108 grains 3/4. Some coins are between 116-31 grains. One of the coins weighing in J. Allan's catalogue is of 155 grains. We also find some coins in copper and lead.

Regulation of Currency

The examiner of coins shall regulate the currency both as a medium of exchange and as legal tender accepted into the treasury. The premia levied on coins paid (into the treasury) shall be 8 Rs. known as *rūpika* 5 Rs. known as *vijājī*, one-eighth *paṇa* known as *pārīkṣika* (testing charge) besides a fine of 25 *paṇas* to be imposed on offenders other than manufacturer, seller, purchaser or examiner.[28]

It obtained its bullion for silver, copper and other metals from the mines. The names of the mines are given in the *Arthaśāstra* but they cannot be located since they bear no resemblance to modern names. The Tutthogata variety from the mountain Tuttha is unknown. Gaṇḍika apparently came from Bengal and probably is indicative of the Burmese sources. The Kāmbu silver, which is said to have come from Kāmbu Mountain, probably indicates the Afghan sources in the Andarab Valley as Kaboj could perhaps be located there. Again the sources of Cakravātika silver coming from the Mountain Cakravāka cannot be identified. It is probable that some came from local sources such as the Kullu Valley and Manbhūm in West Bengal while the remainder was imported from Persia and Afghanistan.

It is clear from the description of the examiner of coins that he not only regulated the currency as a medium of exchange but also received bullion into the treasury. That his operation related to the supply of scrap silver (coins and ornaments) from the public is indicated by the statement that the treasurer (*sanidhātā*) should only receive such coins or money (*hiraṇya*) which was declared genuine and that he should cut the bad coins. Of the levies mentioned, *parīkṣika* was probably a small charge made for testing the silver brought to the examiner. When the bullion was accepted by the examiner, he supplied in return newly minted coins. The *rūpika* was probably the fee charged for this service which would help to cover the cost of manufacture. The term *vijājī* may have been a charge to compensate for the loss of weight of worn coin submitted as bullion.

The examiner of coins is said to regulate currency as medium of exchange. The practice of adding miniature marks on the reverse of coins in circulation was followed for about fifty years or more earlier than the time of Kauṭilya, the author of *Arthaśāstra* (*c.* 320-300 BC). It is very probable that the regulation mentioned in the *Arthaśāstra* refers to this practice. On the other hand, the step to eliminate all bankers' marks by the addition of bold marks should be sought in the text. The *Arthaśāstra*[29] mentions coinage and the mint, and indicates that bullion was obtained from the public as well as from mines, the examiner of coins was probably responsible for the miniature marks.

Debasement of Coins

Before the Mauryas, some silver punch-marked coins contained silver 82 per cent, while others from 72 per cent to 80 per cent silver. The debasement during the Maurya period is mentioned by Kauṭilya[30] when the sanctions alloying 25 per cent copper and one *māṣa*, i.e., 6 ¼ per cent of other base metal with silver for making these coins. The metallic analysis of Mauryan coins has shown that this proportion is roughly correct. According to Durga Prasad[31] these early Mauryan coins showed 79 to 68 per cent silver and 20 per cent to 28 per cent copper. A few coins from Barwani hoard analysed by Gairola showed that they have 67.01 per cent of silver, 29.36 per cent copper and 3.59 per cent lead. From the study of the symbols, it seems that these coins belonged to the reign of Aśoka.

D.D. Kosambi[32] looked for its explanation in terms of greater bureaucratization, expansion in the army and proliferation of trading activities, which combined to produce an acute shortage of currency which had to be met by debasing it.

The greater debasement of the *kārṣāpaṇa* in the Mauryan period is attested by some late tradition, as for example by Dharmapāla commenting on the *Mahāvaṁso* (*Mhvs.*, 5.16 ff.) who ascribes to the Minister Cāṇakya. Patañjali refers in passing to the cults established by the Mauryas for the sale of money (on *Pāṇ*, 5,3. 99). According to Jaina tradition, Cāṇakya issued eight million debased silver coins called *kārṣāpaṇa* to fill treasury.

Counterfeiting of Coins

There can be little doubt that the counterfeiting of punch-marked coins had begun by the time, the *Arthaśāstra* was written towards the end of the fourth century BC. While describing the suppression of the wicked, Kauṭilya refers to a person who often purchased metals, alkalis, charcoal, bellows, clippers, hammers, anvils, dies and crucibles. These are of course the instruments for coin manufacture and the author is alluding to counterfeiters. A spy was to be appointed to detect counterfeiters, who were to be banished on conviction, a heavy fine was imposed for accepting or exchanging counterfeit coin. In this respect, the *Arthaśāstra* does tally with the numismatic record, as several contemporary forgeries have come to light. They betray themselves through their low weight, poor metal and stylish eccentricities. Forgeries produced during the Nanda and Mauryan periods seem to have been manufactured by the normal punching process, but late Mauryan forgeries also used the casting technique, which was introduced into tribal copper coinage in the third century BC.

The manufactue and use of coins in such a large scale led to the deterioration in the quality of coins. As a consequence, debasement and counterfeiting of coins are noticed. People no longer had confidence in the prevailing monetary system, and it affected both internal and foreign trade. Thus financial stringency caused by it was one of the important factors for the downfall of Mauryan Empire.

A critical estimate of the chapter will not be out of place here. D.D. Kosambi is one of the view that there was far greater pressure on currency than in the period of Nandas. It was due to the fact that there was greater bureaucratization, expansion in the army and proliferation of trading activities in the background of which the impact of iron culture and centralisation of administration was in existence. Besides, Aśoka made large grants for various welfare activities and also spent wealth in constructing Buddhist *stūpas*. All these required large sum of money and as the necessary metal could not be availed of immediately, it led to heavy debasement of currency. It created a financial crisis for the Mauryan empire and led to the downfall of it as advocated by D.D. Kosambi.

No doubt, due to reckless increase in home and foreign trade, there was an extraordinary demand for money in commercial circle. During the early Mauryan period, the military sector also pressurised the state by its increasing demand for funds. But it is difficult to agree with his view that financial stringency was the cause for the downfall of Mauryan empire. It seem that money economy made considerable headway during the Mauryan period, because of its expansion in different spheres. The credit for the introduction of legal tender money in the economy goes to the Mauryas. Debasement was not done due to the financial crisis but actually due to the expansion of money economy. As the debasement was linked with the legal tender system, it proved to be successful due to heavy demand for money.

Thus, it is not reasonable to say that this policy of money economy was the important cause for the downfall of the Mauryas. On the other hand, it seems that the revolutionary monetary policy of Mauryas actually collapsed after the downfall of Mauryas as it was exclusively state based.

Notes

1. Bhandarkar, D.R., *Ancient Indian Numismatics*, p. 9, Calcutta, 1921.
2. Murthy, A.V. Narasimha, *The Coins of Karnataka*, p. 20, Mysore, 1975.
3. *JNSI*, XXXV, p. 48 f.
4. *Ibid.*
5. *Ibid.*, XV, pp. 27-41.
6. Bhandarkar, D.R., *Ancient Indian Numismatics*, p. 18, Calcutta, 1921.
7. Chakraborty, S.K., *A Study of Ancient Indian Numismatics*, p. 16, Delhi, 1973, Second edn.
8. न धर्मार्थौ पीडयेव। शत्वि आचार्यमन्त्रिपुरोहित सेनापति युवराज मातृराजमहिष्योऽष्ट चत्वारिंशत्साहस्राः ।।4।। एतावता भरणे नानास्वादत्वमकोषकं चैषां भवति।।5।। . . . कुशीलवास्त्वर्ध तृतीययाताः ।।16।। द्विगुणवेतनाश्चैषां सूर्यकराः ।।17।। कारुशिल्पिनो विंशतिशतिकाः ।।18।। चतुष्पदद्विपदपरिचारकपादिकर्मिकोपस्थायिकपालिकविष्टिक बन्धकाः परिवेष्टनाः ।।19।।
9. *Hindu Polity*, p. 136, Bangalore, 1955, third edn.
10. *Mauryan Polity*, p. 151, Madras, 1932.
11. *Ancient Indian Polity*, pp. 44-45, Madras.
12. *History of Dharmaśāstra*, pp. 120 ff., Poona, 1930-53.

13. *Ibid.*
14. पणानां द्वे शते सार्धे प्रथमः साहतः स्मृतः।
    मध्यमः पञ्च विज्ञेयः सहस्रं त्वेव चोत्तमः।।
15. *NIA*, IV, pp. 1-35.
16. *MASI*, No. 59.
17. *Ancient Indian Silver Punch-Marked Coins of the Magadha-Maurya Kārṣāpana Series*, p. 16, Bombay, 1985.
18. *Ancient Indian Nimismatics*, p. 102, Calcutta, 1921.
19. *MASI*, No. 59.
20. Murthy, A.V. Narasimha, *The Coins of Karnataka*, p. 31, Mysore, 1975.
21. *Coins*, New Delhi, 1969.
22. Bhandarkar, D.R., *Ancient Indian Numismatics*, pp. 124 f., Calcutta, 1921.
23. Allan, J., *BMC AI*, London, 1936, pp. xc, xci and 140-44.
24. *ASI AR*, 1925-26, p. 154.
25. *JNSI*, XXXV, pp. 1-39.
26. *Ibid.*
27. *Ibid.*
28. रूपिकमष्टकं शतम्।।30।। पञ्चकं शतं व्याजीम्।।31।। पारीक्षिकमष्टभागिकं शतम्।।32।। पंचविंशतिपणमत्यर्यं मान्यन क्रतृक्रेतृपरीक्षितृभ्यः।।33।।
29. लक्षणाध्यक्षश्चतुर्भागताम्रं रूप्यरूपं तीक्ष्णत्रपुसीसाञ्जनाना मन्यतमं माषलीजयुक्तं कारयेत् पणधर्मपणं पादमष्टभागमिति।।27।। पादाजीवं ताम्रल्यं माषकमर्धमाषकं काकणीमर्धकाकणीमिति।।28।। रूपदर्शकः व्यावहारिकीं कोशप्रवेश्यां च स्थापयेत्।।29।।
30. *NS*, XLV and XVII.
31. Gupta, P.L., *The Amaravati Hoard of Silver Punch-Marked Coins*, p. 3, Hyderabad, 1963.
32. *Indian Numismatics*, p. ix, New Delhi, 1981.

5

Money Economy During Post-Mauryan Period (c. 186 BC to AD 300)

THE disintegration of the Mauryan empire in the second century BC considerably influenced the money economy of India. The rule of foreigners such as Indo-Bactrians, Indo-Scythians and Indo-Pārthians in the north-western India must have closed the *kārṣāpaṇa* mints in these areas. By the first century BC, the issue of silver punch-marked coins in this region had probably ceased but their use continued up to the second and third centuries AD. The hoarding and melting of these coins also took place. In north India, there arose a large number of small states both monarchial and republican, and they issued large number of coins, mostly in copper. Besides, during this period, city *nigamas*, *śreṇīs* or corporations also issued their coins generally in copper. With a few exceptions, these states did not continue the use of punch-marking technique, instead used first the casting method and later Indo-Greek, die-striking. The main exception was in the Avantī region where Mauryan punch-marked coins were imitated in great abundance.

The gold coins were issued for the first time in India by the Kuṣāṇas in order to facilitate their trade with Rome. The Western Kṣatrapas, who ruled over Avantī and Saurāṣṭra, issued the silver coins for the purpose of trade. Most of the states, the Kuṣāṇas and the western Kṣatrapas lost their importance in the fourth century AD with the rise of Guptas.

In south India, the punch-marked coins seem to have been issued and remained in circulation for three or four centuries longer than in the north. Roman coins and their imitation were in circulation in the market for a long time. The Sātavāhana rulers of the Āndhra dynasty, who ruled over a considerable portion of the Deccan from the latter half of the first century BC down to the first quarter of the third century AD, issued their coins.

From the monetary point of view, this period seems to be very sound in India. Gold coins were introduced in large number for the first time. Besides, coins of different metals, their types and denominations were used. The large number of copper coins proves that they served as medium of exchange even for ordinary transactions. Besides they penetrated in large parts of our country. The literary sources also confirm the different varieties of coins.

COINS OF FOREIGNERS

Indo-Bactrian Coins

The Indo-Bactrian coins[1] began to be issued from about 250 BC when Diodotus became independent from Seleucid emperor of Syria. The early Indo-Bactrian rulers first ruled over Bactria but gradually, they extended their dominions in the East which also included Indian territory. About fortyfive Indo-Bactrian rulers are known from the coins. Among them, the important rulers are Demetrius, Eucratides, and Menander. The last Indo-Bactrian ruler is Hermaeus.

The coins of the Greek kings of Bactria were modelled on those on Seleucid monarchs of Syria. They are on all aspects — basically the Greek money, in fineness and weight, purely of the Attic standard and are die-struck and round in shape. The obverse of the gold and silver coins as a rule bears within a circular border the bust of the king and the bust being executed with meticulous care, is always characterised by a refined realism. The coins of Euthydemus and his successors confirm a high artistic standard; the realistic depiction of the royal portraits in a refined manner. The reverse of all the gold and silver Bactrian coins bears the figure of a Greek deity as well as the name and title of the king in Greek together, almost invariably, with a monogram, the types taken from the Greek mythology. The coins of the Bactrian kings underwent changes for the newly conquered Indian territories though they remained Hellenistic in features. These coins underwent an appreciable change in their fabric and appearance as well as in their weights and sizes, and sometimes in their shapes. Besides, some degeneration is noticed in the artistic quality of coins. Gold coins were issued by Diodotus, Eucratides and Euthydemos, but they were confined to Bactria and never issued in India. A few legendless gold coins are attributed to Menander on the basis of their types If they were really issued by Menander, then they may be the earliest gold coins issued in India. Silver was abundantly used for coining standard money by all kings of Bactria and India. Copper was the important metal for minor Greek coins. Nickel was used by three kings namely Euthydemous, Pantaleon and Agathocles. These are the earliest coins in the world issued in this metal. Strabo II had used lead for some of his coins.

The Greek kings of Bactria first issued the Attic standard of the Seleucids. The gold coins were known as *staters* which weighed 132 grains. Diodotus, Euthydemous and Eucratides are known to have issued the gold coins. Later, Bactrian rulers discontinued the gold coins and the silver coinage was quite common in their times. The standard unit of silver coinage was 66 grains and it was known as *drachm.* It was half of the gold *stater.* The ratio between gold and silver being 1 to 10, twenty of these *drachms* would be equal to a gold *stater. Hemidrachm* weighing 33 grains was half of the *drachm.* Obol was a tiny silver piece weighing 11 grains. A *drachm* was equal to 6 *obols. Tetradrachm* was equal to 4 *drachms,* weighing 66 × 4 = 264 grains. Of the three denominations known — *tetradrachm* (4 *drachms*) *drachm* and *obol* (1/6 *drachm*) — *tetradrachm* and *drachm* were widely struck by all Bactrian kings. *Obols* are known only of six Bactrian kings, viz., Demetrius, Euthydemus, Pantaleon, Agathocles, Antimachus and Eucratides. Unique Attic *hemidrachms* are known of Antimachus and Agathocles.

During the reign of Eucratides, there was a change in metrology. The heavy silver pieces are seen weighing only 150 grains and their quarter weight is about 37 grains. Scholars attributed different causes for this change.

A. Cunningham[2] thought that this had been due to the change in the ratio between the values of gold and silver from 1:10 to 7:11 caused either by rise in the value of gold or by a fall in that of silver. P. Gardener[3] observed that this new standard appears to be identical with that called by metrologists the Persian notably the *sigloi*. As in the Persian standard, the unit weighs 84-86 grains. P. Gardener called the heavier Indo-Greek pieces which weigh a maximum 160 grains as *didrachms* and the smaller pieces which weigh up to 40 grains as *hemidrachms*. A.N. Lahiri[4] who mainly follows A. Von Sallet and R.B. Whitehead[5] has observed that "144 and 36 grains Indo-Greek silver coins were Indian *tetra drachms*" and Indian *drachms* respectively. These *tetra-drachms* were struck on an Indian weight standard of 20 *rattīs* and the *drachms* were struck on that of 80 *rattīs*. Economic and commercial reasons favoured the innovation of the light weight Indian currency. It was meant for the commercial convenience of the people. When Eucratides I saw that his newly conquered Indian subjects were accustomed to use small punch-marked coins, found it profitable to introduce in India an arbitrary and hybrid standard of coinage of which the *drachm* would be readily acceptable to his Indian subjects and allies and the *tetradrachm* to his Greek subjects and Western neighbours. According to B.N. Mukherjee,[6] the Indo-Greeks introduced a sort of Hellenic-Persian standard in north-western India. The standard weight of these so-called *tetradrachms*, which was 160 grains or even more, can be very closely compared with that of a silver *stater* of the Persian empire which was 172-90 grains. This Persian weight standard might have been popular or at least well-known in north-western India and its borderlands, parts of which had been under the Achaemenids for some time before the advent of the Indo-Greeks. This was probably necessary partly to meet local demand to have coinage based on known standard and partly to adjust the intrinsic value of silver coins of Bactria with that of silver species in north-western India where that metal might have been dearer in relation to gold than in the area to the north of the Hindukush. The successors of Eucratides adopted this new weight standard.

According to A. Cunningham,[7] however the Greek copper unit was *chalkon* which was equal in weight to a *drachm*. In value, eight such *chalkons* were equal to an *obol* and forty-eight of them to a *drachm*. The ratio between silver and copper was 1 to 50 in Indian at that time. The copper coins of the Greek kings of Bactria adhered to the Greek or Attic standard, with those struck in India would seem to have been raised to the India standard. Thus, the *chalkon* of the Attic standard weighing 67.2 grains was raised to 70 grains in order to unify the Greek and Indian systems by making the Greek *chalkon* exactly equal to half an Indian *paṇa*. Copper coins are believed to have been issued on the standard of the local coins of Taxila.

A. Cunningham[8] thought that nickel coins were substituted for *obols* (equal to eight *chalkons*). Nickel coins of the weight of Attic *didrachms* (134.4 grains) are called by A. Cunningham *obolus*, while those with half their weight (67.2 grains) were called *hemi-obolus*. A. Cunningham's nomenclature seems to be appropriate, as the double unit coins were struck by all the three, nickel issuing kings, viz., Euthydemus II, Pantaleon, and Agathocles while the single unit coins are known of Agathocles alone. It is also interesting to note that nickel was used only by those three Greek princes who struck *obols* very sparingly. In an event of scarcity of silver, it seems, the three rulers took course to the alloys of copper and nickel and substituted silver *obols* by nickel or rather cupro-nickel *obolus*. Greek gold and silver coins are round. The Bactrian copper coins of the Greeks are always round. When these Bactrian rulers conquered Indian territories, there was change in their shape. The Indo-Greek copper coins are generally square, though some Greek princes of India struck some round copper pieces along with square money. Being Bactrian money, nickel coins were always round.

The obverse and reverse devices of Greek gold and silver

coins of Bactria and India were throughout the same in principles. The obverse in Bactria bore the bust of the king and the reverse name and title as well as the figure of Greek deity. Only in India, the reverse Greek legend was transferred to the obverse. While its literal Prākṛt translation was written on the reverse instead. On the obverse, we find the head or bust of the king. Sometimes, we find royal diadem, the head-gear, the elephant scalp, the Kausia and the helmets. We also find conjugate bust. On the reverse, there are three deities concerned with Greek mythology — Zeus, Artemis, Heracles, Poseidon, Apollo, Dioskouroi, Nike, Athena, Pallas, Demeter, Hekate and Helios. Animals, like bull, elephant, horses and panther, appear on large number of coins. Of birds, we find eagle and owl.

Besides the regular series of gold and silver types, there are commemorative of pedigree coins, the victory coins, the joint coins and overstruck coins. Antimachus, Agathocles, and Eucratides are known to have issued the commemorative or pedigree coins. Being struck in Bactria, they are in the Attic standard generally *tetradrachms* in denomination. Eucratides issued only a unique gold coin of 2593.5 grains. It is regarded as victory coin. Similarly the Indo-Greek Amyntas struck at least two types of victory coins of silver. Joint coins were also issued. Queen Agathocleia and her son Strabo issued joint coinage. Similarly Hermaeus and his queen Calliope issued the joint coins. There are some rulers who overstruck the coins. These coins were sometimes issued of the contemporary ruler. The coins of the conquered rulers were also overstruck. The coins of Appllodotus are found overstruck by different rulers.

Coins of Bactria bear Greek legend on the reverse only, while those of India show Greek legends on the obverse and Kharoṣṭhī legends on the reverse. The Greek legends on these coins invariably had three words : (i) Basileos meaning king, (ii) One of the following titles — *Sotoros, Megalon, Aniketou, Nikephorou, Philapatros, Epiphanou,* and *Dikaiou* and (iii) the name of the issuing king. The same was translated into Prākṛt on the bilingual coins. On the coins of early Bactrian rulers, the legends are simple consisting of royal titles and name of the king such as Basileos, Diodotou or Euthydemou. Antimachus adopted the lofty and unique epithet *theos* (divine). Eucratides imitated the old Persian emperors in assuming the title. Great king (Basileos *Megalou*) on his coins. In his later issues, this was translated as *mahārājā* which became the popular regal title among later Indian rulers. Eucratides was also possibly the world's first ruler to issue a bilingual currency both in Greek and Kharoṣṭhī script. He also used both Greek and Prākṛt legends. Eucratides was however the first king in India to call himself the *mahārājā*. Pantaleon and Agathocles used Brāhmī on their coins. Agathocles again used exclusively the Kharoṣṭhī legends on both sides of their coins. These coins are of regional types confined to Taxila, and we find mention *hiraṇyāśrame* meaning golden hermitage.

Almost all the coins bear curious marks/symbols commonly referred to as Monograms. One Monograms may be found on different coins of more than one king. On the other hand, one and the same type of coins often shows different monograms on different specimens. Their precise meaning is unknown.

A. Cunningham[9] pointed out that all the mint monograms which are common to a number of different princes can only be the name of the cities and cannot possibly be the names either of magistrates or a mint-master or any other functionaries. P. Gardener[10] acknowledged the possibilities that many of the Greek monograms may stand for the names of the mints. According to Rapson[11] these monograms were closely connected in some manner either locally or chronologically. Whithead[12] thinks that these should be regarded as the names of the mints. Tarn[13] believes that the monograms on the coins of Bactria and India represent the names of moneyers, mint-masters or city magistrates.

Indo-Scythian Coins

The Śakas occupied Bactria in about 135 BC by seizing power from Indo-Bactrian ruler Heliocles. Then they gradually extended their supremacy over the northern and north-western regions of Ancient India by ending Indo-Bactrian rule. The last Indo-Bactrian rulers, whom they destroyed in about 75 BC, were Hippostratus and Hermaeus.

The coins of the Scytho-Parthian[14] kings resemble those of the Indo-Greek rulers to a large extent. They adhered to their weight standard of their coins. The reverse of these coins represents numerous divinities which are generally Hellenic but occasionally Indian. The Greek and Kharoṣṭhī legends are found on coins. The coins of joint issues are found in greater number. They bear the name of the reigning king in Greek on the obverse while the reverse shows in Prākṛt the name and title of the heir apparent. Some of the heir apparents known as Kṣatrapas issued coins.

Two main lines of these Śaka invaders are known from their coins. One is that of Maues in the Punjab and its adjoining lands and the other of Vonones and his associates in Kandhāra (Arachosia) and Baluchistan (Godrosia and Drangiana). It seems that Maues and Vonoes are more or less contemporary rulers.

Maues is known to have issued twenty-two types of coins and they are found both in silver and copper. He assumed the simple title *Basileos* on his early coins of bow in the bow-case and elepahnt and Caduceus type. When Maues became more and more powerful by the addition of larger and larger territories, he assumed the titles — *Basileos, Basilion Megalon* (the Great king, of kings) and their Prākṛt equivalents *Mahārājāsa Moasa* and *Rājādhirājas, Mahatasa, Moasa* respectively in Kharoṣṭhī.

The devices of his coins are extremely varied and complex. Some of his coins show nomadic traits also. His most significant type is king with a spear on horseback. This became the charcteristic device of Śaka coinage. On another coin type, a man seated cross-legged is identified by some scholars with Buddha but actually, it is the portrait of the king. A striding male figure with club and, trident on some coins is identified as Śiva but it is not certain.

The coins of Vonones are comparatively few. His silver coins bear on the obverse a king on horseback to right with spear and on the reverse, Zeus standing with a long sceptre and thunderbolt. On the copper coins, standing Herakles crowning himself is shown on the obverse and Pallas Athene standing left with shield and spear on the reverse. His joint issues with his brother Spalagadama and his son Spalahora are also available. After Vonones; Spalyris became the ruler who issued joint issues with Spalagadama and Azes. All his coins have the horse-rider on the obverse and on the reverse is seen Zeus or Heracles.

Soon after, Azes became the ruler and issued *tetradrachms* and *drachms* and round and square copper coins in his own name, independent of any other ruler. His most common coins, both in silver and copper, have the king on the horseback with a spear on the obverse and Zeus, Nike, Pallas or an unidentified deity holding a palm and lamp on the reverse of silver coins and a humped bull or Herakles on the copper coins. He also introduced a new device on his coins — a king riding on two humped Bactrian camel, holding an *arikuśa* (goad) which is an interesting reflection on his nomadic life. Azes I was succeded by Azilises. He issued an extensive series of coins following his two predecessors, Maues and Azes I, and at the same time, he introduced a striking original Indian device — *Abhiṣeka* Lakṣmī. This is the first Indian divinity which could be unmistakably identified on the coins of the foreign invaders. Azilises was followed by Azes II whose coins are characterized by the king on horseback holding a whip. His coins are crude and the metal used in them is highly debased. He also issued some coins in association with one Indravarmā and then with his son Stratagos Aspavarmā in the western area of his domain.

Indo-Pārthian Coins

Azes II was succeeded by Gondophernes I, a Pārthian. He became a great king with a vast domain including Arachosia, Seistan, Sindh, Gāndhāra and the Kābul Valley. He issued coins of copper. The obverse of his coins bears a king on horseback. Nike, Pallas and Zeus are familiar Greek deities that appear on the reverse. He also issued the coin-type in which Śiva is facing and holding in right hand trident and in left hand palm. Coins of Gondophernes in association with Aspavarmā and his nephew Sasa are also found. Gondophernes was succeeded by his nephew Abdagases. After him, Orthagnes, Pacores and others are known from coins. During Śaka-Pārthian occupation of north-western India, the institution of Kṣatrapa was quite popular. These Kṣatrapas were subordinate rulers but some of them issued their own coins. One of them was Zeionises who issued coins in base silver and copper.

Indo-Kuṣāṇa Coinage

After the Indo-Scythians, and the Indo-Pārthians, the Kuṣāṇas established their supremacy in India. Among the Kuṣāṇas, Kujula Kadphises sometime in about AD 50 extended his empire from Persia to the Indus and it included Sogdiana (modern Prokharā) with probability all the territory in modern Afghanistan. He issued many copper coins and very few silver coins. The earliest of them bears the bust of Hermacus, the last Bactrian ruler on the obverse and Herakles on the reverse. This coin type indicates that even after century of the death of Hermaeus, his coins were imitated by the Kuṣāṇa rulers. It also shows that they were current in the newly conquered territory by Kujula Kadphises who had to issue such coins.

Kujula Kadphises also imitated diademed head of the Emperor Augustus (*c.* 31 BC-AD 14) on Roman coins. This imitation of coinage of Augustus by Kujula Kadphises indicates some trade with India and Rome during his time. His coin type bull on the obverse and a double-humped Bactrian camel on the other probably reflects the nomadic habits of the Kuṣāṇas. His coin type of the helmeted head of the Macedonian soldier shows that it was inherited from the Indo-Greek coinage, through his Persian predecessors. All these coins are bilingual having Greek inscriptions on the obverse and Kharoṣṭhī on the reverse.

Wima Kadphises, successor of Kujula Kadphises, is said to have conquered the territory inside India up to Benāras. He was the last Kuṣāṇa king to issue the bilingual coins. His reign is landmark in the history of Kuṣāṇa coinage because he introduced the extensive gold coins for the first time in India. Gold coins of three denominations were issued by him — double *dīnāra* and quarter *dīnāra*. The last one is rare. The main reasons for the introduction of gold coinage seems to be the demand for gold pieces for international trade between India, Roman empire and China. Through trade and commerce, a fabulous amount of Roman gold flew to India. His copper coins are of three sizes — large, middle and small. The large size coins weigh 260 grains, middle 128 grains and small size coins 60 grains.

Wima Kadphises is portrayed on the obverse in various attitudes — seated on a couch, seated cross-legged, seated at *jharokhā* (window), riding on an elephant, driving in a biga and standing sacrificing at an altar. This latter type, i.e., standing on an altar, appears only on copper coins. This became the basic theme of the royal portrait on the later Kuṣāṇa coins. On some coins, Wima is shown floating through or rising from the clouds and a flame is shown blowing from his shoulders. These distinctly indicate that he claimed divinity for himself.

Another feature of coinage of Wima Kadphises is the representation of Indian God Śiva on the reverse of his coins. Probably, Wima Kadphises was connected to Śaiva faith as his title. 'Maheśvara' used on coins indicates Śiva with his long trident and sometimes accompanied by his bull is invariably seen. On a few coins, Śiva is represented by his trident-battle-axe.

The nameless king had a series of local coinages copying the types, denominations and format of his predecessors coinage. His Mathurā-type copper *drachms* on the Attic (Bactrian) weight standard were copied from Yue-Chi copies of the coins of Heliocles with legends in Greek alone. His western Gāndhāra billion *tetradrachms* and *drachms* on the Indian weight standard of horseman standing Zeus type with legends in Greek and Kharoṣṭhī copied the Pahlava coinage of these types and denominations in Western standard. The helmeted head copper coins of Kapisa or Bactria are probably *hemiobols* of the Attic (Bactrian) standard derived from the helmeted type of the house of Eucratides, and using the same red and pellet border with legends in Greek alone. But the nameless king also had a general coinage which is extremely common and is found in large numbers throughout north-west India, Afghanistan and Southern Russia—which has legends in Greek only and which combines the obverse head of the later Indo-Greek issues with the obverse horseman of the Śaka series in a denomination which is an Attic *didrachm*, i.e., metrologically constituting part of the Attic (Bactrian) system but in a denomination and size that reflected the general size of the base billion and copper *tetradrachm* of the Indian standard. This nameless bears the title *Basileus Basileon Soter Megas* on these coins.

According to Vincent Smith, the nameless king was a viceroy of Wima Kadphises. The extensive distribution of coins of the nameless king is conclusive evidence against Vincent Smith's[15] view. Mukherjee[16] regards the nameless king as the earlier phase of Wima Kadphises. David W. Macdonall[17] has argued that nameless king is an independent Kuṣāṇa sovereign the successor of Kujula and predecessor of Wima. There can be no doubt that in general context the nameless king marks the important period of transition from the multiplicity of coinages of the later Indo-Greeks, Śakas and Pahlavas who had a different system of denominations and types in each province — the same pattern that we see in the varied coinages of Kujula Kadphises to the single unified system.

KANIṢKA COINS

Kaniṣka, successor of Wima Kadphises, issued coins only in gold and copper. On the obverse, he preferred only one type for his portrayal. The king clad in coat and trousers is standing at the altar wearing helmet and diadem with spear in his left hand. The legend is in Greek script and language — *Basileus, Basileon* and *Kaniṣkou*, i.e., coins of Kaniṣka, king of kings. On the reverse of these coins, he introduced three deities with Greek names — Helios, Salena and Hephaistos.

Kaniṣka also introduced a new language — the middle Iranian (Bactrian) or Khoṭanese Śaka on the other side of his coins. From now on Kaniṣka's coins bear the legend *shāhonāno shāo kaneṣkī koshāno,* Kaniṣka, the Kuṣāṇa king of kings. On the reverse of these coins are placed a number of deities — Male and female bearing the Iranian names — *Mihira* or *Mithra* (Sun), *Mao* (Moon), *Oado* (*vāyu,* wind) *Orlagno* (Vṛthragna, the national God of Iranian in arms), *Luhraspa* (Druvaspa, the guardian of the health of animals), *Athsho* (Fire), *Pharro* (Khvareno, the Iranian concept of imperial greatness, *Manao Bago* (Personification of good mind), *Mazalah* (Supreme Zoroastrian deity), *Nana* or *Nana Shāho* or *Naina* (Nature goodness) and *Ārdokṣo* (counterpart of Indian Lakṣmī) Kaniṣka also retained Śiva of his predecessors' coins under the name Oesho (Bhaveṣa or Haveṣa) and introduced the figure of Buddha with the legend *Boddo* or *Sakamano Boddo* (Śākyamuni Buddha).

The natural explanation of the diversity of deities is that these various classes of coins were current in different provinces of large empire with different religious traditions. Rapson[18] holds the view that the deities shown on the reverse are no other than tutelary gods of numerous mint cities. Kaniṣka used Greek script for his coins in connection with the commerce of Greeks who had been in Bactria for considerable time. Further Greek was the *lingua franca,* the language of different countries. Kaniṣka's gold coins were minted for foreign trade only. Hence, Kaniṣka used Greek script on his coins.

J. Allan[19] thinks that there is no reason to doubt that the gold coinage of Kaniṣka was suggested by the Roman Solidus. Some of the reverses are direct copies of Roman types. The Kuṣāṇa monarch can hardly be placed before Titus (AD 79-81) and Trajan (AD 98-117).

HUVIṢKA COINS

Huviṣka is known to have enjoyed long reign as his inscriptions are dated with regnal years ranging between 28 and 64. The long reign of Huviṣka is attested by the large number of gold and copper coins left by him. His coinage is characterised by varied obverse as well as reverse devices. Large number of coins depict the kings bust on the obverse in numerous designs. The obverse of his gold coins bears the imperial bust wearing garments decked with jewels, and a high or flat topped ornamental headdress, with a sceptre in hand. The obverse of his copper coins depicts him in various attitudes such as riding an elephant, and reclining on a couch.

The reverse of the coin bears like Kaniṣka's coins, the figures of deities belonging to various pantheons, Greek, Indian and Persian. All the Iranian deities, seen on the coins of Kaniṣka are also seen on the coins of Huviṣka bearing *Orlagno*. He added to the list of these deities a number of new ones—*Ahura-mazuh* (Supreme Zoroastrian deity), *Asheinsho* (Asa Vahista, embodiment of truth) *Oanindo* (Vanainti goddess associated with Vṛthragna), *Oasho* (river God of Oxus), *Reshno* (Riṣṇu, personification of Righteousness) and *Shaoreora* (Shahvevar, the genius of imperial might, good of metal). *Mao* (Moon) and *Miro* are placed together on some coins which is an innovation. Huviṣka's coins also have a few non-Iranian deities. They are *Herakles*, the Greek God; *Serapis*, a synthetic Graeco-Egyptian deity; *Oros* (Egyptian *Horus* or *Oron* — Varuṇa). Among the Indian Gods, Huviṣka has retained Śiva (Oesho) on his coins, and he is most common. On some coins, Śiva is shown with his consort Umā (Umma). Besides Śiva and Umā, his son Kārttikeya also finds a place on the gold coins. He is shown there along with the name Maasena (Mahāsena); in pair with the label *skanda kumāro-vizāga* (Skanda-Kumāra and Viśākha) and in triad with the legend *skanda kumāro-maaseno-vizāgo* (Skanda Kumāra Mahāsena and Viśākha), Skanda Kumāra Mahāsena and Viśākha are the different names of the same God Kārttikeya but these coins suggest that in those days, they had their separate entities.

VĀSUDEVA COINS

After Huviṣka came Vāsudeva. He issued both in gold and copper. His coins are common all over the Punjab and north-west India. The dates of his inscriptions range from the year

67 to 98. He adopted the obverse device of Kaniṣka, i.e., king standing in profile, sacrificing at the altar, but the king now holds a trident in place of spear as held by Kaniṣka in his left hand. His dress is a long tunic, with trousers and tartar boots. He wears a conical helmet and sword at his left side. The usual legend on the obverse is *shāonano shāo bazodeo koṣāṇa.* The reverse devices were reduced to two deities — Nana and Oesho (Śiva). Nana is seen on a few coins but Oesho is quite common.

The symbols appearing on the coins of Kaniṣka II is that of Vāsudeva I and not Kaniṣka I. So he must have come before or after Vāsudeva I. But the correct Greek script and the introduction of Brāhmī letters on the coins of this Kaniṣka, make it impossible to place him before Vāsudeva I. The coins of Kaniṣka II are fairly numerous, hence, he may have reigned for a fairly long period. They are found in the Punjab, Seistan and Afghanistan, which may have been included in his kingdom.

Later Kuṣāṇa Coins

The coins of the later Kuṣāṇa rulers probably constituted the currency of both the Kābul Valley and the Punjab from the date of Vāsudeva I's death until the settlement of the Kidāra-Kuṣāṇas in Gāndhāra. The obverse of the Later Great Kuṣāṇa coins presents the same uniform type: King nimbate to left with peaked helmet and complete suit of chain mail making an offering with right hand over a small altar and long trident or spear in left hand. The inscriptions on the obverse are all in debased Greek characters, which when nearly complete, give the names and Kuṣaṇa titles of Kaniṣka and Vāsudeva — *śāhonāno śāo kaneṣko kuṣaṇo.* Along with the principal Greek legends, there are minor ones in Brāhmī. The reverse of these coins has the Oesho type and Ārdokṣo type.

Among the later Kuṣāṇa rulers, Kaniṣka is well-known from his coins. As his coins are numerous, he might have ruled for a long time from AD 180 to 210. His coins are found in the Punjab, Seistan and Afghanistan, which must, therefore, have been included in his kingdom. He finds the names of the

Governors such as Vāsu(deva), Virupākṣa and Mahī(śvara) written in Brāhmī on the obverse. Vāsudeva was ruling in Seistan for the coins of Kaṇiṣka III with the name of this governor are obtained mostly from that province. There appears on the coins of Kaniṣka III some additional letters like *pa, na, ga, chu, khu, tha, vai,* etc. whose exact significance is not yet known. It is, however, likely that some of these may stand for the initials of the names of cities from which the coins were issued and others for the initials of the names of the provinces or tribes among whom they were current. Thus *pa* may be standing for *Paruśpura* (Peśāwar), *na* for Nagrahāra (Jalālābād) and *ga* for Gāndhāra country. His coin type Śiva is usually found in Bactria and Afghanistan, and those Ārdokṣo type in Gāndhāra, Seistan and the Punjab.

Kaniṣka III was succeeded by Vāsudeva II who was probably his son, governing the important and turbulent province of Seistan. The coins of Ārdokṣo type with the legend *Vāsu* were probably issued while he was the Governor of Seistan under his father. Coins of Vāsudeva as a king are very rare and show only the Śiva and Bull type which was prevailing in Bactria and Afghanistan. It is thus probable that Vāsudeva II could control only those provinces and his Governors in the Punjab and Seistan had become independent.

The Kuṣāṇa coin type of 'king standing and sacrificing at an altar' on the obverse and 'Enthroned Goddess Ārdokṣo' on the reverse was also imitated on the coins of the tribes of Śāka, Śilāda and Gadahāra who ruled over the portions of the Punjab in about the middle of the third century AD.

Kuṣāṇo-Sassānian Coins

The Sassānids occupied the territories of these Later Kuṣāṇa some time during the reign of Ardarshir I (AD 212-41). In course of time, the Sassānian emperor Varhhran II succeeded in annexing N.W. Frontier Province, Seistan and Sind to the Sassānian empire by AD 284. The subdued territories were governed by the princes of the royal family. These princes issued their own coins in gold, silver and copper. The early coins have Kuṣāṇa influence but gradually, they took the form of Sassānian fabric. Hence these coins are known as Kuṣaṇo-Sassānian coins.

The Kuṣāṇo-Sassānian gold coins are evolved from the gold coins of Vāsudeva, the last of the Great Kuṣāṇas. The coins of Vāsudeva were prevalent in Bactria and Afghanistan which were newly conquered by the Sassānians. These Sassānian coins issued in this region have the king standing and sacrificing at an altar. These coins bear *Oesho* (in Greek) on the reverse with type of Śiva and bull Nandī. On the obverse of the coins of first Kuṣāṇo-Sassānian coin series is found corrupt Greek legend *śaohāno śāo-bazodeo kuṣāṇo.* The coins bearing *Ārdokṣo* (in Greek) on the reverse with type of Enthroned Goddess belong to the more eastern portion of the Kuṣaṇa dominions. These princes enjoyed the privilege of using the title *kuṣāṇa śāh* the king of Kuṣāṇas on their coins. From the middle of the third century onward, this title was changed into *kuṣāṇ śahanśāh* that is the king of kings of the Kuṣāṇas. In these early coins, the Kuṣāṇa cursive script was adopted.

In the next stage, the obverse device was changed into 'Bust of the king with peculiar crown' but the reverse device Śiva and Bull' was retained. The legend Kuṣāṇa cursive was accompanied by Pahlavī in the second stage. In the third stage, 'the Bust of the king' device was retained on the obverse but the 'king standing and sacrificing of at an altar type was placed on the reverse with a deity either enthroned or standing. The inscription is marked by the use of Pahlavī only.

Kidāra-Kuṣāṇa Coins

The territories of the Kuṣāṇas that were under the Sassānid Governors passed on to the kings of another dynasty known as Kidāra or Kidārites after the name of the first ruler Kidāra. In the beginning, Kidāra was the feudatory of the Sassānians with his capital Peśāwar in about *c.* AD 340. He conquered Kashmir and Central Punjab and became independent. Kidāra was succeeded by his son Piro in about *c.* AD 375. These rulers appointed their Satraps to rule over these conquered provinces. The coins of Kidāra dynasty were influenced both by the Kuṣāṇas and the Sassānians. Their gold coins bear Kuṣāna type and Brāhmī inscriptions and very few traces of Pahlavī legend. On the obverse of these coins, busts of kings are represented in Sassānian style. Copper coins bearing Brāhmī legends have both Kuṣāṇa and Sassānian influence. The Kidāra-Kuṣāṇa became so popular that it continued to be imitated even after the death of the ruler.

The content of gold coins of the Kidāra-Kuṣāṇas seems to be considerably less than that of the Imperial Kuṣāṇas. The cause for this deterioration in Kidāra-Kuṣāṇa coinage may be found in the decline of trade and commerce after the disruption of Kuṣāṇa empire. The Hūṇa invasion and the Sassānids in Persia which brought some parts of north-western India under their sway must have disturbed the normal activities of trade and commerce with Central Asian territories. This is probably the reason for the deterioration of the gold coinage of the Kidāra-Kuṣāṇas.

Purī-Kuṣāṇa Coins

The series of copper coins commonly designated as Purī-Kuṣāṇa coins[20] were issued in a small territory confined only to Orissa and the adjoining fringes in Bihar and Andhra Pradesh. These coins consisted of two distinct varieties. The first variety was composed of die-struck coins. The second variety consists of cast coins. These coins are crude imitations of Kaniṣka's coinage with the well-known figure of the king with his right hand extended over fire altar and holding a staff or spear in his left hand on the obverse. The figure of the male-moon God is present on the reverse. These coins belong to the third and fourth century AD because these were issued in association with the copper issues of the Imperial Kuṣāṇas.

It has been suggested that the South Zone was ruled by the Kuṣāṇas through their Viceroys, and these Viceroys issued the Purī-Kuṣāṇa coins. Had these coins been issued by the Kuṣāṇa Viceroys, they have been distributed throughout the entire South Zone. They are conspicuously absent from all the finds in this region. Had these coins been issued by the Kuṣaṇa Governors, they should have been exactly of the type of the Kuṣāṇa coins and not merely their imitations, having just resemblance of the motifs.

It is reasonable to assume that the Purī-Kuṣāṇa coins were issued by some local ruler or rulers who had hold over a small territory, confined only to Orissa and adjoining territory in Bihar and Andhra Pradesh. They borrowed the idea from the motifs of the Kuṣāṇa coins, then current there, but at the same time, they had their own innovations in the matters of technique, fabric and weight. This makes it evident that the Kuṣāṇa coins were current there during this period or just before it. These Kuṣāṇa coins came there only through trade and travel because this region must have been a great trading centre during this period. The Kuṣāṇa contact of this region is clear from a unique gold coin found in the course of excavations at Śiśupālagaṛh in Orissa, which bears on the obverse the Kuṣāṇa motif, king standing like along with the legend read as *mahārāja rajadhasa dharmada-madharasa* (i.e. *mahārāja rājādhirāja dharmadama-dharasya*) in Brāhmī characters of the third century AD and on the reverse a Roman head with Roman legend.

The Tibetan and Chinese works, Jaina traditions and the *Purāṇas* mention the rule of the Maruṇḍas in northern India during the third century AD. These Maruṇḍas might have been alien people with kinship to the old Kuṣāṇa dynasty. It is possible that these coins might have been issued during the reign of the local ruler of the Maruṇḍa dynasty. The traders might have minted these coins for meeting their local needs. These were prepared in large number and readily available. These traders might have been selling or exchanging these copper coins at some premium and thus making a good profit for all the troubles they took to bring them from the west.

The Kuṣāṇa coins are of importance from the money economic point of view. Wima Kadphises is known to have started the gold coins of the Roman standard of 123 grains prevalent during the time of Augustus. Wima Kadphises was the powerful ruler and established vast empire. He was not only the ruler of India but also of outside territories such as

Yarkand, Kashgar and Khoṭān. The Romans at this time established vast empire and their coinage assumed international recognition for the purpose of trade and commerce. Wima Kadphises started the golden coins for external trade with the Roman empire as well as with other countries. Even his successors Kaniṣka, Huviṣka, Vāsudeva, Later Kuṣāṇas, Sassānians and Kidāra Kuṣāṇas continued the gold coins. The Kuṣāṇa and Roman coinages seem to have been exchanged in large scale commercial transactions of international trade.

Though originally, Kuṣāna gold coins started equal to the standard of Roman coins, they were not always imitated from the Roman aureus in point of weights. If that were so, then the weight of the Roman coinages of the first and second centuries AD should have been changed. On the contrary, the standard weight of the Kuṣāṇa coinage was maintained throughout the whole period from the time of Kadphises II down to the end of Vāsudeva's reign.

It has been shown by S.K. Maity[21] that the gold content of the Kuṣāṇa coins gradually decreased. Wima Kadphises 121.1 (1.19), Kaniṣka 120.45 (1.17.5), Huviṣka 123.6 (1.15.3, II. 1.19.7), (1.10.7) grains. It is clear from the specific gravity analysis published by S.K. Maity that the percentage of pure gold, that the Kuṣāṇa *dīnāras* contained, was very slightly but progressively reduced in the time of successors of Vāsudeva. Regarding the Sassānians, their gold coins are even purer than Vāsudeva of the Imperial Kuṣāṇa dynasty. But in this connection another economic implication should be profitably remembered, i.e., with the decline of the political fortunes of a dynasty, the gold content of its coinage declined. With the exception of Kuṣāṇa chief Pāsaka, the average content of the gold of the Kuṣāṇa chiefs are higher than the economically depressed little Kuṣāṇas. The analysis of coins leads to the classification of the coins of Huviṣka in two groups (A and B) which may suggest the existence of two Huviṣkas. But from the point of view of design and fabric, we cannot group them as such.

There were fluctuations in the weight of the Roman coinages of the first and second centuries AD. On the contrary, the standard weight of the Kuṣāṇa coinage was maintained throughout the whole period from the time of Kadphises II down to the end of Vāsudeva's reign.

Copper coins[22] were issued in large numbers by the Kuṣāṇa rulers with variation in their weight. The weight of the coins of Kujula Kadaphises is 42-167; Kadphises II 59-260; Kaniṣka 30.5, 64-260; Huviṣka 189-260; Vāsudeva 54-5-130 gms.

The unit of copper coinage in ancient India was called *paṇa* and according to Manu, its weight was like *suvarṇa* (gold coins) 144 grains — 16 *māṣas* — 80 *rattīs*. The *Agni Purāṇa* refers to a *paṇa* of 24 *māṣas*.

From the study of the copper coins of the Kuṣāṇas, it becomes that these may be divided into three classes on the basis of average weights.

(a) Coins weighing 260 grains — one *paṇa* of 28 *māṣas*.

(b) Coins weighing 130 grains — 1/2 *paṇa* of 14 *māṣas*.

(c) Coins weighing 65 grains — 1/4 *paṇa* of 7 *māṣas*.

CHANGING WEIGHING OF THE CURRENCY

The Kuṣāṇas may be given the credit for adjusting the weight of their currency to the changing ratio between gold and copper. Perhaps the value was determined by gold standard which came into vogue from the time of Wima Kadphises. The gradual reduction in the intrinsic value of gold in their coinage and the progressive reduction of the weight of their copper *tetradrachms* may be considered as the monetary policy of the Imperial Kuṣāṇas designed to solve some economic problems faced by them.

Roman Coins

Roman coins were found in the Deccan, Andhra Pradesh, Maharashtra, Gujarat and Madhya Pradesh. The gold coins were known by the term *aureus* and silver by *dīnārī*. These coins were brought into India by Roman traders for the purchase of Indian commodities, such as, precious stones, pearls, scents, spices, perfumes, silks and muslin. In the first century AD, these coins first remained confined to Coimbator District, Madras and Cītaldurg in Mysore but later spread to the entire Peninsula. In the second century AD, Roman coins shifted to Āndhradeśa, Maharashtra and Gujarat. Fine imitations of the Roman coins were current along with the genuine ones. These finds of Roman coins throw welcome light on the Indo-Roman trade.[23]

The Roman contacts with India began only in the time of Augustus (31 BC to AD 14) as it is clear from the finds (3, 5,10,14,15 and 30) which are confined to Coimbator District, Madras town and Cītaldurg in Mysore. The expansion of Roman contacts in the time of Tiberius (AD 14-37) is borne out from the five finds (3, 31, 38, 47 and 52). They show that the Roman trade was flourishing not only in Madras but had extended to the entire Peninsula from the West to the East. This expanded trade continued flourishing in the reign of Claudius (AD 41-54) as it is clear from three finds (6,12 and 29). The Roman trade continued even later in the time of Naro (AD 54-68) as known from four finds (13,17, 22 and 41). Most likely, the tempo of the Roman trade lasted only for about a three-quarter of a century. After Naro, only one find (21) is known of the time of Vespesian (AD 69-79).

The finds of the Roman coins thus indicate that Roman trade in the first century AD was carried out from the ports of Malabar like Tondi and Muziris (Carangore) on the Western coast and from the ports of Coromandal like Kurkai and Kaveripattanam on the eastern coast. As most of the coin finds of this period are centred round the region of Coimbatore, and thereby, they indicate the area around it had keener trade relations with Romans than any other parts of Peninsula. Most likely, this was to the great extent due to the beryl mine at Padiyur in Dharapuram *Tāluka*. Pliny seems to refer to this very mine.

No less than ten finds (32, 33, 34, 36, 37, 39, 40, 42, 43 and 44) indicate that the Roman trade activities in the second century AD had shifted from the lands of the Colas to the lands of the Āndhras. The Roman ships were now coming to the ports of Sopara and Bhṛgukaccha (Barygaza of the Romans) on the western side, and on the eastern side they anchored on the coastal emporium of Āndhradeśa. We have two finds (34 and 36) of the time of Hadrian, Trajan's successor (AD 111-38). Then we have six finds of the time of Antoninus Pius (AD 158-61), and they indicate that the Andhra country had a brisk trade relations with Rome. The trade relations with Rome seem to have ended by the first quarter of the third century AD because we do not have any Roman coin after Caracalla (AD 211-12) anywhere in the eastern and central regions of Āndhradeśa.

FAVOURABLE BALANCE OF TRADE

The import of the products of the Roman empire was negligible in comparison to the Indian exports. So the balance of trade was very unfavourable to the west. It resulted in a serious drain of gold and silver coins from the Roman empire. This was recognised by the emperor Tiberius. Writing to Senate in AD 22, he complained that the empire was being drained of its treasure which was being sent to foreign lands. Pliny (VI.25) complained a little later of the drain amounting to no less than 5,50,000,000 Sestertius flowed every year from Rome to India to pay for the Indian products, which were sold at fully one hundred times their original cost. This statement is not much rhetoric and is proved by the actual discovery of Roman coins in India.

The Roman coins discovered in the south were approximately of the same weight as the indigenous silver punch-marked coins, so they were converted into Indian coinage. For this purpose, first the Roman Imperial authority was cancelled by putting a chisel out over the Imperial efficy on the obverse, and they were authenticated by punching minute marks, similar to those seen on the punch-marked coins.

Fine imitations of the Roman coins were also current along with the genuine coins. These imitations are so finely eccented that they hardly differ with the original Roman coins so far the portrait of the emperor and the figure of the Goddess on the reverse is concerned. It is only the legends, where the imitations have failed. On the obverse, the legend is meaningless scribblings and on the reverse the inscription is erroneous.

Some small copper coins of pseudo-Roman type are also found at some places round about Madura. They closely resemble the early copper issues of the local mints but are Roman in their character. On one side, they bear the Imperial Roman head, very much worn out, sometimes with faint traces of an inscription; the other side shows three Roman soldiers standing with spears. These pseudo-Roman coins were probably struck in this country by the Roman settlers for their own use.

Finds of the Roman coins are also known from Maharashtra, Gujarat and Madhya Pradesh. We have a few coins of Caracalla (AD 198-217), Carirus (AD 283-85) and Diocletion (AD 284-304) from Mathurā (Find 56), Allāhābād (Find 54) and Mirzāpur (Find 55). How these Roman coins of the third century AD reached the Gaṅgetic plain, without leaving any trace of their way either by land or sea, we are unable to explain.

Coins of Western Kṣatrapas

A dynasty of the Śakas known as western Kṣatrapas came into prominence in western India. They belong to two groups — one is called Kṣaharāta and the other Kārdamaka. The former comprised only two rulers and the latter no less than twenty-seven. They ruled in Gujarat, Saurāṣṭra and Mālwā for more than two and a half centuries till AD 310. They issued mostly silver coins as regards size, weight and fabric of Roman *dīnārī* type for convenience of trade with the Western world. The *Periplus* mentions that Uzene was a great emporium from where semi-precious stones were exported to the West via Bharoch on the Narmadā estuary Rudradaman is known to have issued a large number of silver coins.

Some sort of uniformity is noticed on the western Kṣatrapa

coins. The average weight of these coins is about 35 grains. Their weight and module appear to have been based on the Indo-Greek or Roman silver money. Actually, they were issued to the weight standard of the Roman *dīnārī*. They also derived the head of the king from the Roman *dīnārī*. In the beginning, it shows changes in features, but later on, it became stereotype. Similarly in the early coins Graeco-Roman characters on their obverse degenerated into a sort of ornamental traces on the later silver coins. Western Kṣatrapas coins as influenced by Roman *dīnārī* are found. It was the circular Brāhmī legend on the reverse that mentions the name and the title, not only of the ruler, but also of his father. The crescented three-arched Hill with the Sun and the Moon on either side is the reverse symbol on the Kṣatrapa coins. In course of time, the Hill in the centre dominated the other two, which dwindled almost into insignificance. The year of issue in numerals was also introduced for the first time on the obverse of these coins during the reign of Rudrasiṁha I.

Only a few copper coins of Bhūmaka, the first member of the Kṣaharāta family, are known from the coastal regions of Gujarat, Saurāṣṭra and Mālwā. An arrow, a discus and a thunderbolt appears on their obverse and a lion capital flanked by a wheel on the reverse. The two sides of the coins bear the name of the ruler in Brāhmī and kharoṣṭhī, the former in Sanskrit and the latter in Prākṛt.

Both silver and copper coins were issued by Nahapāna, son and successor of Bhūmaka. The reverse type of the silver coins is the obverse type of Bhūmaka's copper coins. In all the coin legends Greek, Brāhmī and Kharoṣṭhī, Nahapāna bears the title Rājā together with his family designation Kṣaharāta. On the copper coinage, the reverse type of the silver coins, somewhat differentially arranged appears in association with a type 'tree' with large leaves, within railing.

The Kārdamaka Kṣatrapas issued coins in silver, copper (very rare) and potin. A few lead pieces are attributable to Svāmī Rudrasena III, a later ruler. The silver coins of Casṭana, the first member of the dynasty, have the royal bust on the obverse with traces of a Graeco-Roman legend. These coins are of two varieties in respect of the reverse. In one, a crescent and a star are placed side by side and in the other, a three-arched hill surmounted with a crescent is introduced in between the two. All the known coins of Rudradāman, the grandson of Castana are of silver, and in all the coin legends he bears the title *mahākṣatrapa*. Rudradāman seems to have been a powerful ruler because even Buddhaghoṣa, author of the fifth century AD in the *Sāratthadīpanī* seems to have mentioned *Rudradāmaka* for the silver coins of the Śakas of western India after him and *Rudradāmakādi* includes the non-Śaka silver coins such as those of the Sātavāhanas and the Guptas.[24]

The copper, potin and lead coins of these rulers are few. They differ from the silver coins only in regard to their obverse where the bust is replaced by an animal. The coins of Castana have a horse, of Jayadāman, Jīvadāman and Rudrasiṁha I, a bull. An elephant is seen on some other coins, which do not disclose the name of their issuers. A few coins bearing the name of Mahākṣatrapa Īśvaradatta with the years one, two and four have been found in some hoards along with the coins of the western Kṣatrapas. They are very similar to the Kṣatrapa coins. He appears to have been some usurper.

In Nasik inscriptions,[25] the coin denominations of the time of western Kṣatrapas, such as, *kārṣāpaṇa, suvarṇa* and *kuṣāṇa* have been mentioned. From this inscription, it is known that 70, 000 *kārṣāpaṇas* were equal in value to about 2000 *suvarṇas* and thus 35 *kārṣāpaṇas* would be equal to one *suvarṇa*. If it is assumed like D.R. Bhandarkar[26] that the silver *kārṣāpaṇas* and the gold *suvarṇas* represented the traditional indigenous currency of the weight of 32 *rattīs* and 80 *rattīs* respectively, then the ratio between silver and gold would be 35 × 32 : 80, i.e., 14 : 1. But this conclusion goes aganist the testimony of *Periplus*, according to which in the first century AD, silver was dearer in India than in the West. The standard of *kārṣāpaṇa* and *suvarṇa* referred to in the Nāsik inscription should not be considered as traditional as mentioned in the *Smṛtis* but actually in vogue during the second century AD. Silver coins were issued by Nahapāna in western India. The silver of Nahapāna is about 35 grains only. If these were the prevailing standards, the ratio between silver and gold was about 10 :1. The ratio might have been even 9 : 1 if the percentage of alloy in the Kuṣāṇa gold coinage of the period were taken into account. In Persia, at that time, the ratio was 13 : 1. It was thus profitable to exchange silver for gold in India as the author of *Periplus* has mentioned.

In the Nāsik inscription of Uṣabhadāta, son-in-law of Kṣatrapa Nahapāna, mention is made of an investment as providing, some resident monks with *kuṣāṇamūla*. The term *kuṣāṇa* has been applied by D.R. Bhandakar[27] to the silver coins of Nahapāna who issued them for his Kuṣāṇa overlord Kujula Kadphises. According to S.K. Chakravarty,[28] 'Kuṣāṇa' used in this context refers to the coins of the Kuṣāṇa emperors. The gold coins of Kaniṣka have the legend, *śāonāno śāo kaneṣki kuṣāṇo* but the copper coins omit the word *kuṣāṇo*. From this, it has been inferred that it is the gold coins of the Kaniṣka which are referred to in the inscriptions as *kuṣāṇamūla*, i.e., the value of a Kuṣāṇa, the gold coins of Kaniṣka, since gold was the standard coinage of the Empire.

INDIGENOUS COINS

After the fall of the Mauryas, indigenous coins were also issued in northern India. These may be divided into two classes — uninscribed and inscribed. Most of these coins are in copper and rarely in silver. Most of the uninscribed coins are found of the cast and die-struck technique but some are of the punch-marked technique. These coins reveal the importance of the local money economy.

Some copper punch-marked coins are attributed to the Śuṅgas. These are square or rectangular dumpy pieces, about one and a half inches long and three-quarters of an inch wide bearing fivebold symbols on one side and four on the other in the punch-marked figure and they have come from various places in Bihar. Quite likely, these coins were issued by Puṣyamitra Śuṅga who usurped the Mauryan throne in about 184 BC. His successors had shifted to Vidiśā. And we find there also the copper coins in the punch-marked technique. They are flat, broad pieces about an inch in size. They bear four or five neat symbols on one side. The other side is blank. These coins in all likelihood belong to the later Suṅga rulers and their successors, the Kāṇvas.[29]

The uninscribed coins of the period are known from Gāndhāra in the North-West Kauśāmbī in the Gangetic plains and Ujjayinī in Central India. Some of the Gāndhāra coins are stamped only on one side and some are stamped on both. The earlier coins used symbols very much similar to those that were used on the punch-marked coins. But soon these symbols were replaced and new devices of animals were introduced. The excavations at Taxila show that the coins of the latter type were current there side by side with the Indo-Bactrian and Śaka-Pahlava coins. The uninscribed coins of Vatsa, whose capital was at Kauśāmbī, are casts. They bear on one side a humbed bull of a lanky type with one or two symbols or the *Abhiṣeka* Lakṣmī, i.e., Lakṣmī standing facing in front with elephants on either side sprinkling water. The other side bears a hill and tree and a few other symbols and may be identified into several varieties.

Ujjayinī Coins

The coins of Ujjayinī are known in a large number of varieties. Most of them bear on one side a single symbol which is popularly known as 'Ujjain symbol'. It is a cross with a circle at the top of each arm. The circle on the coins is mostly plain, but in some cases, it is double circle. The other side of the coin has two to seven symbols, similar to those seen on the punch-marked coins. But on some coins, a striking figure of a standing man with a long stick is seen who in some cases is three-headed. He is identified as Śiva or Kārttikeya. Occassionally, a female figure is also seen on these coins and she is taken to be Lakṣmī.

Abundance of Uninscribed Coins

It was only after the Mauryan period that uninscribed coins were abundantly issued and widely in circulation. According to some scholars, the Indians learnt the fashion of putting the name of the issuing authority or legends on the coins from the Indo-Greeks : Bela Lahiri[30] does not agree to this view. She is of the view that Eran coin with the legend *dhamapālasa* furnishes the earliest example of India's incribed coins and is undoubtedly earlier than any Indo-Greek coin.

Inscribed Coins

The stratigraphical evidence of coins in various excavations in different places of India such as Hastināpur, Kauśāmbī, Rājghāṭ, Śrāvastī, and a Sahgaura, clearly indicates that inscribed coins started later than the uninscribed ones.

The inscribed coins may be divided into three classes (1) City coins, (2) Tribal coins and (3) Monarchical coins.

CITY COINS

City coins seem to be the earliest of the inscribed monetary coins of India. These are found in many places in association with the punch-marked and uninscribed cast coins from layers datable to about the third and second centuries BC while they are rare in later layers. In Kauśāmbī again the city coins which are cast and closely connected with the early uninscribed cast pieces of that place were presumably followed by the die-struck coins bearing rulers' names. Moreover, the cryptic Brāhmī legends of the city coins, consisting of the Prākṛt forms of the names of the cities in the nominative, are in sharp contrast with those of the Dynastic or Tribal Issues which are in the genitive, and indicates an earlier date of mintage for the former. City coins seem to have started about the second half of the third or the beginning of the second century BC.

NO FOREIGN INFLUENCE ON COINS

The city coins are generally of purely indigenous fabric and character, betraying no sign whatsoever of any foreign influence. The coins so far known are made of copper or some alloy of it. Both round and square-shaped coins are known. The cities of this period known from the coins are : Vārāṇasī,

Śrāvastī, and Kauśāmbī in the Gangetic plains, Uddehika and Sudavapa in eastern Rajasthan, Ujjayinī, Erakaṇya, Māhiṣmatī Kurara, Bhagila and Tripurī in Madhya Pradesh and Hiraṇya Śrama, Puṣkalāvatī, Kapiśā and Taxila in Gāndhāra. The coins of these cities continued for a short period. In most cases, monarchy prevailed in them. Coins of some of these states particularly in the region of Rajasthan bear both name of the place and the ruler.

The important city coins are described below :

(i) *Vārāṇasī Coins* : The coins of the city Vārāṇasī are rectangular in shape. The obverse shows the figure of a horse to left while the reverse has traces of the so-called Ujjain symbol. The legend Bārāṇasī in characters of about the first century BC appears on the reverse above the device.

(ii) *Kauśāmbī Coins* : Kauśāmbī was the capital of Vatsa *Janapada*. A few coins bearing the legends *kosabī, koshavī, kośabikanam*, etc. are known.[31] These coins were issued by a corporation of traders who had their establishment in Kauśāmbī. A round coin,[32] bears the circular legend *gandhikānam* in bold Brāhmī characters of about the third-second century BC on the obverse and a square with four compartments on the reverse, and was probably issued by the *gandhikas* or the Guild of dealers in perfume of the city of Kauśāmbī and is in the nature of guild-tokens. The donations made by the *gandhikas* are referred to in various early inscriptions from Bharhut, Mathurā, Karle, Pitalkhora, Amarāvatī, etc.[33] All these show that the *gandhikas* played an important role in ancient Indian economic life.

(iii) *Vidiśā Coins* : The commercial importance of Vidiśā is proved by the discovery of some coins,[34] with the name of the city. They are described as bearing on the obverse the figure of an eight-spoked and on the reverse the legend *vidiśā* or *veddasa* in Brāhmī characters of the early second century BC. These coins were found in association with punch-marked coins.

(iv) *Erakaṇya Coins* : Some coins with the legend *erakaṇya*[35] have been found. The commercial importance of Erakaṇya is evident from the number and variety of coins from that area. Some coins with the legend dug up from recent excavations at Eran prove that they may be dated about the beginning of the second century BC.

(v) *Bhāgila and Kurakura Coins* : The coins with the legend *bhāgilaya* may be issue of the city of Bhāgila which has not been identified.[36] The coins bearing the legend *kurarāya* have been found near the find-spot of the Bhāgilāya coins.[37] This place name, Kurarāya, has been mentioned in the votive inscriptions of Sāñcī.[38]

(vi) *Ujjayinī Coins* : The coins with the legend *ujeni* are found at Ujjain. On the obverse, there is elephant while on the reverse is Ujjayinī symbol with the legend *ujaniyi*.[39] The characters are of the first half of the second century BC. These city coins are found from the mid-level of Period II of Ujjain excavation (500 to 200 BC).

(vii) *Māhiṣmatī Coins* : On some coins, we find *Māhiṣa* identified with the ancient city of Māhiṣamatī.[40] Maheśwar not Mandhāta appears to represent the site of the ancient city of Māhiṣmatī coin with Brāhmī characters *Mahisati*. The coin found in a stratified condition would furnish us with a strong ground for identifying Māhiṣmatī with Maheśwar-Navadatoli. The stratigraphy of the coin indicates a date about the third or second century BC which also seems to be the date of the inscribed city issues.

(viii) *Tripurī Coins* : Tripurī is now known as Tewar. Some coins bearing the legend *tripurī* in early Brāhmī characters are ascribed to this city.

(ix) *Vachaghoṣa, Uddehika and Sudavapa Coins* : Some coins found in the region of the eastern Rajasthan bear the names of the place and ruler both. The coins with the legend *senāpatisa vachaghoṣa* written in the early Brāhmī characters about the second century BC were discovered at Rairh in the excavations.[41] In the opinion of K.K. Dass Gupta,[42] Vachaghoṣa was the name of the Mint-town where from the coins in question were issued by one — *senāpati* who was either a provincial Governor of some unknown king or perhaps

Puṣyamitra Śuṅga.

Some coins of Sūryamitra and Dhruvamitra of the first or second century were also found at Rairh. On the reverse of these coins, there is the representation of a menandring river with fish. On the obverse of the coins of Sūryamitra, there is bull and on the coins of Dhruvamitra elephant.[43] K.N. Dikshit[44] thinks that these are Uddehika coins because the same name of the ruler and symbols are found. On these coins, the name of Sudavapa is found. Uddehika and Sudavapa seem to be the place names.

(x) *Kapiśā and Puṣkalāvatī Coins* : In Gāndhāra, city coins were issued. The Indo-Greek ruler Eucratides issued the coin of city divinity of Kapiśā with the legend *kavisiya nagara-devatā.*[45] The unique gold piece bearing the figure of Goddess and the legend *pakhalavadidevatā* (the city divinity of Puṣkalāvatī) on the obverse and Greek legend Taurus on the reverse, was probably struck by Indo-Scythians. These two are not indigenous city coins.

(xi) *Taxila Coins* : Taxila was the capital of eastern Gāndhāra. The inscribed issues may be divided into three classes according to their legends (1) The *negamā* series, (2) The *pañcanekame* series and (3) The *hiraṇsame* series.

That the guilds or corporations of traders were empowered to issue coins is attested by the *negamā* coins from Taxilā. The word *negamā* (Skt. *naigamaḥ*) here should be taken to mean "the *śreṇīs* or corporations of merchants. The Taxila *negamā* coins bear several other words *dojaka, atatalaka, rālimasa, kedara,*[46] etc. These terms probably refer to the merchants localities where respective coins were minted. Some, Taxila coins bear the legend *pañcanekame* meaning probably that they were issues of a joint body of five *nigamās* or of a guild called *pañcanigama*. This would indicate in the Gāndhāra region during the third, second centuries BC, there existed several guilds of traders who were authorised to issue coins bearing their particular names. The appearance of the weighing scale on several coins signifies the correctness of weight.

Another class of inscribed coins from Taxila bears the legend *hiraṇyasame*[47] (golden hermitage) : According to K.D. Bajpai,[48] this interpretation appears to be far from satisfactory, and he suggests that this legend, which is in the nominative form, may be taken to mean *hiraṇyasvāmī* (the owner of the coined money). The word *hiraṇya* does not mean gold only but it also stands for coined money. This possibly refers to the corporation of traders responsible for the manufacture of these coins. There are some other coins with curious legends, like, *kādasa, vatasvaka, upagodasa, upātikyā, madavika,* etc. but we are not in a position to ascertain those names referred to cities or tribes.[49]

IMPACT OF CITY COINS ON MONEY ECONOMY

It appears that these city coins are of great significance from the point of view of money economy. With the collapse of the imperial authority of the Mauryas in northern India, trade was localised within limited areas in India. With the disappearance of a central minting authority, the regional authorities and the main trade centres took upon themselves the initiative of striking their own coinages for purpose of local transactions. It is significant that most of the cities that issued coins during the early post-Mauryan period were situated in the belt of land between the Gaṅgā-Jamunā and the Narmadā Valley. As known from the literary sources also, the cities of Vārāṇasī, Kauśāmbī and Erakiṇa lay in the route which connected Ujjayinī with Pāṭaliputra while another route from Pratiṣṭhāna to Vaiśālī went through the cities of Māhiṣmatī, Sāketa, Śrāvastī and others. The busy trade that passed throguh these ancient cities naturally necessitated the issuing of monetary tokens as mediums of exchange and this led to prosperity and some amount of autonomy for the cities. The Śuṅgas, successors of the Mauryas, are not so far known to have struck any coins in their own names and do not seem to have interested with the issue of local coinages.

TRIBAL COINS

Tribal coins began their appearance after the disintegration of the Maurya empire. Most of these tribes were located in Punjab. The tribes, that issued coins in the second century BC, were the Agreya, Rājenya, Śibi, Yaudheya, Kṣudraka, etc. In the first century BC were known the tribes —Auḍumbaras, Kuṇinda, Vṛṣṇī, Rājanya and Vemaka and in the frist century AD we hear of Mālava and Kalūta. In the second century AD a tribe known as Ārjunāyana is known. Of all these tribes, only Mālava, Yaudheya and Ārjunāyana are mentioned in the Allāhābād Pillar inscription of the Gupta emperor—Samudragupta. Some of these tribes stayed on in the Punjab and others moved to Rajasthan and elesewhere, probably under the pressure of foreign invaders.

DIE-STRUCK COPPER COINS

The tribal coins may be regarded as representing an advanced stage in the development of Indian coinage. Early coins were punch-marked but now die-stricking coins began to be issued. Another important new feature is the introduction of coin legends. They refer to their names, and in few cases the place also, on their coins in the Brāhmī script. Copper was the prime issue of all these republics. Each tribe seems to have its own weight for the coins, and a number of them had issued coins in more than one weight as multiples or submultiples.

A few tribes issued coins in silver also, but these coins are extremely rare. These silver coins follow the weight of *hemidrachm* of the Indo-Bactrian rulers. In module too, these coins are akin to the Indo-Bactrian coins. The well-executed copper coins of the Yaudheyas of the later period show Kuṣāṇa influence in their type and style. Following the Indo-Bactrian and other coins, Gods and Goddesses were introduced on some of these coins.

The coins of these tribal states are as follows :

(i) *Agreya Coins* : Coins generally bearing the legend in early Brāhmī characters; *Agodaka* (or *-e*) *Agāchajana-padasa*, i.e., *Agrodakāt* or (*Agrodake*) *Agratya janapadasya* is to be attributed to a tribe called Agra.[50] The *Janapada* named Agra, whose chief city appears to have been known as

Agrodake, the region being represented by the modern village of Agroha, the find-spot of the coins. Agroha is situated at a distance of 21 km from Hissar. Coins of this tribe are made of copper and mostly of rectangular or square shape. The symbols tree, bull, lion and Laksmī are engraved on these coins.

(ii) *Rājanya Coins* : Coins of the Rājanya *Janapada* with the legends either in Brāhmī or in Kharoṣṭhī have been discovered. The Rājanyas probably lived somewhere in north or north-eastern Rajasthan, where both the scripts were in use.[51] G.H. Ojha locates them in the region of Mathurā because their Lakṣmī and bull type of coins resemble those of the Kṣatrapa rulers of Mathurā.[52]

(iii) *Śibi Coins* : Coins[53] of the Śibi tribe found in the area round Nāgarī near Chittor in Rajasthan have the legend *mājhamikāya— śibi-janapadasa*, i.e., coins of the Śibi state struck at Madhyamikā. The territory of the Śibi State is located round about Chittor in Rajasthan.

(iv) *Yaudheya Coins* : The Yaudheyas[54] were great powers occupying eastern Punjab. They extended their power which included north Rajasthan and part of Uttar Pradesh. They began to issue coins from the second century BC. Allan attributes the Potin coins without the name of the tribe to the Yaudheyas. The Yaudheyas also issued the coins of the bull and elephant type with the legend *yaudheyānām*. On some coins, we find the name *bahudhāñyake* meaning rich in corn. They issued the Brāhmaṇya Deva type with the six-headed Kārttikeya on the obverse and the Lakṣmī standing between the tree and hill with the legend *bhāgvata svāmino brāhmaṇya yaudheya*. It is clear that Brāhmaṇya is the national God Kārttikeya to whom they dedicated their coins. The Yaudheyas also issued the warrior type with the legend *yaudheyanām gaṇaśya jayaḥ*. There is Kuṣāṇa influence on these coins. The coins of Brāhmaṇya type and warrior type are mostly of copper and only a few of silver.

(v) *Auḍumbara Coins* : Most of the coins are found in the district round Paṭhānkoṭ in the Punjab. Most of these coins are found in copper but a few in silver. These coins bear the name of the tribe. The types issued are tree within railing and two-storeyed domed *stūpa*, humped bull and elephant, and male figure standing holding spear and elephant with rider. Among the rulers, Dharaghoṣa is important.

(vi) *Kṣudraka Coins* : Coins bearing the Brāhmī legend Kṣudrakas[55] have been discovered at a small village Pandusar in a *Tehsil* Nohar, District Śrī Gaṅgānagar, Rajasthan. These coins have tree in railing.

(vii) *Kadasa Coins* : The Kadasa coins,[56] which are rude copper cast coins, bear the legend *kadasa* in Brāhmī characters. They belong to the Kaṭha tribe of Punjab which prominently figures in the accounts of Alexander's invasion. At that time, they occupied the territory between the Rāvi and Beās rivers.

(viii) *Kuṇinda Coins* : The coins of the Kuṇindas[57] fall into two main groups, one issued around the end of the first century BC and the other was resumed in *c.* AD 200. The former bears the name of Kuṇinda and its ruler Amoghabhūti both in Brāhmī and Kharoṣṭhī scripts in Prākṛt. Silver and copper coins are similar in type. The nodule of the silver coins was suggested by *hemidrachms* of the later Greek kings but the types are purely Indian. Economically, the silver coins of the Kuṇindas represent an attempt of an Indian ruler to issue a native silver coinage which would compete in the market with the later Indo-Greek silver. We find the symbols such as the six-arched hill, tree in railing, banner, Lakṣmī and Cobra. The Kuṇindas occupied the territory between the upper courses of the Beās and the Sutlej.

The coinage of the Kuṇindas then disappeared for three centuries till the end of the second or third century AD. We find coins again issued by a Kuṇinda republic. These coins bear a general resemblance to the Kuṣāṇa coinage in weight and fabric. The standing king on the obverse is, however, replaced by the figure of Śiva, holding the trident in his hand. The symbols on the coinage are of earlier type. The Brāhmī script replaces the Kharoṣṭhī. The average weight of the copper coins of the Kuṇindas is about 160 grains.

(ix) *Vṛṣṇī Coins* : Vṛṣṇī coins[58] have been discovered at Sunet in District Paṭiālā in the Punjab. There are silver coins, and have the legend *vṛṣṇirājajā-gaṇasya tratarasya* in Brāhmī on the obverse and Kharoṣṭhī on the reverse. The obverse is a pillar surmounted by an animal, half lion and half elephant, above which is a *nandīpada*. The reverse is an elaborate wheel, probably to be interpreted as a *dharmacakra*.

(x) *Vemaka Coins* : Vamaka coins[59] probably came from Hośiārpur District, Punjab. On the obverse, we find the legend *vamakisa* in Brāhmī and Kharoṣṭhī.

(xi) *Mālava Coins* : Mālava coins have been discovered at Nagara near Uniyara in Jaipur District. J. Allan[60] dates these coins between the second century AD and the earliest part of the fourth century. The heaviest of them do not exceed 40 grains in weight and the lightest are as light as 1.7 grains. These Mālava coins are divided into three groups. Group I bears the legends *mālavānām jayah* or *mālavagaṇasya jayaḥ*. The coins have the vase, lion, bull, king's head, fan-tail, peacock and other objects as their reverse design. The two other groups of coins are ascribed to the Mālavas primarily because they were found along with the Mālava coins and resembled the latter in fabric. The coins of the second group do not bear any legend, while those of the third category have meaningless legend in which the name of the Mālava cannot be usually traced. V.A. Smith[61] regarded these coins as the most curious and enigmatical in the vast range of Indian coinage. This is partly due to the meaningless legends of the third class of the coins, and partly also to the light weight and small size of many coins J. Allan thinks that they are not names but in many cases meaningless attempts to reproduce parts of *mālavānam jayaḥ*, D.C. Sircar[62] does not regard these coins as the genuine monetary issues of the Mālavas but they were minted by the local goldsmiths in imitation of the Mālava coins in order to meet the needs of the people.

(xii) *Kulūta Coins* : The Kulūtas were the ancient inhabitants of the Kulū valley in the Kangrā District of the Punjab. The only known coin[63] however, is of much earlier date, probably of the first or early second century AD. It bears the legend *virayaśasya rājña kulūtasya* of the Kulūta king Virayaśa in Brāhmī. On the obverse there is a wheel surrounded by a circle of dots. The reverse type is made up of a number of symbols all well-known, a mountain with a river below, a *svastika*, a *nāga* symbol and an elaborate *nandīpada* symbol. The coin is a *didrachm* of the standard of the later Greek and Pārthian kings of India who do not, however, strike his denomination.

(xiii) *Ārjunāyana Coins* : Coins of the Ārjunāyana bear the full legend *ārjunāyanām jaya* victory of the Ārjunāyanas are rare and they are known in several varieties.[64] We find the bull on the obverse, and on the reverse, there is a standing female figure identified with the Lakṣmī. They occupied the area of eastern Rajasthan.

MONARCHICAL COINS

In the Gangetic Doab, there sprang up monarchies during this period. Among them, four are important. One was the Sūrasena with its centre at Mathurā, the other was of the Pañcāla with its capital at Ahichatra (Rāmnagar, District Bareilly), the third was of the Vatsa with its headquarters at Kauśāmbī and the fourth was of Kośala. It had its capital either at Śrāvastī (District Goṇḍā, U.P.) or at Ayodhyā (District Faizābād).

MATHURĀ COINS

The coins attributed to Mathurā[65] fall into two main series : Those struck by local Hindu dynasties in the second and first centuries BC and those struck by Śaka Satraps. The earliest ruler of the Sūrasena kingdom known from his coins was Gomitra. He was followed by Sūryamitra, Brahmamitra, Dṛḍhamitra and Viṣṇumitra. The coins of Gomitra bear the figure of Lakṣmī holding a lotus in her up-lifted hand, and on the reverse, there are three elephants facing each with a rider. The coins of these other rulers also bear symbols similar to those that were used earlier for the punch-marked coins such as the tree in railing, river with fishes and Ujjayinī symbol. The Mitra dynasty was supplanted by the kings having names with the suffix 'Datta'. The kings of this dynasty were Śeṣadatta, Puruṣadatta, Uttamadatta, Rāmadatta, Kāmadatta and Bhavadatta. Thereafter ruled two other rulers Balabhūti and Apalata. These rulers are known on their coins as bearing the regal title *rājā* and Apalata bears *mahārāja*. The coins of these rulers follow the types of the preceding Mitra rulers.

Among the Śaka rulers of Mathurā, the earliest of them is Rajuvula, who was originally the ruler of some parts of the Punjab as known from his earliest coins. These coins are *hemidrachm* of silver, highly debased with lead and closely resemble those of the Indo-Bactrian ruler Strata. The portrait on the obverse shows the king facing to the right, the legend in blundered Greek gives his name with the title *basileos basilion sotoros*. The reverse shows Pallas, Athene and the Kharoṣṭhī legend. He issued another type in lead showing a lion on the obverse and Herakles on the reverse with Greek and Kharoṣṭhī legends. When Rajuvula occupied Mathurā, he issued coins similar to the coins of the earlier ruler of that place, with a standing Lakṣmī on the obverse and an *Abhiṣeka* Lakṣmī on the reverse. On them, the inscription is in Brāhmī. Rajuvula was followed by his two sons Sodāsa and Toranadāsa. Then Hegama and Hagamaṣa ruled jointly for some time, thereafter Hagamaṣa ruled alone. They were followed by two other rulers Śivadatta and Śivaghoṣa. While Rajuvula and Sodāsa had the title of Mahākṣatrapa on their coins, the others bear only the title of Kṣatrapa.

PAÑCĀLA COINS

The Pañcāla coins[66] form one of the largest and most uniform series of ancient Indian coins. These remarkable series of coins were found at Ahicchatra, Aonla, Badaon, Eastern Oudh and Bastī Districts. These are of copper and round in shape. On the obverse, we find the three symbols: tree in railing, trident with base and Mauryan "ẏ" mounted on ^ with the king's name below and on the reverse, there is some deity connected with the king. No less than twenty-one rulers are known to have issued these coins. On the coins of there is a deity on the reverse identified with *agni.* On the reverse, we have the deities such as Lakṣmī, Sun, Earth, Dhruva, Indra, Phālguni, Rudra and Viṣṇu of the respective rulers. Towards the end, some coins from Pañcāla are known to be of quite a different series showing a wheel on one side and the name Acyu on the other These coins are taken to be the coins of Acyuta, who is mentioned in the Allāhābād Pillar inscription.

VATSA COINS

Vatsa coins bear a bull with a symbol on one side and tree in railing with some other symbols on the other with the name of the king. The coins with these devices are uniformly found for about eighteen rulers[67] such as Vavaghoṣa, Aśvaghoṣa, Parvata, Indradeva and Sudeva. Soon after them, the coins of a new dynasty are known. They also retain the above devices with a slight modification; but the fabric is quite different. These coins bear the names Bhadramagha, Vaiṣṇavana, Bhīmavarman, Navika, Puṣvaśrī and Dhanadeva. Lastly, we have coin bearing the name Rudra on one side and Śiva standing by the side of the bull on the other. Most likely Rudra, the issuer of the coin, was Rudradeva who is mentioned in the Allāhābād Pillar inscription.

KOŚALA COINS

The Kośalas issued by the cast coins in the beginning. These coins have a bull or an elephant before a standard and the reverse bears five or six symbols of the type issued on earlier punch-marked coins. The issuers of the coins were Mahādeva, Vāyudeva, Viśākhadeva and Dhanadeva. Another series of cast coins were issued by Navadatta, Jyeṣṭhadatta and Śivadatta. These coins are similar to the above but smaller in size. Śivadatta issued some other coins showing an elephant on one side and an *Abhiṣeka* Lakṣmī on the other. Some die-struck coins bearing the name Śivadatta are also known. Perhaps, he was different from the issuer of the above coins. Such coins have a bull before a tree-railing. His coins were followed with certain modifications by Haradatta, Śivapalita, Kumudasena, Ajavarman, Sanghamitra, and

Vijayamitra. Vijayamitra issued a new type. On it, while he retained the bull on the obverse, the reverse has a *haṁsa* (swan) before a palm tree. This type was also issued by Sūryamitra, Devamitra and Āryamitra.

NĀGA COINS

Nāga coins have been discovered at Vidiśā, Kāntipurī (Kutwar) and Padmāvatī (Pawāyā).[68] Vṛṣanāga is known to be the Nāga ruler of Vidiśā. Sometime in the second century AD, there arose the dynasty of the Nāgas which lasted in all probability up to the fourth century AD. The rulers of this dynasty known are Bhīma, Skanda, Vasu, Bṛhaspati, Ravi, Prabhākara Bhava, Deva and Gaṇapati. The coins of Gaṇapati are found in large number, and he is identified with the name Gaṇapati mentioned in the Allāhābād inscription of Samudragupta.

These Nāga coins are die-struck. Most of them are round but some are rectangular. On one side, of the coins, there is a symbol in a circle of pellets, one group bearing the figure of a peacock, and the other of a humped bull. Some of the Nāga rulers issued coins with an additional recurring symbol. These symbols are—a trident, a crescent, a lion and a wheel. Except the last one, all are Śaivite emblems. The other side has a fragementary Brāhmī legend—*mahārāja, adhirāja* and *śrī.* These are of copper and confirm to the standard of thirty six, eighteen and nine grams representing respectively a *kākiṇī,* a half *kākiṇī* and greater *kākiṇī* respectively.

A few silver coins issued by the Auḍumbaras, Kulutas, Kuṇindas and Yaudheyas are all based on the *hemidrachms* of the later Greek and Śaka kings and are of the later Indo-Greek standard. It was due to the influence of the foreign powers in the neighbourhood of which they were situated. They might have some trade relations with them. These states are known to have issued numerous copper coins. It is difficult to generalize about the weight of these copper coins. In the first place, they were not struck or cast so carefully as the silver coins, and secondly they have suffered much more in course of time. These copper coins prove that their issuing state authorities were not so prosperous. These coins served only the local ordinary transactions. They were not meant for outside trade and commerce.

EARLY COINS OF SOUTH INDIA

After the disintegration of the Mauryan empire, many subordinate and feudatory families who were serving the Mauryan emperor faithfully, all of a sudden declared independence. The centralised money economy was shattered, and it was replaced by the local one. The local governors and feudatories called Mahārāṭhīs established their own kingdoms in many parts of the Deccan. They began to issue die-struck coins. Their early coins were uninscribed and are of copper. In course of time, they started to issue inscribed coins. Among the inscribed coins, lead coins are found in large number. The credit of inaugurating of minting coins in lead goes to these Mahārāṭhīs. After the Mahārāṭhīs, Ānandas ruled and their coins are also available. The Sātavāhanas ruled for a considerable time and over wide territory. Their coins are the richest in the Deccan both in variety and quantity. The money economy of the Sātavāhanas is regional in characteristic. It is indigenous and it played dominant role in the development of coinage of South India.

Uninscribed Coins

After the fall of the Mauryas, the local governors and feudatories in the beginning issued the die-struck uninscribed coins for sometime all over the Deccan paticularly in the Pāṇḍyan and Āndhra areas. The Pāṇḍyan die-struck copper coins are rectangular in shape and invariably have a big elephant either alone or associated with a few other symbols smaller in size. Most of these symbols are similar to those which are found on the north Indian early die-struck uninscribed coins.

The Āndhra die-struck coins have been found only in excavations and are not many in number. They generally have one symbol on each side, occassionally, some of them have one or two small symbols accompanying them. The symbols found on these coins are mostly hills of different types *nandīpada, svastika,* bull and tree in railing.

MAHĀRAṬHĪS

The Mahāraṭhīs ruled over Mysore Kanara region. They might have issued some above uninscribed coins, but they soon issued coins inscribed with their names. Only three members of the family are known so far through their coins. Their coins bear the Brāhmī legends *sadakaṇa kalaya mahāraṭhīsa, sadakaṇa cunekanha mahāraṭhīsa* and *sadakaṇa kanasa mahāraṭhīputasa.* This family is called Sadakaṇa by the surname. The credit for minting the coins in lead goes to these Mahāraṭhīs. They might have preferred this metal because it was easily available to them in the neighbourhood. It remained the prime metal of south Indian coinage for a considerable time. These coins are circular and thick with a diameter ranging from 1.5" to 0.95". Most of the specimens measure about an inch in diameter. The lowest weigh about 67 grains and the highest weigh about 221 grains. These coins have a standing bull on the obverse and a tree in railing and a six-arched hill with or without a few small symbols on the reverse.

ĀNANDA COINS

The Sadakaṇa family was followed by another family which may be called Ānanda Cutukulananda and Mulananda the only members of the family who are known from their lead coins. These coins have a big symbol of nine-arches — two rows of four small arches each one over the other and over them a big arch. Over the symbol is an inscription. The reverse has a tree in railing with a few small symbols. These are the earliest south Indian rulers who adopted the title of *rājā (rājña)* on thier coins. Their coins are known from the Kerwar area and the excavations at Candravallī.

KURA COINS

Another Mahāraṭhī family famous by the name Kura ruled round about Kolhāpur in Maharashtra. The Kura rulers known from the coins are Varithiputra Vilivāyakura, Māḍhariputra Śivalakura and Gotamiputra Vilivāyakura. This is the earliest metronymic on the Indian coins and reveals that matriarchal family system was followed by the people to which the Kuras belonged. All these rulers had their coins in lead and introduced copper or potin (copper-lead alloy) also. These coins uniformly bear a bow and arrow along with the inscription on the obverse. On the reverse is found a bull symbol either alone or associated with a tree. An interesting feature of the Kura is that they are mostly restruck. A number of Kura coins have been found amongst the Brahmapurī (Kolhāpur) hoard, cut into a half, one-third and a quarter. Perhaps, they were cut to serve the purpose of fractional coins.

There was another Mahāraṭhī family with his kingdom in the heart of Āndhradeśa but their inscriptions on the coins cannot be deciphered. A new kingdom in the region of Vidarbha issued coins bearing the name *rājño dimbha* and *rājño sebaka.*

SĀTAVĀHANA COINS

Thousands of Sātavāhana coins have come to light in the whole of India. They are mostly discovered in Mālwā, Kṛṣṇā-Godāvarī area in Āndhra, Maharashtra and Karnataka. The Sātavāhana kings minted potin, lead, copper and silver coins. Silver coins are, however, not prolific as the lead and potin coins. The Sātavāhanas developed the technique of coinage which was locally available in the country itself. These coins do not show any foreign influence in the early period. These coins, though exhibit originality in their execution, do not show high artistic merit. Generally, the figures and even the legends are crude. But still, the Sātavāhana coinage played a dominant role in their development of coinage of south India and the Deccan. They have somehow influenced the subsequent coins.

The Mahārathī and other rulers were followed by the kings of the dynasty which is styled in the *Purāṇas* as Āndhra, Āndhrajati or Āndhra-bhṛtya and is called Sātavāhana or Sātakarṇi. According to the Purāṇic traditions, the Āndhra

Sātavāhana dynasty began with Simuka who destroyed the remains of the Śuṅga power and killed the Kāṇva king Susarman. Simuka Sātavāhana is also known from the coins. 29 or 30 rulers of this family are known from the *Purāṇas*. The first 21 rulers of the Purāṇic are unknown in numismatic history but it is only the last nine rulers of the Purāṇic list whose historicity is supported from coins. The coins show that these rulers were of some considerable importance. It appears from the coins that the Sātavāhanas came into prominence as independent rulers only after the fall of Śuṅga and Kāṇva rulers in 27 BC. The early rulers known from the coins are Śrī Sātakarṇi. These rulers may conveniently be identified as Śrī Svāti and Gautamīputra Sātkarṇi of the *Purāṇas*. Besides the above two, six of them are Śrī Pulumāvi, Śiva Śrī Pulumāvi, Skanda Sātakarṇi, Śrī Yajña Sātkarṇi, Vajaya Sātakarṇi and Pulahamāvi of the Purāṇic list, the successors of Śrī Sātakarṇi in regular order. Besides them, the coins are also known of four others who do not find mention in the *Purāṇas* — Śaka Sātakarṇi, Rudra Sātakarṇi, Śaka Kumbha Sātakarṇi and Karṇa or Kṛṣṇa Sātakarṇi.

Motifs depicted on Sātavāhana coins include certain broad devices like the figure of elephant, lion or horse and some traditional Indian symbols such as tree in railing, Ujjain symbol, hill symbol and river symbol. The largest number of the Sātavāhana coins are found having an elephant on the obverse. The ship symbol may indicate the naval strength of the Sātavāhanas as well as the sea borne trade. It is only the rare silver coins that depict on the obverse the issuer's head, but even there the reverse depicts a group of indigenous symbols like the crescent-topped hill, wavy line (or river), star, etc.

The Sātavāhana coinage consists of the minor metals namely copper, lead and potin. It is the earliest and popular from Sātakarṇi I and the Sātavāhanas exploited this metal for the vast majority of coins. The Sātavāhanas also issued the coin of potin which is an alloy of copper, zinc, lead and tin. Lead was used extensively for coining purposes in different localities by the Sātavāhana rulers. A special liking for lead as a metal for currency was due to its malleability in manufacturing the coins of various shapes. It might have been easily available for manufacturing as lead mines are known at Zawar in Rajasthan, Kurnool and Agnigundala in District Guntur. Large quantities of lead appear to have been available by import also as indicated by the statement in the *Periplus*.[69] As the Sātavāhanas had to maintain the great quantum of currency in order to govern the large territory; so they chose lead, copper and potin. Rare silver coins of some Sātavāhana kings are known. These are modelled on the characteristic silver coins of the western Kṣatrapas since they are of the same weight and fabric as those of the latter rulers.

The coins bear on one side short or fragment any Prākṛt legends written in early Brāhmī characters. Rare silver pieces on the contrary bear Brāhmi bilingual-Prākṛt on the obverse and old Telugu on the reverse.

The money economy of the Sātavāhanas was based on regional characteristics[70] because coins with special fabrics, motifs and metals were prevalent in different parts of their kingdom. In the Vidiśā region, Śrī Sāta and Sātakarṇi issued the square inscribed punch-marked copper coins with four symbols on the reverse. In other regions, die-struck coins and cast coins were issued. In the region round about Tripurā, the above two rulers issued the copper and lead coins with standing human figure prominently on the obverse and four different symbols on the reverse. In north Maharashtra, Śrī Sātakarṇi and Śrī Sātavāhana issued bull type in copper and lead. These two rulers also issued the copper and lead coins in this region having elephant on the obverse and the tree as the prominent reverse symbol.

A few coins are known as having lion as the prominent symbol on the obverse. They may be classified into three distinct groups A, B and C. The coins of group A are chiefly known from Gujarat and the adjoining territories of north Maharashtra. The coins of group B lion having six-arched on the reverse were issued in eastern Deccan and they were issued by Sātakarṇi and by Sāta coins of group C having Ujjayinī symbol on the reverse were issued by Pulumāvi, Yajña Sātakarṇi and Gasada in eastern Deccan.

In Deccan, different types of coins were issued in large

numbers by the Sātavāhana rulers. The coins of Elephant group B have Ujjayinī symbol on the reverse. The copper coins are square while lead coins are round. About thirteen rulers are known to have issued this group of coins in this region and it seems to be the most popular. Like elephant, arched hill is seen on many lead coins in the Deccan. There are three distinct forms — (A) Three, (B) Six and (C) Ten. These have Ujjayinī symbol on the reverse. Six rulers namely, Śrī, Sāti, Pulumāvi, Sātakarṇi, Vijaya Sātakarṇi, Vāśiṣṭhiputra Śrī Pulumāvi and Gautamīputra Śrī Yajña Sātakarṇi issued the three type coins in the Deccan. Either Gautamīputra or Gautamīputra Yajña Sātakarṇi issued the coins of six-arched. The ten-arched hill type was issued by Gautamīputra Sātakarṇi, Vāśiṣṭhiputra Pulumāvi and Gautamīputra Yajña Sātakarṇi, Vāśiṣṭhiputra Sātakarni, Pulumāvi and Gautamīputra Yajña Sātakarṇi issued the round lead coins of horse type on the obverse and tree in railing and Ujjayinī symbol on the reverse, Vāśiṣṭhiputra Pulumāvi issued the wheel type in this region.

Svāmī Pulumāvī and Yajña Sātakarṇi issued the lead coins of ship type on the obverse and Ujjain symbol on the reverse on various places on the Coromandal Coast.

In north Maharashtra, Gautamīputra Sātakarṇi counter-struck the silver coins of Mahākṣatrapa Nahapāna with three-arched or six-arched on the obverse and Ujjain symbol on the reverse. On the eve of the destruction of the Kṣaharāta house, Gautamīputra restruck the silver coins of Nahapāṇa as a measure of his suzerainty over the conquered treasure.

Gautamīputra Sātakarṇi added the silver coinage to the already widespread lead, copper and potin coinage of the Sātavāhanas. He also issued the six-arched hill silver coin type in Ujjain. Besides, he is the first Indian monarch to issue an independent silver portrait coin as one such protrait coin was found at Belāpur, almost near the borders of Orissa and some were acquired at Indore. The above standardised portrait type was faithfully continued by the Imperial rulers[71] Vāśiṣṭhiputra Sātakarṇi, Śivaśrī Pulumāvi, Skanda Sātakarṇi, Yajña Sātakarṇi and Vijaya Sātakarṇi.[72] All the issues were found in the northern and western territories of the Sātavāhana empire — their find spots being Bombay, Sopara, Nāsik Paithan, Barodā, Tripurī, Besanagara, Indore, Hyderabad and Dhulikatta. The selection of Telugu by the Sātavāhanas on the reverse was undoubtedly to proclaim their nativity and mother tongue to the subjects. That these coins at least from the time of Pulumāvi were minted in the Āndhra region at Nāgārjunkoṇḍa is established. This coin type was not intended for official circulation in their home province.

During the time of Gautamīputra Sātakarṇi, the kingdom of Sātavāhanas became extensive. It became necessary for the imperial Sātavāhana rulers to issue coins for trade purposes. At the same time, these coins reveal some prosperity of their kingdom. The marked variations in the weight standards of several groups, their wider circulation and long duration of their currency pose problems for specific grouping and defies any empirical classification based on weights. The Nānāghāṭ inscription of queen Nāganikā and the Kānheri dated inscription of the sixteenth year of Gautamīputra Yajña Sātakarṇi clearly reveal that the sums of money were estimated in *kārṣāpaṇas*. The coins in case of silver might be 32 *rattīs*, (3.823 grains) and in copper 38 *rattīs* (9.460 grains). The Sātavāhana silver issues however showed no more than 2 grains and thus corresponds to *ardha. Kārṣāpaṇa* standard or *hemi-drachm* of the western Kṣatrapas.

The later lead and copper coins appear to confirm to the *purāṇa* or *kārṣāpaṇa* standard (80 *rattīs* or 146.4 grains equal to 9.460 grains) and its multiples ascending by a process of reduplication or descending like the *ardha* or *pāda kārṣāpaṇa*. The least weight standard thus could originally be of 1.666 grains just half of the *pāda kārṣāpaṇa*. All the available examples come under a scale 1.666 to 2.397 to 4.794 to 9.460 to 18.920 to 28.380 to 37.840. The minimum weight noted among the entire series is F (*cakra*) 28 : 1.600 and rarely B (elephant) — 50 : 712 which are copper rectangular ones and much worn out examples put in general the minimum weight standard should have been originally 1.666 (10 *rattīs*) and its multiples. The maximum weight is regarded as in E (lion) 11 and C (hill) — 24 : 39 grain which is again very abnormal single specimen put a perusal of the entire series show that the weight never exceeded 37.840 E ((lion) — 13) but frequently the lead and potin issues ranged between 9.460 and 28.380.[73]

Impact of Sātavāhana Coins on Trade and Commerce : The discovery of several coins in the different parts of the kingdom of Sātavāhanas reveal prosperity. This is also clear from the different occupations, crafts and industries as known from the donative inscriptions of western India such as traders in corn[74] (*dhāṇikas*), drugs[75] (*gandhikas*), jewellers[76] (*maṇikāras*), garland makers[77] (*mālākāras*), iron-smith[78] (*lohavaṇijakas*) or (*karmāras*), goldsmiths[79] (*suvarṇakāras*), braziers (*kāsakāras*), stone cutters (*salavañjakas*) *Suvarṇakāras*[80] artisans (*avasanīs*), carpenters (*vaḍhikas*), weavers[81] (*kolikas*), potters[82] (*kulārikas*), hydraulic workers[83] (*udayantrikas*) oil mongers[84] (*tilāpiśakas*). These were organised into guilds. The sound money economy is clear from the fact that under the Sātavāhanas cash endowments were made to the guilds of artisans for meeting the religious needs. These guilds used to do banking functions by the payment of interest and to spend it according to donors wishes. Besides, the Nānāghāṭ inscription mentions numerous *kārṣāpaṇas* given in charity in connection with the sacrifices performed by Nāganikā, wife of Sātakarṇi.

Bodhi Coins

As known from the coins found both from the surface and excavations, the Bodhis[85] ruled over Ḍāhala *Maṇḍala* with Tripurā as their capital between the close of the second century AD and AD 300. Most of the coins are of lead. Only few of them have an alloy of zinc in them. They are round. Their weight varies between 7 and 40 grains. The Bodhi coins were primarily meant for circulation in Tripurā region, where Bodhis ruled. The name of the first ruler of this dynasty was most probably Bodhi. The names of the rulers now known from their clay sealings and coins are (1) Bodhi, (2) Candra Bodhi, (3) Vasu Bodhi, (4) Vīra Bodhi, (5) Śiva Bodhi and (6) Dharma Bodhi. The symbols on their coins are akin to those found on the Sātavāhana coins. Apart from the deity, (a crude representation of Lakṣmī, the other symbols on the Bodhi coins and scalings are three-arched hill, tree in railing, etc. Both used Prākṛt language and minted lead coins.

Punch-Marked Coins

After the political and economic disintegration of the Mauryan empire, the manufacturing of silver punch-marked coins in northern India generally ceased but their circulation continued even up to second or third century AD along with the Indo-Greek, Indo-Scythian, Indo-Parthian, Indo-Kuṣāṇa and Indo-Sassānian coins. This is borne out from a number of finds of these coins. They have been found with the coins of Kujula Kadphises, Wima Kadphises, Kaniṣka, Vāsudeva and the Sassānian coins of the third to fourth century AD in a monastery at Taxila.[86] In the lower city of Taxila, they are found along with the Indo-Greek coins of Appolodotus, Philoxenus, Indo-Scythian coins of Maues, Azes, Gondophernes, Soter-Megas and Kujula Kadphises I and Wima Kadphises.[87] Again more than 4000 coins of this type were found at Mazakah, 60 km east of south of Kābul, along with Bactrian, Indo-Greek, Indo-Scythian and Kuṣāṇa coins. Three *kārṣāpaṇas* were found in the deposit at the foot of the Vajrāsana, the throne of Buddha, in the temple of Mahābodhi at Gayā, which were placed during the reign of Huviṣka.

The *kārṣāpaṇa* coins are also known associated with Indo-Greek coins in a number of hoards. A hoard of these coins was found in 1853 in Kāṅgrā along with the coins of Indo-Greek rulers Antimachus II, Philoxenos, Lysias, Antialkidas and Menander.[88] Another small hoard of nine coins found at Thatta (Distt. Atter) had a coin of Philoxenen.[89] A hoard from Bairat included eight punch-marked coins along with 25 Indo-Greek coins of Heliodes, Apollodotus, Menander, Antialcidas and Hermaeus.[90] These unmistakably indicate the currency of the *kārṣāpaṇa* coins in the second-first century BC along with the Indo-Greek coins.

Moulds of Kuṣāṇa period have been found in which copies of *kārṣāpaṇas* were cast. The post-Mauryan tribal states and the Kuṣāṇa rulers in India managed virtually without their own silver coinage in period c. AD 150-200 and it is clear that the *kārṣāpaṇa* passed as currency during this period. This is also varified from an inscription of the Mathurā.

During this period, the Mauryan punch-marked coins were imitated in great abundance in the Avantī region. Most of these are of copper and only a few coins bear silver coating. The excavations at Ujjain, Vidiśā and Eran brought the copper punch-marked coins in a pretty large number. Period II B of Eran has yielded apart from stray early coins a hoard 3,268 punch-marked coins, assignable to the second-first century BC.[91]

In north India, punch-marked coins were gradually replaced by foreign coins. This was not in the south where these coins continued to be issued for three hundred years more than in the north. Nārada remarks that in the south, *kārṣāpaṇa* was a silver coin. Some silver punch-marked coins of a local type were issued in the Pāṇḍyan territory.[92] They have five symbols just like the Mauryan coins—the sun and six-armed symbol—with the difference that the sun has only twelve rays instead of sixteen found in the Mauryan symbol. The third symbol on these coins is the representation of a *stūpa*-like architecture; the fourth is a leafy tree and the fifth is a trident-battle-axe in railing. The reverse bears a symbol like fish drawn in lines. These coins weigh 16 to 30 grains and appear to be half of the Mauryan *paṇa*.

These *kārṣāpaṇa* punch-marked coins have been found associated with number of Roman coins in south India. 270 punch-marked coins were found at Mambalam (Madras) along with the coins of Augustus. Twelve *kārṣāpaṇas* were found at Eyyal, 33 km north-west of Trichur (Cochin) along with twelve gold and fifty Roman silver coins. Eight *kārṣāpaṇas* were found along with 39 Roman silver coins at Nasthutapur, in the District of Karīmnagar.[93] Besides these finds in hoards, a number of *kārṣāpaṇa* coins were found with Roman coins at several places in south India in tumulis.[94] These show that these coins were current in south India along with the Roman coins during the early centuries of the Christian era.

The Roman silver coins have approximately the same weight as the local silver punch-marked coins. There are some Roman silver coins which are countermarked with minute punches of symbols, very similar to those known on the silver punch-marked coins. These punches show that the local authorities authenticated the silver pieces as their own by putting their own authority symbols or testing marks.[95]

MONEY ECONOMY FROM LITERARY SOURCES

From different literary sources, we know about money economy during the post-Mauryan period. It included old coins as well as recent ones. The *Periplus* (AD 80) mentions that old *drachmai* bearing the Greek inscriptions of Apollodotus and Menander were current in Barygaza.[96]

The *Periplus* of the Erythrean sea also throws light on the metals imported in the first century AD. It tells us that tin[97] was imported from the west and Spanish lead[98] was imported in some quantity in the port of Barygaza and Muziris. The Roman gold and silver coins were imported in great quantity at Barygaza and Muziris as their exchange with the indigenous coins yielded profit.[99] Arabian gold came from Onumans to Barygaza.[100] The *Periplus* also refers to gold mines in the vicinity of Bengal.[101] The currency of gold coins named *Caltis* is also mentioned though its exact identification is rather difficult.

The *Aṅgavijja*,[102] a text originally compiled during the Kuṣāṇa period, furnishes important data of the money in circulation. The gold, silver and copper coins were current. The *kārṣāpaṇa* was used in general term, and it seems to have included gold, silver and copper coins, as well as old and recent coins. This work mentions *uttama* (high), *madhyama* (middle), and *jaghanya* (inferior) *kārṣāpaṇas*. It is very likely that *uttama kārṣāpaṇa* means *dīnāra* or *suvarṇa* (i.e., gold coins). The *madhyama kārṣāpaṇa*, refers to coins of silver and *jaghanya* to those of copper, viz. the *nāṇaka* pieces. This work also refers to the sub-multiple pieces.

Gold Coins

The gold coins *dīnāra*, *suvarṇa*, and *sateraka* have been mentioned. The name *dīnāra* was derived from Roman *denarius*. It appears that the name was introduced in the realm of Indian coinage during the reign of Imperial Kuṣāṇas who applied it to their gold issues. The *dīnāras* also known as *suvarṇas*. *Sateraka* is derived from the Greek term *stater*, a gold coin weighing 133.2 grains at the time of Indo-Greek period. *Sateraka* continued to be current during the Kuṣāṇa period.

Silver Coins

The silver coins known as *ādimūla kahāpaṇa* and *khattapaka* have been mentioned. The *ādimūla kahāpaṇa* is explained by the *Aṅgavijjā* itself as denoting the *purāṇa* or ancient punch-marked silver coins which were still current as standard money. These coins were known as of substantial value. They have been referred to as a square or irregular shape. Owing to the presence of variety of symbols, they have also been described as *citta*. Manu also, mentions the coin under the name *rajata purāṇa*, i.e., a *purāṇa* coin of silver which was equal in weight to 16 *raupya-māṣakas*.[103]

During the Śaka-Kuṣāṇa period (i.e., first century BC third century AD), they served as the standard money and public endowments were made and recorded in terms of the *purāṇa* or ancient *kārṣāpaṇa* of the punch-marked variety. In the *Puṇyaśālā* pillar inscription of Huviṣka at Mathurā, an endowment of 1100 *purāṇa* coins was deposited with two guilds which undertook to make certain provisions of public benefaction in consideration of the interest accruing on the original sum.[104]

The *khattapaka* mentioned by *Aṅgavijjā* denotes the coins issued by the Kṣatrapa rulers of Ujjain and western India. The Pālī commentaries such as *Sāratthadīpaṇī* mention *rudradāmaka* and *rudradāmakādi* coins. *Rudradāmaka* coins were minted by Rudradāman, the Great Satrap who ruled in AD 150. *Rudradāmakādi* coins, i.e., others which were minted by his successors on the model of the original *rudradāmakas*.

They were identical in weight, fabric and value. Their value was three-fourth in the value of old *kahāpaṇa*. The general name for all such coins of western *kṣatrapas* must have been *khattapaka* as revealed by *Aṅgavijjā*. These *khattapakas* come under *bāla-kahāvana* or *nava-Kahāvana* (young or recent ones).

Copper Coins

The new copper coins of the Kuṣāṇas were known as *nāṇaka*. These were much inferior in value (*asāragata*). One who counterfeits coins is called *kūṭakṛta nāṇakasya* and an examiner of coins as *nāṇaka parīkṣī* in the *Yājñavalkyasmṛti*.[105] This evidence may almost have been of the same age as the *Aṅgavijjā*. The *nāṇaka* coin of lesser value as pointed out above was the name for the copper money of the Kuṣāṇas which according to the commentator of the *Mṛcchakaṭika* was also called *śivāṁkaṭnaka*, i.e., the money bearing the figure of Śiva.

Sub-Multiples

The sub-multiples of the standard gold, silver and copper coins have been mentioned in the *Aṅgavijjā* and they were minted. There were *suvarṇa māṣaka* and *dīnāra māṣaka* which were of five *rattīs*. *Suvarṇa kākaṇī* was of 1.25 *rattīs*. *Suvarṇa guñja* signifies a *guñja* or one *rattī* of gold. *Rayaya māṣaka* is obviously the silver *māṣaka* coin which Manu[106] mentions as *raupya māṣaka*. Its weight was 2 *rattīs*. Punch-marked specimens of the silver *māṣaka* are well-known and it may be taken for granted that they were current at author's time. *Māṣaka kākaṇī* seems to refer to *kākaṇī* coin related as a sub-multiple to the silver *māṣaka* coin. These were names of the sub-multiples of the copper *nāṇaka*. The *māṣaka* would be 5 *rattīs*, *ardha māṣaka* 2.5 *rattīs*, *kākaṇī* 1.25 *rattīs* and *ardha kākaṇī* and *atthā* (i.e., one-eighth *māṣaka*) 5/8th *rattī* or 1.125 grains. Of course, they were very minute coins but their existence may be taken for granted.

Other early Jaina works also refer to these different coins. A false (*kūḍa*) *kāhāvaṇa* is referred to in the

Uttarādhyayana Sūtra,[107] *māṣa*, *adhamāṣa* and *ruvaga* are mentioned in the *Sūtrakṛtāṅga-sūtra*.[108] *Uttarādhyayana Sūtra*[109] further refers to a *suvarṇamāṣya*.

Thus, just as *kahāpaṇas* of gold, silver and copper were in use, smaller denominations, called *māṣa* were also available in gold, silver and copper. *Rāvaga* was probably a silver punch-marked coin. *Kahāpaṇas* are also referred to by the *Vasudevahiṇḍi* where a wood cutter is seen getting with great labour, one *kahāpaṇa* at the end of a day. Here the *kārṣāpaṇa* may be a copper *kārṣāpaṇa* as also in another story from the same text where a *ṭiṭṭirī* bird was sold for a *kārṣāpaṇa*. We are told that a partridge could be bought for one *kahāpaṇa*. Actually we do not know much about the purchasing power of money in those days. In the *Mahābhārata*, there are references to coin names such as *niśka*, *suvarṇa*, *śatamāna*, *śāṇa* and *prati*.[110] As among the punch-marked variety of coins, not a single gold coin has up to now been found. It seems that *niśka* and *suvarṇa* refer to the golden coins of the Kuṣāṇa period. Manu and Yājñavalkya refer to the *śatamāna* weighing 320 *raktika* but actually there is no evidence of finding such a coin. In the *Mahābhārata*, *śatamāna* has been referred equal to eight *śāṇa* coins. Actual specimen of *śāṇa* coins have been discovered in Orissa and a big hoard of 60,000 coins from Singavaran in the Krishna district of Andhra also consisted of the *śaṇa* coins. *Prati* of the *Mahābhārata* is also mentioned in the Nāsik cave inscription of Uṣavadāta recording on *pratīka* interest on 2000 and 3/4 *pratīka* on 1000 *kahāpaṇas* deposited with some guilds.[111] *prati* is another name of *kārṣāpaṇa*.

The early *Dharma Śāstra* writers such as Manu (VIII. 138), Viṣṇu (IV.10) and Yājñavalkya used the copper coin *paṇa* and silver coin *kārṣāpaṇa* in the sense of payment to be made as pay, taxes and fines for offences. Here the *paṇa* was meant in the sense of 80 *rattīs*. Sixteen *paṇas* make one *kārṣāpaṇa*. In other context, these writers have also mentioned the coins. Manu[112] says that two *kṛṣṇalas* or *rattīs* make one silver *māṣaka* and sixteen such *māṣakas* make one *dharaṇa* (VIII.135-36). A *dharaṇa* or *purāṇas* is equal to 32 *rattīs*. Manu ordains that a hired servant or workman who without being ill, out of pride fails to perform his work according to the agreement, shall be fined eight *kṛṣṇalas*. *Kārṣāpaṇa* was called *dharaṇa* probably meaning a handful of sixteen copper *paṇas* from *dhri* to hold. The name *purāṇa* given to it meant that the coins were not current but were old issues. They were called *purāṇa* (old) to distinguish them from the new or the current coins of the Indo-Greeks. The term *purāṇa* used by Manu may refer to lighter coins of earlier period.[113] The term *purāṇa* is no doubt known in the sense of a coin, and probably the punch-marked coins in the inscriptions of Kuṣāṇa period, but if *dharaṇa* was ever known to be a coin, is nowhere mentioned. In the *Manu Smṛti* in course of the prescriptions to pay, fines and taxes, it is not mentioned even once, while *kārṣāpaṇa*[114] and *paṇa*[115] are referred to at several places and clearly bear testimony that these were the current coins and not the *dharaṇa*.

According to the *Yājñavalkya Smṛti*, the *śatamāna* otherwise called *pala* is a money weight of silver equal to 10 *dharaṇas* or 160 silver *māṣas* or 320 *kṛṣṇalas* (*rattīs*). The same view is expressed by *Manu Smṛti*.[116] The only difference between the two authorities is that *Manu Smṛti* does not apply the name *pala* to the *śatamāna* although it applies the name to the gold measure or currency weighing 320 *rattīs* in the same context.

The Bakshi Manuscript (text composed in AD 200), a work of Indian Mathematics refers to the following coins while citing examples — *dramma*, *dīnāras*, *stater*, *māṣaka*, *dhānaka*, *amdikā*, *yava*, *kāla*, *pāda* and *mūdrikā*.[117] The relation in their calculation is as follows :

1 *dīnāra* = 12 *dharaṇa*

1 *dharaṇa* = 4 *aṁsa*

It also confirms that the daily wages of a coolie amounted to one *dramma*.

Like earlier Mauryan period, the science of money economy continued to be of great importance. The *rūpa* in the sense of coin was known in the time of Patañjali. Patañjali causes a *rūpatarka* to examine a *kārṣāpaṇa*.[118] *Rūpatarka* of Patañjali is identical with the *rūpadarśaka* of Kauṭilya. From the commentary of *Mahāvagga*, it is known that *rūpasutta* means a science of coins which was studied by the individual in order to become either *rūpadarśakā*, *lakṣaṇādhyakṣa* and *sauvarṇika*. From the Hāthigumphā Jaina inscription,[119] it is known how Khāravela as a *yuvarāja* is represented to have mastered *rūpa*, i.e., the science of coinage.

IMPACT OF MONEY ECONOMY

Money economy during the post-Mauryan period seems to be sound. This is confirmed by the fact that a large number of gold coins were issued and also in different metals and denominations.

This resulted in all round development or progress of the economy. It gave impetus to international trade. It brought prosperity. This money had easy acceptability in foreign countries. The productivity of capital increased as capital was transferred from less productive to more productive uses. This, led to large scale production and distribution. It gave choice to the consumers in the marketing of goods and enable them to secure maximum satisfaction.

The introduction of other metals besides gold and silver facilitated small payments in small transactions. It economised the use of valuable metals and thus with smaller metallic basis, the state was in position to issue large number of coins of such metals. It also checked the tendency among people melting down the coins on account of rise in the price of metals and disposing off the bullion in the market at a profit. Coins of other metals served as subsidiary to standard money of gold and silver. They were much more elastic. Supply of it could be easily adjusted to demand as metal used in manufacture was lighter and cheaper.

Concentration of coins in particular regions was no longer there. Coins of other metals which were issued in large numbers penetrated in larger parts of the country.

Finally it may be said that there was sound money economy during this period. Punch-marked coins seems to be no longer issued in north India but its use continued. Gold coins were issued for the first time and in large number. Copper coins were used for ordinary transactions. Other metals also served the purpose of exchange.

We find a large number of foreign coins such as Indo-Bactrian, Indo-Scythian and Indo-Pārthian which were basically of Greek technique. Then, we have Indo-Kuṣāṇa, Kuṣāṇa-Sassānian, Kidāra-Kuṣāṇa and Purī-Kuṣāṇas which were in imitation of the Roman coins. Roman coins were issued in connection with Roman trade in gold and silver. Western Kṣatrapas imitated silver coins of Greek and Roman.

Besides foreign coins, there were large number of indigenous coins. They are generally copper and produced by die-struck and cast technique. It can be classified as inscribed and uninscribed coins. In inscribed coins, we have city, tribal and monarchical coins.

Notes

1. Lahiri, A.N., *Corpus of Indo-Greek Coins*, Calcutta, 1965.
2. *Coins of the Indo-Scythians*, p. 19, London, 1869.
3. *BMC, GSK* London, 1886, p. lxviii.
4. *Corpus of Indo-Greek Coins*, p. 16, Calcutta, 1965.
5. *NC*, 1923, p. 297.
6. *JNSI*, XXXII.
7. *Coins of the Indo-Scythian*, London, 1869.
8. *Ibid.*
9. *Ibid.*, p. 51 f.
10. *BMC, GSK*, London, 1886, p. vi.
11. *JRAS*, 1905, p. 788.
12. *NNM*, B. pp. 26-27.
13. *The Greeks in Bactria and India* (Appendix) Cambridge Reprinted, 1951.
14. Gupta, P.L., *Coins*, New Delhi, 1969.
15. *The Early History of India*, p. 268 & footnote, Oxford, 1924.
16. *Kuṣāṇa Genealogy*, pp. 51 ff.
17. *JNSI*, XXXVII, Part I-II, pp. 44-71.
18. *Catalogue Coins of Andhra Dynasty*, Introduction, pp. xi-xii, London, 1908.
19. *Cambridge Short History*, p. 77.
20. *JNSI*, XXXVI, p.2.
21. *Ibid.*, XX, pp. 162-64.

22. Chattopadhyay, B., *The Age of the Kuṣāṇas*, pp. 204 f., Calcutta, Second Edn. 1979.
23. Rapson, E.J., (ed.), *Ancient India*, Cambridge, 1922 No. 2, pp. 116-20; Gupta, P.L., *Roman Coins from Andhra Pradesh*, Hyderabad, 1965.
24. Sircar, D.C., *Studies in Indian Coins*, p. 98, Delhi, 1968.
25. Sircar, D.C., *Sel. Ins.*, pp. 164-66, Calcutta, 1965.
26. *Ancient Indian Numismatics*, p. 200, Calcutta, 1921.
27. *Ibid.*, p. 205.
28. *A study of Ancient Indian Numismatics*, pp. 98-100, Delhi, Second Edn. 1973.
29. Gupta, P.L., *Coins*, p. 35, New Delhi, 1969.
30. *JNSI*, 1976, Part II.
31. Bajpai, K.D., *Indian Numismatic Studies*, Delhi, 1976.
32. *Ibid.*
33. See *Luders* Nos. 37, 68, 1090, 1187, 1210 and 1230.
34. Allan, J., *BMCAI*, London, 1936, pp. xci-xcii.
35. *JNSI*, XV, p. 70, XVII, p. 94.
36. *Ibid.*, XIV, p. 9.
37. *Ibid.* p. 9.
38. *Ibid.* XXIII, p. 303.
39. Allan, J., *BMCAI*, London, 1936, p. cxvi.
40. *JNSI*, XV, p. 70, XVII, p. 94.
41. Puri, K.N., *Excavations at Rairh*, p. 50, Jaipur, 1995-96 (AD 1938-39).
42. *JNSI*, XXVIII, p. 50.
43. Allan, J., *BMCAI*, London, 1936, p. 240.
44. *JNSI*, III, p. 47.
45. Lahiri, A.N., *Corpus of Indo-Greek Coins*, p. 126, Calcutta, 1965.
46. Allan, J., *BMCAI*, London, 1936, pp. 214-19.
47. *Ibid.*, pp. 131-32.
48. *Indian Numismatic Studies*, Delhi, 1976.
49. *JNSI*, XXXVIII.
50. *Ibid.*, XXXII, p. 19.
51. Majumdar, R.C., *The Age of Imperial Unity*, p. 160, f.n.1, Bombay, 1951.
52. *Ojhā Nibandha Saṁgraha*, p. 24, Udaipur, I.
53. Allan, J., *BMCAI*, London, 1936, p. cxxiv.
54. *Ibid.*, cxcvii; *JNSI*, xxxv.
55. *JNSi*, 1975, p. 16.
56. *Ibid.*, XL, 1978, pp. 9-12.
57. Allan, J., *BMCAI*, London, 1936, p. ci; *JBORS*, XX, p. 153 f.
58. Allan, J., *BMCAI*, London, 1936,p. civi.
59. *Ibid.*, p. civ.

60. *Ibid.*, p. cvi.
61. *CCIM*, Oxford, 1906, p. 162.
62. *JNSI*, XXIV, pp. 3-4.
63. Allan, J., *BMCAI*, London, 1936.
64. *Ibid.*, p. xxxii.
65. *Ibid.*, p. cviii.
66. *Ibid.*, pp. cxvi-cxx.
67. Gupta, P.L., *Coins*, New Delhi, 1969, pp. 39-40.
68. Trivedi, H.V., *Catalogue of the Coins of the Nāga Kings of Padmavati*, Gwalior, 1957.
69. Scoff, W.H., *The Periplus of the Erythrean Sea*, p. 42, 1912.
70. Shastri, A.M., *Coinage of the Sātavāhanas and Coins from Excavations*, p. 4, Nagpur, 1972.
71. Sarma, I.K., *Coinage of the Sātavāhana Empire*, p. 109, Delhi, 1980.
72. *Ibid.*
73. *Ibid.*, pp. 60-61.
74. *EI* X. Luder's list of Ins.
75. *Ibid.*, No. 1210.
76. *Ibid.*, No. 1005.
77. *Ibid.*, No. 1061.
78. *Ibid.*, Nos. 1032, 1055.
79. *Ibid.*, Nos. 986, 1177.
80. *Ibid.*, II, No. 190.
81. *Ibid.*, No. 1133.
82. *Ibid.*, No. 1137.
83. *Ibid.*
84. *Ibid.*
85. *JNSI*, XXXVII, *Prācya Pratibhā*, VII, p. 55.
86. *ASIAR*, 1923-24, p. 26.
87. *BMCAI*, London, 1936, Intr. xliv.
88. *N.C.*, 1873, p. 209.
89. *ASIAR*, 1926-27, p. 229.
90. *JNSI*, VIII, p. 24; Sahani, Dayarama, *Archaeological Remains and Excavations at Bairat*, Jaipur.
91. Bajpai, K.D., *Indian Nimismatic Studies*, p. 6, Delhi, 1976.
92. Gupta, P.L., *Coins*, p. 43, New Delhi, 1969.
93. *JNSI*, XIX, p. 1.
94. *Transactions of International Congress in Prehistoric Archaeology*, 1968, p. 225, *Numismatic Gleanings*, p. 10.
95. Gupta, P.L., *Roman Coins from Andhra Pradesh*, p. 69, Hyderabad, 1965.
96. *Periplus*, 47 (McCrindle; *IA*, VII. 43).
97. *JNSI*, XIX, p. 49.

98. *JNSI*, p. 56.
99. p. 49.
100. p. 56.
101. p. 63.
102. *JNSI*, XIX.
103. VIII, pp. 135-37.
पलं सुवर्णाश्चत्वार: पलानि धरणं दश।
द्वे कृष्णले समधृते विज्ञेयो रोप्य मासकं।।135।।
ते षोडश स्याध्दरणं पुराणश्चेव राजत:।
कार्षापणस्तु विज्ञेयस्ताम्रिक: कार्षिक: पण:।।136।।
धरणानि दश ज्ञेय: शतमानस्तु राजत:।
चतु: सोवर्णिको निष्को विज्ञेयस्तु प्रमाणत:।।137।।
—*Manu Smṛti*, Ch. VIII.
104. *Sel. Ins.* p. 151.
अयं पुण्य-शाला प्राचिनीकन सरूकमान-पुत्रेण खरासलेर-पतिन वकन-पतिना अक्षय-निवि दिन्नतु तो वृद्धि . . . मे पुराण-शत 500 (+) 50 समितकर श्रेणी — व च पुराण-शत 500 (+) 50.
105. *II*. 240-41.
106. *VIII*, 135.
107. 20.42; *JUPHS*, p. 67.
पोल्से व मुद्‌ठी जह से असारे अवन्तिए
कूडकहावणे वा। —20/42
108. 2.2.
109. जहा लाहो तहा लोहो लाहा लोहो पवड्ढई।
दोमास-कयं कज्जं कोडीए वि न निठ्ठियं।।
— 8/17
110. *JNSI*, XVIII, pp. 143-56.
111. *Sel. Ins.* p. 164-65.
. . . दत चानेन अक्षय-निवि काट्टापण-सहस्रानि त्रीषि 3000 संघत चातुदिवस ये इमस्मिं लोणे क्सातान।.। 2 भविसंति विषरिक कुशाणमूले च ।1। एते च काहापणा प्रयुता गोवधनं वाधवासु प्रेणिसु।1। कोलीक-निकाये 2000 वृद्धि पडिकशत अपर-कोलीक-निकाये 1000 वधि पा ।य। न-। ए। डिक्-शत्-।1। एते व काहापणा ।अ। पडिदातवा वधि-भोजा।
112. VIII, 215.8. 330; IX.84; XI.137.
113. VIII, pp. 135-36.
114. Sircar, D.C., *Sel. Ins.*, Vol. I, pt. I, p. 152, Calcutta, 1965.
115. VIII, 274, 366, IX.282; X.120.
116. I.364.
117. *JNSI*, XVI, pp. 231 ff. Satyaprakash and Rajender Singh, *Coinage in Ancient India*, New Delhi, 1968, pp. 299-308.
118. Patañjali's Commentary in the *Mahābhāṣya* on Pāṇini's *Aṣṭādhyāyī* (5.1.27-30; 5.1.34; 8.1.12; 5.2.120).
119. ततो लेख-रूप-गणना — व्यवहार-विधि-विसारदेन सव-विजावदातेन नव-वसानि योवराज।प। सासितं।
Vasudeva Upadhyaya, *op. cit.*, p. 26

6

Money Economy During the Gupta Period (*c.* AD 301-500)

AFTER the Kuṣāṇas, money economy suffered because of the barbarous invasions of the foreigners. However, there was revival of trade between India and Byzantine empire. It is for this reason that the Guptas issued the gold coins of the Roman standard which was already adopted by the Kuṣāṇas. As the Kuṣāṇa money was well established and popular among the masses, the Gupta rulers took the wise step by continuing the same type of coins for the convenience of the people. Gradually, we find the attempt of the Gupta rulers towards Indianization in style, metrology and fabric. The gradual rise in the weight of the gold coins is noticed from king to king in succeeding generations. When Candragupta II annexed Gujarat and Kāṭhiāwāḍ to his empire, he issued the silver coins of the western Kṣatrapa type. Candragupta II is also known to have started copper coins. The scarcity of Gupta coins in comparison with the earlier coins suggests that money economy was becoming weaker at this time. Besides Buddhaghoṣa, his commentators and others give useful information of other coins current during the fifth century AD.

GOLD COIN TYPES OF INDIVIDUAL RULERS

Coinage of Candragupta I

Among the early rulers, Candragupta I (*c.* AD 319-50) was the powerful ruler because he assumed imperial title of *mahārājādhirāja*, and it seems that he started the golden coinage. The view of J. Allan[1] that coins bearing the figures of Candragupta and his queen Kumāradevī on the obverse are — commemorative medals struck by his son Samudragupta is untenable. Candragupta I owed his imperial status to a considerable extent to the valuable assistance that he has received from the Licchavis relations of his wife. It was, therefore, but natural for him to issue throughout his reign a joint coinage whose type would be acknowledging the Licchavi help in a suitable manner. Had Samudragupta issued these coins as a commemorative medals, the name of commemorator would naturally have appeared somewhere upon them, as it is in the case of commemorative issues of the Indo-Bactrian rulers Agathocles, Antimachus and Eucratides. As Samudragupta's own name is conspicuous by the absence on these coins, these coins cannot be commemorative medals.

On the obverse of the coins of Candragupta I, we see the king and his queen Kumāradevī standing and facing each other, the king is probably giving the marriage ring to his consort. The names of both are engraved by their sides. On the reverse, there is Durgā seated on a lion. The legend is *licchavayah* which is probably in acknowledgement of the help the Guptas had received from their Licchavi relations.

Conservatism was a very strong force in money economy in ancient times. The early issues of the Guptas, therefore, closely resembled those of the later Kuṣāṇas to whose imperial position they succeeded in the North. The obverse of the Kuṣāṇas proto-types the king standing and offering incense at the altar is very common in the earlier stages of the Gupta coinage. The Gupta king is also to be seen wearing the Kuṣāṇa overcoat and trousers. His name is written perpendicularly under the arm as on the Kuṣāṇa prototypes. The reverse is again a close copy of the Kuṣāṇa type which has Ārdokṣo seated on a high backed throne. The Kuṣāṇa monograms also reappear with only slight variations.

There was, however, a definite move to Indianise the type soon afterwards. The Greek legend on the Kuṣāṇa proto-type was replaced by the Brāhmī one from the very outset. The peaked Kuṣāṇa cap was never put upon the head of the Gupta emperor. Ārdokṣo on the reverse was Indianised usually by transforming her into the Goddess Lakṣmī and seating herself on a lotus. Lakṣmī, that was introduced on the reverse, was destined to figure on the Indian coinage for more than a millennium as we find her not only on the coins of Cedis and Gahadavālas, but also on some coins of Muhammed Bin-Sam.

Coinage of Samudragupta

The Kuṣāṇa proto-types, the king offering incense at the altar lingered on for a few decades but side by side with it the Gupta Mint-masters introduced a number of original artistic types. Candragupta I's son Samudragupta (*c.* AD 350-70), who made extensive conquests, made his influence felt over the rulers of the south-eastern coast as well as over the rulers beyond his frontiers in the north-west, introduced the standard type, *aśvamedha* type, Battle Axe type, Lyrist type, Archer type and Tiger Slayer type. Kācha, who seems to have ruled for some time as usurper, issued only *cakradhvaja* type. From the type of coinage, he seems to be the near contemporary of Samudragupta.

Coinage of Candragupta II

Samudragupta's son Candragupta II (*c.* AD 376-414) who extended still further the boundaries of his empire, by annexing Gujarat and Kāṭhiāwāḍ to his empire by defeating the Śakas, issued the (1) Archer type; (2) Couch type; (3) the Lion slayer type; (4) the horseman type; (5) the *chatra* type; (6) *cakra vikrama* type; (7) the standard type; and (8) the king and queen type. As the gold coins of Candragupta II are found in the larger number in comparison with the other Gupta rulers, it seems that his reign was of great prosperity. The coins of the most of the types of Samudragupta and Candragupta II are quite original in their conception and show no foreign influence whatsoever. Their execution is generally very fine and high water mark of Indian-numismatic art may be seen in the *aśvamedha* type of Samudragupta and the lion slayer type of Candragupta II which are by far the best specimens of coins struck in ancient India.

Coinage of Kumāragupta

Candragupta II's son Kumāragupta I (*c.* AD 415-50) who is known to have performed the *aśvamedha* sacrifice, must have extended the empire by his new conquests. He continued the coin types of his father, namely, the Archer type, *chatra* (umbrella) type, Lion slayer type and the Horseman type. He also revived the coin types of the earlier rulers. The coin types of Samudragupta revived by him are *aśvamedha* type, Tiger slayer type and Lyre type. He also revived the coin types of Candragupta I. The new coin types introduced by him are Elephant type, Elephant Rider type, Lion slayer type, Rhinoceros type, Kārttikeya type, swordsmen type and *apratigha* type. His closing years were of serious disturbances. In the Narmadā Valley, we find a rebellion of the Puṣyamitra tribe. The struggle with the tribe of the Puṣyamitras must have put the heavy strain upon the resources of the empire, and it might have influenced his money economy.

Coinage of Skandagupta

Skandagupta (*c.* AD 455-67), son of Kumāragupta I, was also occupied with military affairs. There was a serious invasion of the Hūṇas during this time and a deadly conflict. He was, however, able to drive back the invasion. It seems that this invasion must have influenced the money economy of the Guptas during the reign of Skandagupta. Hence, Skandagupta remained contented to issue coins of two types only — the king and Lakṣmī type and the archer type.

Coinage of Buddhagupta and Others

Soon after Skandagupta, the empire began to decline. By the time of Buddhagupta (*c.* AD 495-500), the western part of the empire was lost, and after him, it remained confined to Bihar, Bengal and some parts of Orissa, and ultimately it went into oblivion by 543 AD. During this period of decline, the rulers were Kumāragupta II, Purugupta, Prakāśāditya, Vainyagupta, Narasimhagupta, Kumāragupta III and Viṣṇugupta. The successors of Skandagupta were usually contented to issue gold coins only of one type — archer type being the favourite one. It is also possible that during the later Gupta period, the trade with the Byzantine empire was stopped and it adversely affected the money economy of the Guptas. They were compelled to reduce the coin types and at the same time, they issued the debased gold coins.

Legends

Samudragupta was the first Indian King to introduce metrical legends on its coins. This practice was followed by his successors. Kumāragupta I introduced the important poetical legends on some of its coins namely *vijitāvaniravanipatit kumāro gupta divamjayati.* This was destined to have a long life of more than two centuries. It was copied with the necessary change of the proper name not only by the later Gupta kings, like Skandagupta and Buddhagupta but also by the Hūṇa invader Toramāna and the Maukhari kings like Iśāna-Varman and Avanti-Varman. Even king Harṣa requisitioned the same line for his coin legend.

Metrology

The weights of the gold coins of the Imperial Gupta kings vary from king to king. The coins of Candragupta I, Kaca and Samudragupta have the average weight of 119 grains. J. Allan has given the weight standard of these coins to be about 121 grains. In the time of Candragupta II, we find coins of three weights 121, 125 or 126 and 132 grains. In the time of Kumāragupta I, we have the coins of 126 and 132 grains. In the time of Skandagupta, coins of two weight standard one of 132 grains and the other of 142 grains were issued. This gradual rise in the weight of the coins from king to king continued in every succeeding generation and reached up to 151 grains in the time of Viṣṇugupta, the last known ruler of this dynasty.

Adulteration

It was specially the rise in the weight of the coins of Skandagupta that led scholars to think over this matter. J. Allan[2] suggested that the standard was changed to the old Hindu *suvarṇa* standard of 146.4 grains. A. Cunningham[3] thought that the heavy weight of Skandagupta's coins was due to adulteration. The depreciation in purity of gold was possibly due to financial drain caused by the Hūṇa War.[4] Had there been any strain on the treasury, the coins would have been debased without raising the weight of the coins. The increase in the weight of the coins and adding base metal to meet the weight would bring no depreciation in the metallic value of the coin. It would rather increase it, as the cost of the additional silver would be added to it. This kind of debasement instead of lightening the burden of treasury or meeting the need of the exchequer, would add an additional burden. On the other hand, if the percentage of the costly metal is reduced, keeping the same weight of coin by adding more base matal, the coin would cost less in metal and reduce the burden of treasury.

B.P. Sinha[5] by classical analysis of eight coins of Skandagupta has proved that the heavier coins were not debased at all in comparison to lighter ones. This fact turns the theory other way. It shows that the latter part of the reign of Skandagupta was more prosperous than the earlier one. It reveals that the gold had gone cheap by 10 per cent and to maintain the ratio between gold and silver coin, it became necessary to increase the weight of the gold coin. As a matter of fact, there was already no basis to postulate any stress of continued war in the reign of Skandagupta. His inscriptions spread in the various parts of his dominion always speak of the rising prosperity.

The chemical analysis of some of the gold coins of the early Gupta kings by S.K. Maity[6] reveals the pure content as follows :

1.	Candragupta-Kumārdevī coins	105 grains
2.	The *Aśvamedha* and Lyrist type of coins of Samudragupta.	101-04 grains
3.	The standard, Battle Axe and Archer type of Samudragupta.	92-98 grains
4.	The combatant Lion, Lion slayer and Umbrella type of coins of Candragupta II	102-104 grains
5.	The Horseman and Archer type of Candragupta II	100-99 grains
6.	The Couch type of coins of Candragupta II	95 grains
7.	The peacock type of coins of Kumāragupta I	105 grains
8.	The Archer, Lion, Elephant rider and the Tiger type of coins of Kumāragupta I.	96-100 grains
9.	The Horeseman type of coins of Kumāragupta I	88 grains
10.	The king and queen type of coins of Samudragupta	122 grains
11.	The Archer type of coins of Skandagupta (*svarṇa* standard of Manu)	122 grains

It can be tentatively suggested that these coin types were perhaps minted in the same order and on the same principle as that of Gresham's law. It states that any type of money that becomes more valuable in some other use than as money will cease to be used as money.

The gold coins of the early Gupta rulers show no debasement with the rise of the weight. If the coins have their weight increased without any debasement, P.L. Gupta[7] is of the view that the increase in weight is indicative of the rising prosperity of Gupta empire from king to king during the reign of early kings.

But this was not the case after Skandagupta. The rise in the weight of the coins of his successors was accompanied with a tendency to reduce the percentage of gold as is evident from the results of the chemical analysis published by B.P. Sinha.[8]

According to him the value of gold was going high and high and to maintain the old metallic value of the gold coins in ratio to the silver coins, the necessity was felt to reduce the gold contents of the coins. And it was reduced in such a quantity that if needed some more silver or the base metal, was added, to meet the deficiency of the value of the coin affected by the reduction. But this debasement and the rise of the weight up to the early part of Narasiṁhagupta's reign was slow. Only a few grams of gold were taken out. This suggest that the scarcity of gold was being felt by the people, but it was not so as to affect the prosperity of the country. It might have been more or lees the same as was in the time of Skandagupta.

But in the later part of Narasiṁhagupta's reign, we find a heavy reduction of 23 grains of gold. Its percentage was reduced from 70 to 54 grains. This suggest that exchequer suffered from a sudden heavy drain due to some unforeseen reasons. We know of Hūṇa menace in this period, and most likely that might have been the cause of economic deterioration.

This condition persisted in the time of Kumāragupta III, but in the time of his successor Viṣṇugupta, we see another heavy fall in the gold percentage with a nominal rise in the weight. This reflects the decaying condition of the Gupta empire leading towards its collapse.

Source of Gold Supply for Coins

How to explain the abundance of the gold coins under the Guptas who issued far more gold money than their predecessors.[9] Although the Gupta empire carried on trade with the eastern Roman empire, the volume of trade was considerably less than what India had with the Roman empire in the beginning of the Christian era. The source of gold does not seem to be indigenous but outside. No doubt, Indians seem to have procured some gold from the south Indian gold fields the high period of whose working correspond with the last century BC and first two centuries of the Christian era.[10] The available archaeological evidence based on Carbon-14 and examination of some objects from the old workings suggest that gold mining continued vigorously in the Raichur District from the first century BC to the third century AD and then, it began to dwindle and finally disappeared. Thus, the local supply of gold dwindled. Even from Africa, it was interrupted by the Arab invasion. In the early centuries of the Christian Era, especially in the Gupta period, China and South East Asia seem to have supplied gold to India in return for some precious stones as beryl, cotton fabrics and sugar. The very names *suvarṇabhūmi* and *suvarṇadvīpa* given to the countries of South East Asia suggest that the Indians went there in search of the yellow metal.

The gold coins issued by the Gupta rulers could be useful for big transactions, such as, sale and purchase of land, in which *dīnāras* were used. In the Sāñcī inscription[11] of AD 450-51 there is a reference to *dīnāras* which were used for charitable purposes.

SILVER COINAGE

Silver coinage was started by the Guptas towards the end of the reign of Candragupta II when they came into contact with the silver currency of western Kṣatrapas. The size, weight and fabric of these coins are closely similar to those of the Kṣatrapa ones and no wonder for they were originally intended to circulate only in those provinces which were once inluded in the Kṣatrapa kingdom. They, therefore, bear the Kṣatrapa bust on the obverse, as also the meaningless traces of the once significant Greek legend. The year of issue is, however, given in the Gupta era and the Garuḍa, the emblem of conquering dynasty, replaces the three-arched hill on the reverse.

In the reign of Kumāragupta I, silver coinage was started also for the home provinces of the Gupta empire and a new type was introduced which was naturally free from all foreign influences. The meaningless traces of Greek letters were discarded and Kṣatrapa bust was discontinued. The Garuḍa on the reverse was replaced by the peacock which is the mount of the God Kumāra after whom Kumāragupta himself was named. Towards the middle of the fifth century, financial stringency compelled the Guptas to issue the silver plated coins. They have trident on the reverse. Among the later Gupta rulers, only Skandagupta and Buddhagupta continued the silver coinage of the peacock variety but both its type and legends were continued by the Hūṇas, Maukharis and the Puṣyabhūtis (i.e., Harṣavardhana).

COPPER COINS

Candragupta II is known to have issued a large number of copper coins with varieties in comparison with other Gupta monarchs. The copper coins of Candragupta II are worn out. Nine types may be distinguished but the general type is same on all. On the obverse, there is a king and on the reverse, there is Garuḍa standing and facing. These coins bear the name of 'Candragupta'. Candragupta II is known to have conquered a large territory from the Kuṣāṇas where copper currency was prevalent. It was, therefore, necessary for Candragupta II to issue the coins in the conquered territory in already existing currency. The copper coins of Candragupta II do not show the close imitation of the later Kuṣāṇas or the Śakas. It is clear that the Guptas were gradually abandoning the Kuṣāṇa motifs, devices and standards. Therefore, Candragupta II, did not imitate the Kuṣāṇa prototypes on his copper coins. Further, he was the follower of Vaiṣṇavism. He gave the portrait of Garuḍa on the reverse of his copper coins.

Candragupta II issued the copper coins in the western conquered territory where the Kuṣāṇa influence was predominant and where people were accustomed to use such coins. Kumāragupta, however, practically discontinued the copper currency of his father. We get very few specimen of it. They were probably issued in the early days of his reign where the people were still accustomed to use the copper currency in the western conquered territory of his father. Their obverse shows either standing king or altar, and the reverse Garuḍa or Lakṣmī.

Cowries as Coins

In course of time, people of his western dominions became accustomed to use of *cowries* in place of copper coins for small daily transactions. Kumāragupta, therefore, thought that the copper currency was hardly worth the trouble and the expense it involved and, thus, discontinued it. It might be possible that Kumāragupta must have lost the conquered territory of his father where the copper currency was particularly confined. The phenomena of extreme rarity of copper coinage clearly shows that ordinary daily small transactions were carried on with the help of barter or *cowries*. The Chinese pilgrim Fahien seems to have been correct when he stated that *cowries* formed the common medium of exchange.

Relative Values of Different Coins

The average gold and silver coins during the Gupta period weighed 120 and 30 grains respectively. Towards the middle of the fifth century, the weight of the gold coins was raised to about 148 grains by the Guptas and a record belonging to this period suggest that 16 silver pieces were equal to one gold coin.[12] This would show that the ratio between the prices of gold and silver was as high as 7 : 1. The Guptà coins of 148 grains were, however, heavily adulterated and contained only about 50 per cent of gold. The ratio between the prices of the two metals seems to have been 7 : 1 which is somewhat higher than in the Sātavāhana age, which was 9 : 1.

Some *Smṛtis* of this period state that 16 copper *paṇas* weighing 144 grains, were equal in value to 16 silver *kārṣāpaṇas* weighing 56 grains. During the Gupta period, the normal silver coins issued by the Kṣatrapas and Guptas weighed only 30 grains, and they may have been equal to 16 copper *paṇas* which weighed about 80 grains. The Guptas, however, issued copper coins, apparently intended to weigh 100, 90,75, 60, 50, 40, 30, 20 and 10 grains. It is not possible to state at present how many copper coins of different denominations were equal to the silver coins of 30 grains. The ratio between the pieces of silver and copper varied between 50 : 1 and 70 : 1.

Copper Coins of Rāmagupta

The copper coins of Rāmagupta have been found at Vidiśā, Eran, etc. in Mālwā. These are of four types (1) Lion; (2) Garuḍa; (3) Garuḍa-*dhvaja*, and (4) Border-Legend type. These coins vary in weight from 20 to 30 grains. These coins are circular in shape and their fabric is similar to the Nāga coins, P.L. Gupta,[13] A.S. Altekar[14] and K.D. Bajpai[15] attribute these coins to Rāmagupta of the Gupta dynasty ruling in the fourth century AD. On the other hand, D.C. Sircar[16] and A.K. Narain[17] are of view that these coins do not belong to Rāmagupta of the Imperial Gupta dynasty. These copper coins were issued after the fall of the Gupta empire in the fifth century AD by Rāmagupta, a local ruler. The type, fabric, weight and provenance indicate that these are local coins and Rāmagupta may have been an independent local ruler.

Besides the local copper coins of Rāmagupta, local copper coins of Jiṣṇu belonging to the fourth or fifth century AD have been found at some sites in Mālwā.[18] On the obverse of these coins, there is the legend, *Jiṣṇu* and on the reverse, there are couches or wheels or *nandīpāda* or vase with foliage. It seems that Jiṣṇu was a local ruler of Mālwā in the fourth century AD.

MONEY ECONOMY FROM LITERARY AND EPIGRAPHIC SOURCES

Literature

BUDDHAGHOṢA AND HIS COMMENTATORS

Buddhaghoṣa and his commentators[19] by mentioning the

different varieties of coins throw light on the money economy during the fifth century AD. The passage from the *Sāmantapāsādikā* together with those from the commentaries of Sāriputra and Buddhanāga yields the names of the following coins:

(A) *Nīla Kārṣāpaṇa*, (B) *Rudradāmaka*, (C) *Rudradāmakādi* (D) *Pāda of Nīlakahāpaṇa* and (E) *Māṣaka of Nīlakārṣāpaṇa.*

NĪLA KĀRṢĀPAṆAS

The *Sāmantapāsādikā* shows that the punch-marked coins called the old type — blue *kārṣāpaṇa* were in circulation as late as the fifth century AD when Buddhaghoṣa flourished. The old *kārṣāpaṇas* were made in accordance with the Purāṇic *Śāstra* by impressing symbols on them and that they resembled the blue *kārṣāpaṇas*. These passages show that the punch-marked coins were manufactured as late as the fifth century apparently as private issues.

RUDRADĀMAKA AND RUDRADĀMAKĀDI

It is also clear that silver coins of the Śakas of western Indian were in circulation at least as late as the fifth century AD. They were known by the name of *rudradāmaka*. The whole class of the Śaka silver coins was known as *rudradāmaka* after the greatest and most famous of the Śaka rulers of western India, viz., Rudradāman I (*c.* AD 130-55). The silver coins of the Śakas of western India are of a single type following the weight standard of the Graeco-Indian *hemidrachms* and weighing between 34 and 26 grains. The later commentators bring out the difference between the old type blue *kārṣāpaṇa* and the new *kārṣāpaṇa* called *rudradāmaka* and state that the latter was 3/4 of the former value.

The coins called *rudradāmakādi* seem to include non-Śaka silver coins of about the same weight standard as those of the Sātavāhanas and the Guptas.

The passages made it clear that both old fashioned and new style *kārṣāpaṇas* were in use side by side and that the manufacture of the old fashioned *kārṣāpaṇa* was going on.

The *kālā kārṣāpaṇa* (black *kārṣāpaṇa*) mentioned by Buddhaghoṣa is derived from the metal of these coins, viz. copper.

PĀDA

The *pāda*, which was one-fourth of a silver *kārṣāpaṇa* (of the older variety and of the new tangled *rudradāmaka* and other varieties) seems to have been usually a coin of a cheaper metal or material, one-fourth of the later in value and of various weights and only rarely a silver coin which was one-fourth of the standard silver coins in weight.

MĀṢAKA

Māṣaka was made of *lauha*, wood, lac, etc. The *māṣakas* were so-called probably not because they were one *māṣaka* in weight, but because they were one-sixteenth in value of the standard silver coin called *kārṣāpaṇa*.

Lauha Coins: The *lauha-māṣaka* furnished by the *Sāmantapāsādikā* has been explained as the *māṣaka* made of *tāmra* (copper), *lauha* and others (i.e., other metals). The word *loha* or *lauha* means iron, copper, brass or any other metal and the expression *lauha* and others has been apparently used in the sense of any cheap metal other than copper which is separately mentioned. It appears that copper *māṣaka* was not so-called because it was only one *māṣaka* in weight but because it was regarded as one-sixteenth of the silver *kārṣāpaṇa* in value. It further explains the omission of the quite common copper *paṇa* or *kārṣāpaṇa* from the *kankhāvitaraṇi* list of coins. Thus the copper *māṣakas* mentioned in the test of *māṣakas* and the copper *kārṣāpaṇas* in the *Sāmantapāsādikā* would appear to have been the same coin or at least similar coins put under different heads. It is believed that the weight of the *māṣakas* of cheap metals like copper, iron, brass, lead, etc. was determined by their intrinsic value (depending on current market prices of the metals) as one-sixteenth of the standard coin. Buddhaghoṣa further informs us that there were other kinds of money which were current in different parts of the country although they were not mentioned by him, and that were of bone or skin or the fruits or seeds of trees and might be with or without any *rūpa* or figure raised on them.

Wooden Coins : Buddhaghoṣa's *Sāmantapāsādikā* explains the wooden *māṣaka* as those made of strong wood and of bits of bamboo and includes in this category even the *māṣaka* that was made by cutting in a figure on a piece of palmyra leaf. Apparently the palmyra-leaf *māṣaka* could not have been one *māṣaka* in weight. As the intrinsic value of the *Māṣāka* made of wood bamboo or palm-leaf could hardly have been one-sixteenth of either the silver or even the copper *kārṣāpaṇa*, they appear to have been of the nature of the modern currency notes.

Lac or Gum Coins : The same appears to have been the case with the lac *māṣaka* explained as those made by providing a figure on a quantity of lac or gum. It is tempting to suggest that the metallic *māṣakas* stood in the same relation to the standard coin of cheap metal like copper. Although there is evidence to show that metallic coins weighing one-sixteenth of the standard money of silver and other metals were not unknown, they were probably not common everywhere.

The subject of *Rūpasūtra*, which we may call in modern terminology by the name money economy, was popular during the Gupta period as it is clear from the writing of Buddhaghoṣa. From the passage of the *Viśuddhimagga*, it is clear that the shroff was well conversant with this subject. Hence, he was in a position to decide after handling the coins in a variety of ways (such as looking at them, hearing the sound they produce, by being struck at, smelling them, licking them and touching them) as to which of them were struck at which village, muffassil town, capital city, mountain and river bank and also by what mint-master.

VARĀHAMIHIRA

Varāhamihira, who lived in the sixth century AD, refers to the coin denominations *kārṣāpaṇas* and *rūpakas*, while giving the tariff of prices of precious stones.[20] *Kārṣāpaṇa* and *rūpaka* are used by Varāhamihira as two different names of one and the same coin. Most probably, he referred to late Gupta silver coins.

Epigraphs

The Gupta epigraphs show that the gold coins of the dynasty were usually known as *dīnāras*, and *suvarṇas*. The Gandhwa inscription probably of the time of Kumāragupta refers to *dīnāra* in line 8, but in line 16, an endowment is made in terms of *suvarṇas*. Official transactions are noted in the Damodarpur Plates[21] are in terms of *dīnāras*. Sub-multiples like half or quarter *dīnāras* were rarely issued from the royal mints. No quarter *dīnāra* or double *dīnāras* have so far been discovered. The Baigram Copper Plate Inscription[22] of this period bears witness to the fact that the Gupta gold and silver coins were respectively known as *dīnāra* and *rūpaka*, and that sixteen *rūpakas* were equivalent to 1 *dīnāra*.

The rate of interest varied between 12 and 24 per cent according to permanent endowments. One *dīnāra* was sufficient for the feeding of one monk throughout the year.[23]

IMPACT OF THE PAUCITY OF COINS

There was paucity of coins of common use during the Gupta period. The scarcity of Gupta coins in comparison with the Indo-Greeks, Kuṣāṇas and the Sātavāhana coins suggests that money economy was becoming weaker at this time. This led to the decline of internal trade and the consequent necessity of producing local commodities to meet local needs. With the decline of the internal trade, the towns which were flourishing during the Kuṣāṇa period, began to decline during the Gupta period as proved by archaeological excavations.[24]

Land Endowments

Under the Sātavāhanas and the Kuṣāṇas, cash endowments were made to the guilds of artisans for meeting religious needs, but under the Guptas, land endowments were made to officials and others for the same purpose. A very early instance is found in Central India in AD 496-97 in a grant made by the Ucchakalpa Mahārāja Jayanātha. A village was granted as an *agrahāra* to a scribe (*dīvāra*) and his son and two grandsons, who were to manage it for religious purposes. The practice of making land grants to the brāhamaṇas started generally during this period. Both religious and secular services had to be paid by land grants because of the paucity of coins. If priest and temples were maintained by land grants, how could have been officers maintained otherwise.

Besides, the issue of seals by Nālandā villages as well as guild of Vaiśālī during the Gupta period indicates that these local mints were emerging not only as politically independent but economically self-sufficient units. From the paucity of coins, it can be inferred that local units of production were coming into existence. This accelerated the process of political disintegration, for issuing coins was an important function of sovereign power.

To conclude the chapter it may be summed up that Gupta period cannot be called the golden age from the monetary point. They issued gold money and of high artistic quality but did not issue many copper coins. Comparative absence of issue of copper coins by central authority shows that there was hardly any easy medium through which masses could enter into exchange relations. People relied on barter or *cowries* for payment of small transactions. Therefore, Indian economy in Gupta times was largely based on self-sufficient units of production in villages and towns. Foreign trade was also not as extensive as in post-Mauryan times. Partial feudalization is noticed during this period. Also there was introduction of credit instruments.

Notes

1. *CGD*, London, 1914, pp.lxiv-lxviii.
2. *Ibid.*, Intro. p. cxxxi.

3. *Coins of Ancient India*, London, 1891.
4. Majumdar, R.C. and Altekar, A.S., *The Vākāṭaka Gupta Age*, p. 179, Benaras, 1954.
5. *The Decline of the Kingdom of Magadha*, pp. 47-48, Patna, 1954.
6. *JNSI*, XX, pp. 162-64.
7. *Ibid.*, XIV, pp. 118-21.
8. *The Decline of the Kingdom of Magadha*, pp. 47-48, Patna, 1954.
9. *JNSI*, XXX. 1, pp. 1 f.
10. Allchin, F.R., "Upon the Antiquity and Methods of Gold Mining in Ancient India", In *Journal of the Economic and Social History of the Orient*, V, Pt. II, 1952, p. 211.
11. Marshall John and Alfred Fouger : *The Monuments of Sanchi*, p. 388.
12. *EI*, XXI, pp. 81-82.
13. *JNSI*, XII, p. 3.
14. *Ibid.*, p. 106.
15. *Ibid.*, VIII, pp. 340-44.
16. *JIH*, XL, p. 533.
17. *JNSI*, XII p. 41.
18. *JNSI*, XIII, pp. 150, 192, XV, p. 89.
19. Sircar, D.C., *Studies in Indian Coins*, pp. 91-106, Delhi, 1968.
20. Shastri, A.M., *India as seen in the Bṛhatsaṁhitā of Varāhamihira*, pp. 328 ff., Delhi, 1969.
21. *EI*, XV, pp. 113-45.
22. Sircar, D.C., *Sel. Ins.*, p. 357, Calcutta, 1965.
23. *CII*, III, 261.
24 Sharma, R.S., *Urban Decay in India*, Delhi, 1987.

7

Money Economy During Post-Gupta Period (*c.* AD 501-800)

THE money economy of northern India declined considerably during the post-Gupta period. The main reason for this was the setback to trade and commerce, both internal and external. Northern India was divided into a number of states, and their mutual struggle led to insecurity which seriously affected trade. The rise of the Hūṇas, their conquest of parts of Central Asia and subsequent invasions of India adversely affected the trade. The silk trade of India with the Byzantine empire came to an end. The rise of Islam leading to the collapse of old empires, such as, the Sassānid (Iranian) empire, also affected India's foreign trade, particularly the inland trade. As India's foreign trade was much favourable earlier, it used to import gold and silver in exchange because these were not mined in appreciable quantities. Because of the decline of the foreign trade, there was shortage of the supply of gold and silver in India. Besides the introduction of the coins of base and inferior metal during this period, there was withdrawal of the earlier costly coins. It naturally led to the paucity of coins. As a result of it, the study of *Rūpasūtra* was no longer pursued during this period.

DECLINE OF MONEY ECONOMY

Gold coins of this period are rare, silver coins are few and copper coins not many in number. No continuity in coin currency is noticed nor are they seen uniformly distributed over the kingdom. All the kingdoms did not issue coins nor did all the rulers of a dynasty or kingdom seem to have their own coins. Most of the coins of this period lack originality. However, Gupta coinage exercised considerable influence on the gold coins of Bengal and on the silver coins of northern India and western regions. The isolation of the southern Peninsula is as marked in the development of the coinage as in political history. With the sole exception of the elephant pagodas of the Gajapati dynasty, initiated by Harṣadeva of Kashmir, there is no certain point of contact between the south and north after the third century AD.[1] The earlier punch-marked coins as well as Roman coins remained current. Besides, the Kadambas of Banavāsī inaugurated the tradition of issuing *padmaṭarikas* in gold. The coins of the south remained independent and superior to the coins of the north.

Hūṇas Coins

The Hūṇas were rude and barbarous people and they overran and conquered many countries. They were past masters in imitation, and they introduced no innovation in any sphere. The main characteristic of their coinage is its absence of originality. Wherever they went, they imitated the coinage of their conquered territories. They borrowed the Sassānian type in Afghanistan, the Gupta type in India and the later Kuṣāṇa type in Kashmir. They issued their coins only in silver and copper. Issue of gold coins is not known.

Toramāna and Mihirakula[2] both issued silver coins of the Sassānian bust-type, showing the bust of the king to right on the obverse. On the reverse, there is — Sassānian fire-altar with its two attendants. The coins of Toramāna bear his title *śāhī jabuvlah* or *jabula* in Gupta Brāhmī and do not disclose his name. The coins of Mihirakula have his name *jayatu mihirakula* in some cases while in some others they bear only the title *jayatu vṛṣadhvaja.* Toramāna also issued silver coins of the two other types. The one followed the Sassānian tradition for its reverse and had the fire-altar with the two attendants and adopted a new obverse showing a horseman. The legend on these coins is *śāhījabula* or *śāhījanabula*. The other type closely followed the Gupta silver coins of the eastern region with the difference that the king is turned to the left. The reverse contains the fan-tailed peacock and the legend is almost the same with the only change of name.

The copper coins, found in the eastern Punjab and Rajasthan and attributed to Toramāna, bear a king's head of the Sassānian type on the obverse, and, the sun wheel with the name of 'Tora' or *zabva* or *jabula* on the reverse. He also issued copper coins of the Gupta archer type, closely copying the obverse and the reverse and only differing in the inscription. Then, there are a large number of copper coins of the Kidāra Kuṣāṇa type, found mainly in Kashmir, where the king is standing with the legend *śrī toramāna* on the obverse and a crudely executed Ārdokṣo holding a lotus with the legend Kidāra on the reverse. These coins have been found along with the coins of the Muslim *sultāns* of Kashmir in the excavations, near the Avantīswāmī temple, Srivara, a chronicler of the fifteenth century AD, also refers to the circulation of Toramāna coins in his period. Thus, this coin type remained current for centuries, and its subsequent copies were made for circulation.

The copper coins of Mihirakula are of three types. The larger copper coins portray the king riding a horse on the obverse and Lakṣmī on the reverse. This appears to have been copied from the Gupta horsemen type. The second type follows the later Kusānas. The third is the Sassānian Type with the king's bust on the obverse and a humped bull on the reverse.

After Mihirakula, some Hūṇa rulers still existed somewhere in the north-eastern region; and they issued coins of the Sassānian type. Of these rulers, Khiṅgila, Udayāditya and Narendrāditya may particularly be mentioned.

Gold Coins in Imitation of the Guptas

After the general devastation caused by the inroads of the Hūṇas, a few rulers of Bengal, because of the remoteness of their kingdoms, could have retained sufficient wealth in their treasuries to imitate the golden coins of the Guptas. In the sixth century AD, Samācāradeva and Jayagupta (Jayanāga) issued coins of the archer type of the Guptas, showing the king standing left in Tribhaṅga pose, holding a bow in the left hand and an arrow in the right and with the name below. The bull-standard is seen in the left with field on the coins of Samācāra and the *cakra*-standard on the coins of Jaya. On the coins of former Lakṣmī seated on a lotus and holding a lotus in her left hand is shown. Lakṣmī is also seen on the coins of the latter, but there an elephant on the lotus is seen in addition in the left field below. Samācāradeva had also issued coins of another type where the king is seated on a couch in the *rājalīlā* pose with female attendants on either side. On the reverse, Lakṣmī is replaced by Sarasvatī, standing with a lotus in both the hands and a *haṁsa* (Swan) standing by her side.

Then after a short gap in the first quarter of the seventh century AD, Śaśāṅka, the king of Gauḍa (east Bengal), issued his coins in debased gold. These coins show Śiva reclining on his bull on the obverse and Lakṣmī seated with an elephant on the reverse. Another coin of this period belongs to Vīrasena. On these, a bull is seen on the obverse and Lakṣmī on the reverse.

Thereafter many crude and debased imitations of the Gupta coins are known from different parts of Bengal and they may be placed in the seventh and eighth centuries AD. The obverse of these coins has a standing king with bow and arrow, and a standing goddess on the reverse and she is shown sometimes as eight-handed. In most cases, the obverse bears no inscription, in a few cases *Śrī* may be seen with some unintelligible scribblings; on the reverse; some traces of legend are also seen and they are not always legible. They disclose some names but they could not be properly deciphered. These coins might have been issued by some local rulers of Bengal about whom nothing is known.

To the eighth century may be assigned a gold coin of the neatly Gupta tradition whereon Avalokiteśvara, a Buddhist deity, is shown seated and before him is sitting a crowned figure with folded hands. The reverse bears an elephant-standard with a flying penon. The name Śrī Vindhyāśakti is inscribed on it. But no king of such name is known so far in the eastern region. Then a solitary gold coin is attributed to Devapāla of Pāla dynasty. It bears a king with bow and arrow on one side and Lakṣmī on the other. The inscription placed on it makes it genuineness doubtful.

The Uttar Pradesh, gold coins are extremely rare. A coin showing Śiva and Pārvatī seated together is attributed to Harṣavardhana, the great king of Thāneśvara and Kānyakubja. Then a few coins are known bearing the names of Vappuka,[3] Keśava and Vatsadāman. On one side of the coins, a cow is depicted showing a calf and on the other side, a Varāha trampling on the demon. These coins are attributed to the Sūrasena dynasty of Bayana. Both from the Kaman[4] and Bayana[5] inscriptions, it is known that Phakka was the founder of Sūrasena family. The Kaman inscription, which may belong to the eighth century AD records the erection of a temple of Viṣṇu during the reign of Vatsadāman, the seventh descendant of a king of the Sūrasena dynasty named Phakka. If we place Vatsadāman in AD 750 or 775, Phakka, the head of the dynasty, will date from about sixth century AD. From the Bayana inscription of VS 1012 (AD 955), it is known that in the family of Phakka, there was a king named Phakka.

Silver Coins

The silver coins of the Gupta dynasty were adopted by a few rulers of this period. The Puṣyabhūtis of Thāneśvara and the Maukharis of Kānyakubja, who were interrelated by marriage, issued the eastern peacock type of Kumāragupta and Skandagupta. A hoard at Bhitora in Faizābād District of U.P. contains the five hundred coins of Maukhari's and Puṣyabhūtis of 37 grains. On the obverse, the head of the king is turned to the left with some dates in numerical figures and on the reverse, there is peacock and circular legend *vinita vanira vanipati* with ruler's name. Īśānavarman (AD 550-76) was the first Mankharī king who started silver coinage. It appears from the Harah inscription that after assuming the title of *mahārājādhirāja*, he might have issued these coins. He was followed by Sarvavarman (AD 576-80) and Avantīvarman (AD 580-600) who are also known to have issued the coins. Harṣa in the name of Śilāditya issued this type of coin. The name Śilāditya for Harṣa has been mentioned by Yuan Chwang. The *Harṣacarita* also refers to the issue of the coin by Harṣa. Harṣa's father Prabhākara Vardhana (Pratāpaśīla) also issued the coins. These coins were later copied by Bhīmasena or Bhīmarāja of an unknown family.

The western silver coinage of the Guptas may have been imitated by some of the powerful Maitraka rulers of Valabhi who asserted their independence at the end of the fifth century AD. The western type of Gupta silver coins were copied by Kṛṣṇarāja of the Kalacuri dynasty in the middle of the sixth century AD. They bear a bull on the reverse on the pattern of Skandagupta's coins.

Tiny silver coins, weighing in the proximity of 6-7 grains, originated towards the end of the eighth century AD in central and western India. They have an elephant walking to right on the obverse and the inscription *raṇa-hasti* on the reverse. They probably belong to the Pratihāra ruler Vatsarāja (AD 778-88). These coins by name of *vṛṣabhas* are found mentioned in the Shergarh inscription[6] of AD 1018.

Hepthalo-Sassānid Coins

Towards the north-western region Sassānid type of coins was introduced by the Kidārites and the Hūṇas in the early period. This same type was continued by a dynasty which was Sassānid itself or acknowledging the suzerainty of Persia. It had established itself either contemporaneously to the Later Hūṇas or soon after their decline. As these coins have the traits of the Hūṇas as well as those of the Sassānids, hence, these were called Heptho-Sassānids.

The chief feature of these coins is that the king wears a headdress which is adorned with a buffalo head and wings on either side. On the reverse, there is fire-altar with attendants. These appear to be restruck because of the peculiar striking techniques. These coins may be classified as (1) Monolingual, (2) Bilingual and (3) Trilingual. The best known and finely executed silver and copper coins of this series are those which bear the name Pahalavī. A few coins have also Brāhmī legend. These coins are of 67 grains and are known as *drammas*. These coins may be regarded as the prototype of Gadahiyā coins.

Indo-Sassānian or Gadahiyā Coins

These coins signify base silver or copper coins with rude imitation of Sassānian bust and meaningless lines or curves on the obverse and lines and dots suggesting the Sassānian fire-altar with or without attendants on the reverse. These coins continued to circulate from the sixth century to the twelfth century AD. These are found in large quantities in Rajasthan, Gujarat and Mālwā with its extension towards Uttar Pradesh and Bihar. They follow the weight of their prototypes, i.e., 66 grains and are named *drammas*.

These coins in their early stage, preserved the thin flat fabric of their prototypes, but they gradually grew thicker and thicker and shrank in size. Ultimately, they became dumpy and appeared like pellets. These later types are popularly known as Gadahiyā coins. Likewise, the motifs on the two sides of the coins gradually degenerated and there remained hardly anything with which to identify the original motifs. These coins bear short inscriptions consisting of one or two letters and perhaps represent the initials or abbreviations of the names of the issuing kings. These initial-bearing coins are predominantly found in Rajasthan with its extension towards Mālwā.

Copper Coins of Punjab

In Punjab, a series of copper coins is found which crudely represent Śiva with the bull in the style of the later Kuṣāṇa coins on one side and the name *kota* or *śruta* with some flanking devices on the other.[7] Some coins show a human figure with a spear or bow and the name Jiṣṇu. They also appear to belong to the above series. But little is known about the issuers of these coins.

Coins of Kashmir

The coins of Kashmir follow the Kidār coins, and have seated Ārdokṣo and the standing king. After Toramāna and Mihirakula, one of the kings named Pravarasena (*c.* AD 580) struck coins of gold and silver. But the economic condition of the country was not favourable to gold and silver coins. The Karkotas, who began to rule from the beginning of the seventh century AD, struck their coins in copper as well as mixed metal containing gold, silver and copper in different proportions. Pratāpāditya, Vinayāditya (Jayāpīḍa), Yaśovarman and Vigraha were the important rulers of the dynasty. The name Pratāpāditya was assumed by the king Lalitāditya himself when he defeated the army of Yaśovarman of Kanoj. This is also confirmed to some extent by the discovery of the big hoard in Bāndā District of U.P. which contains the coins of this ruler. These coins must have been issued on the conquered territories. The conquering expeditions of Lalitāditya and his son Jayāpīḍa were probably responsible for the creation of an Indian market for Kashmir goods. These rulers established trade relations with China, Tibet and other countries. The result of this trade is reflected not only in the magnificent temples and buildings of this period but the mixed coinage of gold and silver.

South Indian Coins

The most striking feature of the South Indian coins is the revival of the punch-marked coins. The coins of this period are different from the coins of northern India. The attribution of these coins is a big problem. The chief device on the coins is common. Inscriptions on the coins are rare and small. Anyhow, the findspots of the coins help for the attribution to any ruler or dynasty.

KADAMBA COINS

The Kadambas of Banavāsī, who ruled from the fourth century to seventh century AD, occupy a prominent place in the history of south. Their gold coins can be dated fifth or sixth century AD.[8] These Kadambas are considered to be the originators of the gold coin known as the *padmaṭaṅka* which remained popular in south India for many centuries. These are round and cup shaped small and thin coins. They have a prominent lotus punched in the centre in addition to various symbols punched on sides. Because of the punches, the flat thin pieces assumed the shape of low cup. These coins weigh 58 grains. On the obverse of this coin is seen a central punch on a lotus and around this are seen punches containing retros-peetant lions. The reverse has a scroll ornament and two indented marks.

COINS OF GANGAS OF TALKAD

As the Gaṅgas had elephant as their royal emblem, some of the uninscribed coins with elephant on their obverse have been ascribed to the Gaṅgas of Talkad.[9] M.H. Krishna has described five types of coins of the Gaṅgas. These coins are in gold and copper. The gold coins vary from 58-59 grains in weight. They may be Varāha coins. Other type of gold coins weigh about 6 grains and they are taken as gold *hanas*. Such gold coins which weigh 1.5 grains represent the quarter *hanas*.

CĀLUKYA COINS OF BĀDĀMĪ

The Cālukya of Bādāmī had the boar (Varāha) on the royal emblem. Hence, it is generally believed that the early gold coins[10] of south India and the Deccan which contained a boar on their obverse were issues of the Cālukyas of Bādāmī. In fact, the tradition of boar coins was inaugurated by the Cālukyas of Bādāmī. Recent inscribed gold coin by Cālukya Vikramāditya (AD 655-81) has been discovered.[11] The obverse of the coin contains a big boar facing right. Above the boar, are symbols of the Sun and the Moon and between them is a floral design. Below the boar is the legend *śrī vikrama*. This gold coin weighs 117 grains. The usual standard of south Indian gold coins is 55-60 grains. Vikramāditya imitated the Gupta standard of 120 grains. In addition to the gold coin, three more electrum coins of this ruler were discovered.[12]

They are round coins. They weigh 153 grains. These coins contained 30 per cent gold and 70 per cent silver.

Two doubtful coins of the Varāha type are ascribed to Pulakeśin I (AD 540-66). These weigh 57.2 grains. On the obverse, there is caparisoned boar to the right with the sun and moon and pellet above. The reverse contains a large eight-petalled lotus. As the reverse contains a lotus which was predominantly a Kadamba symbol, Krishna thinks that this coin might have been issued by Pulakeśin I to commemorate Kīrtivarman's victories over the Kadambas of Banavāsī.

Coins Known from Literature and Inscriptions

The *Bṛhatkalpa-Bhāṣya* composed in AD 600 or earlier throws interesting light on the current coins.[13] The couch shells (*kava daga*) were most ordinary coins. *Kākiṇī* was the name of a copper currency in the Dakṣiṇāptha. *Dramma* was a silver coin current in Bhillamāla (west of Ābu, in Rajasthan), the golden *dīnāra* was in use in the eastern parts of India. *Kevadika*, also known as *ketava* was a current coin of eastern India.

The *Bṛhatkalpa-Bhāṣya* further gives exchange vlaues of different coins in the following *gāthās* :

Thus, 2 *sābharakas* of Dvīpa

1. Silver coin of Uttarāpatha.
2. Uttarāpatha coins — 1 silver coin of Pāṭaliputra.
3. Silver coin of Dakṣiṇāpatha — 1 Neaka of Kāñcipurī in Draviḍa country.
4. Nelakas of Kāñcipurī — 1 silver of Kusumapura (i.e., Pāṭaliputra).

The location of *Dīva* or *Dvīpa* to the south of Saurāṣṭra in the sea may be noted. The *Sābharakas*, current in *Dvīpa* were pre-Islamic silver coins known as *sabean* coins.

In the *Vyavahārabhāṣya*[14] written in about AD 600, there

is a reference to *paṇṇika* which may be the same as *paṇa*. Haribhadrasūri,[15] author of the eighth century AD, mentions *payarika* which seems to stand for the *pāda*. False *ruvagas* were known to Jinadasa Mahattara, the author of the *Āvaśyaka-Cūrṇī*[16] in *c.* AD 676. *Ruvaga* was probably a silver punch-marked coin. In the *Āvaśyaka-Cūrṇī*[17] and in the *Āvaśyaka-ṭīkā*,[18] *suvarṇa* is mentioned separately. Here *suvarṇa* refers to the gold coins current at that time. From the *Niśīthacūrṇī* written in AD 676, it is known that the silver coins current in Śrīmāla at that time were known as *varmalāta-dramma* after the name of the ruler who issued them. R.C. Agrawal considers *vyāghramukha* as the title of Varmalāta and the coins of *vyāghramukha* with a lion on the reverse are actually of Varmalāta.[19] From the *Niśīthacūrṇī*, it is also known that *mayurāṅkita dīnāra* discovered in treasure trove was nothing but the peacock type coins of a Gupta ruler Kumāragupta. An officer arrested a person carrying out them for business transaction because it was illegal. From this, it is clear that treasure trove was the property of the state.[20]

From the *Āvaśyaka-ṭīkā* of Haribhadra Sūri, it is known that goldsmiths (*heraṇṇiya*) could detect false coin (*rāvaga*) in darkness. Sometimes, we come across the purchasing power of money or the prices of ordinary commodities in those days. The *Āvaśyaka-cūrṇī*[21] mentions a cow for fifty coins. In the *Bṛhatkalpa-Bhāṣya*,[22] the price of a blanket varied from 18 *rūpakas* to a hundred thousand *rūpakas*. The *Āvaśyaka-cūrṇī*[23] also refers to a *naulavo* or money bag filled with the *dramakas*. That the import of gold from central Asia or Tibet continued from early times is supported by a reference in this work.[24] Asahāya, the commentator of the *Nārada Smṛti*, who flourished in the eighth century AD has specially referred to one lakh *drammas*.[25]

The Gotha-Mangloda (Rajasthan) inscription[26] of the time of Druhlana dated AD 608 refers to the *drammas* as many as *triṁśatiśatam* and *sahasram* in number. The only Pāla grant, which mentions the use of *drammas* in an inscription of Dharmapāla, refers to the construction of tank at the cost of 3000 *drammas*. The Pālas ruled for about 300 years but no coins can be attributed to any Pāla king. Similarly, the reign of the Rāṣṭrakūṭas was of great prosperity but not a single coin is attributed to them. Our knowledge of the coins current in the Rāṣṭrakūṭa empire rests on their inscription which mention *drammas*, *suvarṇas*, *gadyāṇa*, *kalanju*, *kasu*, *mañjadi* and *akkam*.[27] The *drammas* were of two types namely gold and silver. One Rāṣṭrakūṭa inscription distinguishes gold *drammas* from ordinary *dramma*. Probably, it was of 66 grains, *gadyāṇa* was a popular gold coin of the south at this time. Probably, it was of the weight of 96 grains. One inscription mentions that *gadyāṇa* was equal to two *kalanjus*. Hence, *kalanju* must have weighed about 48 grains. From an inscription, we come to know that twenty *kasus* were equal to 7 *kalanjus*. Hence *kasu* must have weighed 15 grains. *Mañjadi* was one-twentieth of a *kalanju*. Hence, the coin *mañjadi* must have weighed two and a half grains. *Akkam* was one-twelfth of a *kasu*. So the weight of *akkam* was about one and a half grams.

IMPACT OF ECONOMY

D.D. Kosambi[28] appears to have been the first writer to have commented upon the significance of the paucity of indigenous coins in the post-Gupta period. This, in his opinion, is pointer to a major change in the economy. The self-contained village was hereafter the norm of production. Taxes had to be collected in kind, for there was not enough trade to allow their conversion into cash.

D.D. Kosambi was supported by R.S. Sharma.[29] Because of the paucity of coins, lands were granted not only to priests, scholars, temples and monasteries but also to the officers of the state. In the time of Harṣavardhana, high officers were not paid in cash for their services to the state, for one-fourth of the royal revenue was earmarked for the endowment to public servants. At one place, Hiuen-Tsang explicitly states that the Governors, Magistrates and officials had each a portion of land assigned to them for their personal support. These high officers, according to Harṣa's inscriptions would include *daussādha sādhanika*, *pramātāra*, *rājasthānīya*, *uparika* and *viṣayapati*.

There was decline of both internal and external trade. Local units of production were coming into existence. There arose the necessity of producing local commodities to meet local needs. Peasants and artisans had to be attached to the village for the purpose. There was prevalence of local weights and measures. There was the transfer of income in cash and kind from trade and industries to the temples. Monasteries and temples formed wide economic units; some of them comprising more than hundred villages. Urban life also began to disappear. All these tendencies gradually led to feudalism.

Thus it may be seen that during post-Gupta period, money economy received considerable setback because of the attack of Hūṇas, decline of silk trade of Indian with Byzantine empire and collapse of Sassānid empire.

Hūṇa rulers, namely Toramāna and Mihirakula issued silver and copper coins but they lacked originality. Coins of the native rulers are also available. Samācāradeva and Jayadeva rulers of Bengal issued gold coins in imitation of Guptas. Silver Gupta coins were adopted by Puṣyabhūtis of Thāneśvar and Maukharis of Kānyakubja. Indo-Sassānian or Gadahiyā coins were popular in Rajasthan, Mālwā, Gujarat and Bihar were issued with base silver or copper. Coins of Kashmir followed the Kidār type of coinage. Among south Indian coins, gold coins known as *padmaṭaṅkas* were popular.

Notes

1. Brown, C.J., *The Coins of India*, Calcutta, 1922.
2. Gupta, P.L., *Coins*, pp. 59-60, New Delhi, 1969.
3. *JASB*, 1927, *Num. Suppl.* XXII, pp. 14-18 and *JNSI*, XXII, p. 279.
4. *JA*, X, pp. 34-35.
5. *EI*, XXII, p. 121.
6. *Ibid.*, XXIII, pp. 133-34.
7. Gupta, P.L., *Coins*, p. 67, New Delhi, 1969.
8. M. Murthy, A.V., Narasimha, *The Coins of Karnataka*, p. 62, Mysore, 1975.
9. *Ibid.*, p. 65.
10. *Ibid.*, p. 67.
11. *JNSI*, XXVI, pp. 244-46 and XXVII, pp. 46-52.

12. *Ibid.*, XXVII, p. 44.
13. *Ibid.*, XIV, pp. 107-10.
14. 3. 267-68.
15. *Āvaśyaka-ṭīkā*, p. 432.
16. p. 550.
17. p. 39.
18. p. 64.
19. *JNSI*, XX, p. 220.
20. *Ibid.*, XVI, p. 2 ff.
21. p. 117.
22. 3.3890.
23. p. 57.
24. p. 120.
25. *ABORI*, IX, p. 75, f.n.4.
26. *EI*, XI, pp. 299 ff.
27. Murthy, A.V. Narasimha, *The Coins of Karnataka*, p. 72, Mysore, 1975.
28. *Indian Numismatics*, p. ix, New Delhi, 1981.
29. Sharma, R.S., *Indian Feudalism*, p. 11, Delhi, Second Edn. 1980.

8

Money Economy During the Early Medieval Period (*c.* AD 801-1200)

THERE was a revival of money economy on a wide scale in western and central India during the early medieval period which again can be linked with the revival of trade and commerce. R.S. Sharma[1] traces this revival from the eleventh century AD but it is more reasonable to place it from the ninth century onwards. The evidence as regards eastern India including Bengal and Bihar is weak. A striking feature of the monetary system of the period is the gradual change from gold to silver, gilt, silver, bronze and finally copper. In the ninth century AD and onwards, *drammas* were issued in large number. Most of the Rājpūt dynasties of this period issued the seated Goddess type of coins introduced by Gāṅgeyadeva of the Kalacuri dynastry of Ḍāhala. In about the second half of the ninth century AD, a dynasty called Śāhī, ruling in the Gāndhāra or Kābul-Ohinda region, issued coins of their own devices, weight and fabric in copper and silver. Their most common type was Horseman and Bull which influenced the coinage of some ruling dynaties and their rulers of the twelfth and thirteenth centuries AD. The coins of Kashmir had a monotony but the only break in these series occurs in the reign of Harṣadeva. The coins of the ruling dynasties of the south such as eastern Cālukyas, Hoysālas, Colas, Pāṇḍyas and Yādavas are available. The inscriptions and literary works of this period also throw welcome light on the revival of monetary system during this period.

Gadahiyā Coins

The Gadahiyā or Indo-Sassānian coins had a long period of existence and a wide range of — circulation. These are found in Rajasthan, Gujarat, Mālwā, Uttar Pradesh and Maharashtra. This coin type has many varieties. Some of these coins are inscribed whereas most of them are uninscribed. It is very difficult to ascribe a particular variety to a definite dynasty or locality or within a definite date. Gadahiyā coins appear some time like silver and some time like copper but mostly they are bullion pieces having different percentages of silver-copper alloy.

Inscribed coins started from the ninth century AD onwards. The coins with the legends *śrī vigraha*, *ādivarāha* and *vināyakapāla* belong to the ninth century AD while others belong to the tenth, eleventh and twelfth centuries. Some coins found in Uttar Pradesh have a bust of the king on the obverse, and in front of the face, there are letters *vigraha*. On the reverse, there are indications of a fire-altar with attendant on each side. The attribution of these coins is difficult to decide. Another coin type known as *ādivarāha* type has the figure of the Varāha incarnation of Viṣṇu to right with the left leg raised. On the reverse, we have in bold characters the legend *śrīmadādi varāha*. There is no doubt that the coins with the legend *śrīmadādivarāha* were issued by the king Mihira Bhoja (AD 837-85) of the Pratihāra dynasty. Similar coins were also issued by his son Vināyakapāla, but they are extremely crude in their fabric and execution. Some of these coins from north Koṅkaṇa have on the reverse the legend *śrī chitarājadeva*. This Chitarāja was the king of Śilāhara dynasty. Some coins found in Rajasthan bear the name *śrī somaladevī*. She was perhaps the queen of the Cahamāna ruler Ajayadev of Sākambharī.

Some coins with the reverse legend *śrī oṁkāra* on them from their provenance appear to have referred to Oṁkāra Māndhata on the Narmada and may have been a local type of Gadahiyā coins for southern Mālwā. The king issuing them put the name of the temple instead of his own out of the honour paid by him to the deity or because of the remarkable influence thought to be weilded by the deity. The Śiva and Bull type has the figure of Śiva and his Bull on the obverse, and on the reverse, there is a very rude representation of the fire-altar with an attendant on each side. On some coins of this type, we have letters *bala* and on others, we have the legand *rudra*. The fighting horseman has been found on some coins discovered in Nimar region. It seems to be a local type.

Coins of Śāhī Kings

In about the second half of the ninth century AD, a dynasty called Śāhī was ruling in the Gāndhāra region with Udbhāṇḍapura (Ohinda) as the capital. The rulers of this dynasty issued coins of their own devices, weight and fabric in copper and silver. A single specimen of a coin of this area has on its obverse a peacock with outspread wings to left and on the reverse, a lion to left with the legend *śrī kamara*. The remaining coins can be classified into two types (i) Elephant and Lion and (ii) Bull and Horseman. We have coins of the first type for the reigns of Śrī Padama, Śrī Vakkadeva and Śrī Sāmantadeva. The Bull and Horseman type belongs to the reigns of Sāmantadeva, Spalapatideva, Khudavayaka, Bhīmadeva and Vakkadeva. The most common type of the Śāhī rulers was the Horseman and Bull type. This type was most likely introduced by Spalapatideva and was continued by several rulers. Amongst them, Sāmantadeva is most important. These coins have a wide diffusion throughout northern India and appear to have gained wide popularity in his name. These coins also influenced the coinage of the subsequent periods.

Coinage of Early Rājpūt Dynasties

KALACURIS OF TRIPURĪ

The seated Goddess type of this period was initiated by king Gāṅgeyadeva (AD 1015-40) of the Kalacurī dynasty of Tripurī. His coins, irrespective of their size and metal, have the same type. On the obverse of these coins inside a circle of dots, the name, of king is given as *śrīmad gāṅgeyadeva* in bold characters covering the face of the coin, whereas on the reverse inside the circle of dot appears the figure of four-armed Laksmī nimbate, sitting cross-legged with lotus in her two upper hands and the remaining two hands spread on at her sides. Gāṅgeyadeva adopted Lakṣmī because it was widely worshipped during this period. Besides, there was the old tradition of representing Lakṣmī on the coins started by the Guptas. The coins of all the three metals gold, silver and copper have the name of Gāṅgeyadeva, and they are all of the seated Goddess type. Regarding the weight of these coins, most of the scholars believe that these coins are *drammas* weighing 675 grains. Acçording to P.C. Roy[2] these coins follow an Indian weight standard of 41/2 *māṣas* (i.e., 66 grains) as mentioned by Ṭhakkura Pheru in the *Dravyaparīkṣā*.

A. Cunningham[3] attributed these coins to Gāṅgeyadeva of Tripurī. Since these coins have been found in all the three metals and in different values, A. Cunningham thinks that the coins of Gāṅgeyadeva form a perfect monetary system. Gāṅgeyadeva was the first king who introduced this type which was afterwards copied by the Candella *rājās* of Mahoba, the Rāṭhors of Kannauj, the Tomaras of Delhi and even by Muhammad Bin Sam, the conqueror of Delhi. These coins were so numerous that the successors of Gāṅgeyadeva did not find it necessary to issue additional coins.

D.W. Macdowall[4] has challenged Cunningham's view that Gāṅgeyadeva's coins from a perfect monetary system. He thinks that all the coins bearing the name of Gāṅgeyadeva were not issued by Gāṅgeyadeva alone, because officially all three metals gold, silver and copper were not used simultaneously; on the other hand, this was the result of the gradual debasement of the whole series spread over a long period. The metal of these coins varies from gold to base gold, silver, giet, silvered copper and the differences in the metal are so small that it is difficult to believe that these coins were issued in gold, silver and copper as of the same monetary system under one king. There is degeneration in the depiction of the deity on the reverse of these coins. The figure of the seated Goddess on the reverse of these coins undergoes innumerable intermediate stages between extremely good representations on one hand and crude and stylized ones on the other.

Pure gold coins are found only with the earliest types, while silver occurs in the middle ranges and the most degenerate forms of the reverse type are found with the silvered copper issues alone. The whole coinage of the Kalacuri of Dāhala was issued by Gāṅgeyadeva and his successors.

P.C. Roy has suggested that Gāṅgeyadeva issued his coins in all the three metals gold, silver and copper. His whole coinage, therefore, comprised three separate units. He issued comprehensive and complete currency. As many as eight variations can be established in his coinage on the basis of the use of the three metals and the four-weight divisions in gold, three in silver and one in copper.

Gāṅgeyadeva ascended to the throne in AD 1075. Shortly afterwards, he took the title of *Vikramāditya* and started his conquests. He defeated the Kośala, Utkala, Candella and Pāla kings. After having defeated the Kaliṅga king, he took the title of *trikaliṅgādhipati*. His extensive empire needed a comprehensive coinage system. Gāṅgeyadeva thus thought of issuing coinage which could easily be popular within his extensive empire. The beginning of the eleventh century AD opened the road to trade and commerce with central Asia. At this time, gold also came from the Far East, Sumātrā, Jāvā and other places. Gold was more easily available in this period than silver in the Islamic countries. Gāṅgeyadeva may have taken the advantage of this supply of gold, and was the first to issue gold coins in this period.

DEBASED COINS

It seems that when Gāṅgeyadeva could not meet the demand of the people of his extensive empire with his pure gold coins, he started issuing debased gold coins in order to increase the number of his gold coins. He issued his silver and copper coins to meet the demand of the people for the coins of lesser market value and they were issued before the debased gold coins, because some silver coins give better representations than some of his debased gold coins. These rapid issues of various series of coins were the real causes of the degeneration of the reverse device on the coinage of Gāṅgeyadeva. Debasement in gold was deliberately adopted to meet the growing needs for coins. Because of his wide conquests, his coins have been found in Prayāga and Benāras. When even the policy of debasement could not meet the demands for his coins in his kingdom, Gāṅgeyadeva started issuing coins in smaller denominations.

THE COINAGE OF THE KALACURĪS OF RATNAPURA

The coins of the Kalacurīs of Ratnapura are found in gold, silver and copper. There are two types (1) Gajaśārdūla type and (2) Hanumān type. On the former type, one figure is of the lion (*siṁha*) and another of elephant (*gaja*). For the Gajaśārdūla type, the Kalacurī rulers of Ratnapura have followed the same weight standard of 4-1/2 *māṣas* for the large sized coins. The small coins are of the quarter size of the large size coins. The gold coins of large size of Jājalladeva (AD 1090-1120) and Jājalladeva II (AD 1165-70) and small coins followed this standard. The gold coins of Ratanadeva (AD 1120-35) were also issued of this standard both in big and small coins. Most of the coins of Pṛthvīdeva (AD 1135-65) followed the big stand while some of 15 grains.

The Kalacurī rulers of Ratnapura also adopted the Hanumān type of coins. These coins are found in copper, but there is variation in standard. One coin of Pṛthvīdeva I (AD 1065-90) is of seven *māṣas* (102 grains). One middle size copper coin of Pṛthvideva weighs 4 *māṣas* 2 *rattīs* (62 grains). His another copper coin weighs 5 *māṣas* 3 *rattīs* (77 grains). Three coins of Pṛthvīdeva weigh respectively 99.5, 99.5 and 68 grains two coins of Jājalladeva (AD 1090-1120) weigh 36 grains, and one coin 43.5 grains and his middle sized coin weigh 44 grains. Three coins of Pṛthvīdeva I weigh about 100 grains.

The lion type was adopted by the rulers of the Kalacurī dynasty of Ratnapura only. The lion type silver coins of Pṛthvīdeva II are very tiny and the available three coins weigh only 6 grains each. The weight of the lion type of copper coin of Jājalladeva I is not known. One coin of Pṛthvīdeva I weighs 73 grains, one coin of Ratnadeva II weighs 100 grains and another coin 102 grains. One coin of Ratnadeva II weighs 22 grains and each of the other two weighs 16 grains. One coin of Pratāpammala (AD 1200-25) weighs 39 grains, one of 22 grains, five thirtythree grains and six of 44 grains.

COINAGE OF THE CANDELLA DYNASTY OF JEJAKA BHUKTI

The seated Goddess type of the coins of the Candellas in gold weigh about 60 grains. The large sized coins of Kīrtivarman (AD 1073) weigh 63 grains. The small sized coins of Kīrtivarman weigh 31 grains. The big size of Sallakṣaṇavarman (AD 1095) weigh 62 grains and the small ones 15 grains. The large sized gold coin of Mādhavavarman (AD 1129-63) weigh 62 grains whereas small ones only 15.5 grains. The weight of a solitary coin of Paramārdi (AD 1195-1221) is 61.4 grains. One coin of Trailokyavarman (AD 1205-41) weighs 61 grains. Two gold coins of Vīravarman (AD 1254) weigh 62.5 and 46 grains respectively.

The seated Goddess type of silver coins of the Candellas give the same weight. Eight silver coins of large size of Madanvarman weigh 60-62 grains whereas his forty silver coins of small size weigh 15 grains.

The Hanumān type of the copper coins of the Candella rulers also follow the weight scheme of 4-1/2 *māṣas* of the large sized coins which was the weight standard for their seated Goddess type of coins. A. Cunningham give the weight of a coin of Sallakṣaṇavarman as 61 grains and of Jayavarman (AD 1117) as 60 grains. Vincent Smith gives the weight of eleven coins of Jayavarman as 62 grains each. One coin of Trailokyavarman weighs 60 grains. Some coins of this type have also been reported in smaller denominations like the gold coins of the seated Goddess type. One coin of Jayavarman weighs 30 grains while that of Madanvarman is 15 grains.

One coin of Pṛthvīvarman weighs 16-2 grains whereas the other coin is of 41 grains.

OTHER RĀJPŪTA DYNASTIES

The Paramāra rulers Udayāditya (AD 1070-86) and Naravarman (AD 1094-1133) also issued the gold coins of the seated Goddess type. Mahipāla (VS 1150-61 AD), the ruler of the Kacchapaghāṭa dynasty of Gwalior, issued both gold and silver coins of this type. Vīrasiṁha, of the Kacchapaghāṭa dynasty, also issued the coins of this type. Govindacandra (AD 1114-54) issued the coins of this type in gold, silver and copper. The seated type of gold coins of Cālukya (Solaṅkīs) of Jayasiṁha Siddharāja (AD 1094) Kumārapāla (1143-45 — 1171-72) and Ajayapāla (1172-76 AD) are available. Six silver coins of Jayasiṁha Siddhirāja weigh 7.715 grains. One gold coin of the seated Goddess of Kunvarpāla of the Yādava dynasty of Bayana weighing 61.29 grains is known. There are some silver coins of the seated goddess type which bear the name of Śrī Ajayadeva.

Horseman and Bull Type Coins

During the twelfth and thirteen centuries, a number of dynasties and rulers issued coins of Horseman and Bull type of the Śāhī rulers of Kābul in silver and bullion. According to P.C. Roy, there might be the weight scheme of 28 *rattīs* (51-52 grains) of these coins. They not only copied the type but also retained the name of Sāmantadeva on the bull side of their coins. They added their names on the horseman side. Some of the rulers prefixed an epithet to the name of Śrī Sāmantadeva of which the real significance is still obscure.

The coins bearing the name of Sāmantadeva without any prefix during this late period were issued by the Tomara rulers Sallakṣaṇa Pāla (AD 978-1008) and Anaṅgapāla (AD 1049-97). Next in chronology may be placed the Gahaḍavāla coins of Medanapāla Deva (AD 1080-15) which bear the legend *mādhava śrī sāmantadeva*. Then came the coins of Cahamāna rulers of Śākambharī-Someśvaradeva (AD 1162-66) and Pṛthvīrāja (AD 1166-92). They have the legend *aśvarī śrī sāmantadeva.* A king named Śrī Pipala of some unknown dynasty issued coins with the name *Kulaman* Śrī Sāmantadeva on the bull side. A few coins of quite a crude fabric bear no inscription on the horseman side and have the name of the issuer on the bull side. In one case, the name is Śrī Mahipāladeva and in the case of the other Śrī Aṣaṭapāla or Śrī Amṛtapāla. The former is attributed to the Tomara dynasty (AD 1103-28) and the latter to the kingdom of Budauis and placed in *c.* AD 1200.

Lastly, in this series are the coins of Malayavarman of the Pratihāra dynasty (AD 1220-30) and Cāhaḍadeva (AD 1235-54), Āsalladeva (AD 1254-79) and Gaṇapati (AD 1291-98) of Jājapella dynasty of Narwar. These coins retain only one of the two motifs of the Śāhī coins. The horseman motif is seen on the coins of Malayavarman, Āsalladeva and Gaṇapati and the bull motif on the coins of Cāhaḍadeva. The other side bears the name of the issuer in both *Nāgarī* letters. Somalekhā, the queen of the Śākambarī ruler Ajayadeva, (*c.* AD 1133) also issued coins with the horseman motif on the obverse and her name on the reverse.

Coins of Kashmir

The Karkoṭa dynasty of Kashmir was followed by the Utpala dynasty in about AD 855. They issued coins exclusively in copper. From the time of Śaṅkaravarman (AD 883-902) onwards, nearly all kings whose names recorded in the *Rājataraṅgiṇī* are represented by copper coins but the uniform degradation of fabric continued. This type of the coin without exception is derived from the standard Kuṣāṇa type with the standing king on the obverse and the seated Goddess on the reverse. Among these are the coins of queens Sugandā and Dīdā (AD 980-1003) the latter chiefly remarkable for an adventurous career. The other rulers, who issued the coins, are Pārtha (AD 906-21), Kṣemagupta (AD 950-58), Tribhuvana Gupta (AD 973-75), Bhīmagupta (AD 975-80) etc. The debasement and degradation of the coins of these rulers may be perhaps due to the conservative nature of the rulers. The one break in this monotonous coin series occurs in the reign of Harṣadeva (AD 1089-1111) who struck both gold and silver. The elephant type, which is found in both metals, was copied from the coins of Karṇāṭa in the south and the 'horseman' type was initiated from the money of the Śāhī kings of Kābul. These two coin types were popular during this period. Harṣadeva might have adopted them for commercial purpose. He also continued the usual type of seated Goddess on the reverse. The standing king coin type of Kashmir thus remained unchanged till Muslim conquest in AD 1339. Thus, the Kashmir coinage offers an almost unique example of a coin type remaining unchanged for so many generations.

Coins of South India

The gold coins current in south India[5] during the medieval period were generally known as *padamaṭarika* and *gadyāṇa* (Varāha-(boar) symbol). These are of 48 *rattīs*. The ruling dynasties are known to have issued their respective coins.

The gold and silver coins of the Cālukyas of Kalyāṇa have been discovered. The Cālukya coins are generally round and punched with various symbols on one side of the coin only. Thus, their reverses are blank. Usually, they contain Kannaḍa legend of the name of the king and Śrī in Kannaḍa characters. The important symbols punched on the coins are Sun and Moon, temple, *gopura*, elephant, lion and boar. Because of the large number of punches on their sheets of metal, they have assumed the cup shape. Kalyāṇa Cālukya coins have been reported from Karnāṭaka, Āndhra, Tamil Nadu and Maharashtra.

The Kalacurīs of Kalyāṇa were the subordinates of the Cālukyas of Kalyāṇa in the beginning but later, they became independent and issued coins. Their gold coins weighing 54.5 grains were discovered in Satārā District. The obverse of the coins contains a human figure advancing to the right. The reverse has a three line legend in Kannaḍa characters of the twelfth century AD.

The Hoysala coins belong to the type of double die-struck coins. They are different from the coins of Kalyāṇa Cālukyas who followed the punch-marked type of coinage. Not only in type but also in weight standard, the Hoysala coins are different from those of the Kalyāṇa Cālukyas. The standard weight of Varāha or Gadyānna of the Hoysala period was 63 grains whereas the Cālukyan coins of the corresponding denomination weighed 58 grains. There is certain amount of similarity between the Cola and Hoysala coins. In fabric and weight, the Hoysalas followed the Colas.

Originally, the Yādavas of Devagiri were the feudatories but later assumed imperial status. They continued the essential elements of the Cālukyas of Kalyāṇa. Their known coins belong to the punched variety as those of the Cālukyas. These coins are cup-shaped with a reverse blank. They look like a low cup because of the punches at the sides and the centre. The lotus or *padma* is punched on the centre and at the margin are seen four symbols made by circular punches. Because of the central punch of the *padma*, the Yādava coins have been called *padamaṭaṅkas*. The usual weight of these coins is 57 grains.

The coins of the Imperial Colas are characterised by three symbols, viz. fish, bow and tiger. Some scholars believe that the tiger, fish and bow were the natural emblems of the Colas, Pāṇḍyas and Keralas respectively and that the coins bearing the aforesaid symbols testify to the Cola occupation of the Pāṇḍyas and Kerala kingdoms. On certain silver issues of the celebrated Cola emperor Rājarāja I (AD 985-1016), we find the deformed bust of the king and the royal name inscribed in the Nāgarī script. Rājarāja introduced his coins in Ceylon after the annexation of Northern Ceylon to Cola kingdom. The Cola coinage served as the prototype for the currency of the indigenous rulers of Ceylon, who flourished at a later date.

Several gold coins of the fish-type, belonging to the Pāṇḍya rulers, have been discovered. In this connection, mention may be made of some silver pieces of king called Vīra-Kerala, which bear legend in the early medieval Nāgarī characters. The eastern Cālukya kings are known to have struck the boar-type coins. Certain light pieces of gold bearing the names of some of the well-known kings of this dynasty, viz., Cālukya Candra or Śaktivarman I (AD 999-1011) and Rājarāja I (AD 1019-61) have been found in the

Cheduwa Island on the Arakan Coast.

Some of the rulers of the later western Cālukya dynasty issued coins bearing the lion and temple symbols. King Permāḍi VI (AD 1076-1127) was a contemporary of the celebrated Kashmirian Monarch Harṣa. The evidence of the *Rājataraṅgiṇī* suggests that Vikramāditya VI struck elephant-type coins which were imitated by Harṣa of Kashmir. Unfortunately, however, no coin of this type bearing the Cālukya king's name has yet come to light. The anonymous gold coins bearing the representation of the forepart of an elephant are known as the *gajapati pagoda* though it would appear from the testimony of the *Rājataraṅgiṇī* that such coins were struck or allowed to be struck by the later Cālukya rulers of Karṇāṭa. A few copper pieces of king Pratāparudra I (AD 1163-95) of the Kākatiyā dynasty of Warangal have been discovered. They have Nandināgarī legend and no symbols.[6]

Coinage Mentioned in Inscriptions and Literary Works

From the inscriptions and literary works of this period, it is known that *dramma* was the common term used for money. Generally, *dramma* used to denote the silver coin. There were several varieties of *dramma*. Different denominations of *dramma* were also known. Copper coins have also been mentioned. Gold coins were rarely used. A number of coin denominations associated with *cowries* clearly prove that they were widely used in various transactions by the people during this period. In south India, we find a number of references to coins, mints and denominations during this period. Silver *pala* or *śatamāna* weighing 320 *rattis* was regarded as the standard of claculation in the monetary transactions in early medieval Orissa. Medieval Orissa inscriptions often speak of a coin called *māḍha* which was both of gold and silver. The monetary system of north India and of south India seem to be independent from each other. Most of those inscriptions of this period refer to coins in connection with religious donations.

Coins in North India

DRAMMA AS GENERAL TERM

In the ninth century AD and onwards, *drammas* were used frequently in the epigraphs of north India. There are instances of their being mentioned as a general term. The Āhaḍa inscription[7] dated the (Harṣa) *Saṁvat* 258 mentions the *drammas* of the illustrious Kañcanadevī. The Gwalior inscription of Bhojadeva dated AD 875 refers to the use of the *drammas*. The Kaman inscription[8] in the year 299 of the Harṣa Era (AD 915-16) refers to the distribution of some *drammas* by Shri Bhojadeva. *Drammas* are mentioned in the Besani stone inscription[9] dated 958 from the Cedi country. *Dramma* also occurs in the Bayana inscription[10] of *VS* 1012 (AD 955). The Harṣa stone inscription[11] of the Cahamana Vigraharāja dated *VS* 1030 (AD 973) refers to the *drammas*. The copper-plate grant[12] of Mummunirāja (Śaka year 971) refers to 2500 *drammas* and the term *dramma* also occurs in the Banakpur inscription[13] of Śaka year 977 of Someśvara. The undated Kalvan plate of Yaśovarman (about eleventh century AD) refers to a donation of 14 *drammas* to the Jaina temple of the illustrious Munisuvratadeva in the company of Śvetapāda. A mortgage deed engraved on a brick found in a village near Jaunpur (U.P.) dated *VS* 1273 records the loan of 2250 *drammas* on the pledge of certain fields.[14]

VARIETIES OF DRAMMA

Ādivarāha drammas : The *Śrīmad Ādivarāha drammas* are mentioned in the Siyadoni inscription.[15] The Somanātha temple inscription of Shergāh mentions that the third donation of Devasvāmin given in *VS* 1084 (AD 1028) was the monthly payment of two Varāhas to be made on the occasion of *Saṁkrānti.*[16] These coins have been identified with the coins of Bhoja I, the great Pratihāra ruler which have on the obverse *śrīmadādi varāha* in two short lines in Devanāgarī and Boar (Varāha) incarnation of Viṣṇu on the reverse.

Vigrahapālīya drammas : The Siyadonī inscription[17] mentions Vigrahapālīya *drammas*, Vigrahapāla *drammas* and

Vigrahatuṅgīya *drammas*. These coins have been tentatively identified with the silver coins of the Sassānian type which bear the name Vigraha on one side and crudely executed fire-altar on the other.

Ajayadeva drammas : The Ajayadeva *drammas* are mentioned in the Menal inscription[18] dated *VS* 1225 (AD 1168). These were issued by Ajayadeva, the famous Cauhāna ruler of Ajmer. The inscription[19] dated *VS* 1238 (AD 1171) existing in the Rūṭhīrāṇī temple at Dhoda (in Mewār) presents interesting information about his coins. His silver *drammas* were put to careful scrutiny and examination, and then became legal tender.

Bhīmapriya drammas : The *Purātanaprabandha-Saṁgraha*[20] mentions *Bhīmapriya drammas* which may be identified with Bhīmapurī coins of the *dravyaparīkṣā*. These were probably struck by the Cālukya ruler Bhīma II of Gujarat who ruled between *VS* 1235 and 1298.

Vīsalapriya drammas : *Vīsalapriya-drammas* might have been issued by the Vāghela ruler Vīsaladeva (*VS* 1301-19). The Sanchor stone inscription[21] of Sāmanta Siṁha of *VS* 1345 records a grant in perpetuity of eight *Vīsalapriya drammas* by Meharas. An inscription of AD 1299 records the award of a few *Vīsalapriya drammas* to the temple of Rāṭā Mahāvīra at Hathuṇḍi. The *Lekhapaddhati* furnishes very interesting information about these coins. These coins were in circulation in the contemporary market and had been tested thrice. This same work also called these coins as *dvi-vallakyai* at one place. C.D. Dalal rightly interprets the phrase as referring to the coins which had a mixture of two *vālas* of a base metal. In the *Guruvāvalī* of Yugapradhānācārya also, these coins are called *dvivallaka drammas*. All this shows that Vīsaladeva issued coins of pure silver as well as of some base metal. At several places in the *prabandhas*, the *ṭaṅkaśālās* (mints) are referred to and some standard coins are mentioned as the *Bhīmapriya*, *Vīsalapriya*, etc. which show that the Cālukya kings of Gujarat had their own mints and that coins of some of those kings, e.g., Bhīmadeva and Vīsaladeva were known through their own names.

Pārupatha Drammas : An inscription[22] of the Śaka year 1106 (AD 1184) of Aparāditya II found at Lonada near Kalyāṇa in Maharashtra refers to a grant of 10 *pārupatha drammas* for the *abhiṣeka* of god Someśvara and another gift of *pārupatha drammas* for the *mahābhoga* of the temple for ten years. The inscription[23] of Silāhāra Someśvara from Chañje (Koṅkaṇa) dated in the Śaka year 1182 (AD 1260) mentions *drammas*.

The *Lekhapaddhati*[24] and the *Purātana Prabandha Saṁgraha*[25] also mention these *drammas*. The *Lekhapaddhati* refers to *Pārulha-drammas* minted at Śrīmālīya mint. The *Purātana Prabandha-Saṁgraha* informs that *pārutthas* were prevalent in the kingdom of Jālor during the reign of Udaya Siṁha. This work further states that one *pāruthaka* was equal to eight *drammas*. In the *Kharataragaccha Paṭṭāvalī*, it is mentioned that Naravarman, the Paramāra ruler of Mālwā (AD 1097-1111) was pleased with *Muni* Jīnavallabha and offered him an option of accepting three villages or 30,000 *pārutha drammas*. Jīnavallabha accepted neither, but requested him for the grant of two *pāruttha drammas* daily from the custom house of Cittor for the maintenance of two Kharatara temples.

These were in circulation in the area of Rajasthan, Mālwā and Maharashtra. Kṣema-Kirtti, (*VS* 1332) commenting on the *Bṛhatkalpa-Bhāṣya*, refers to the silver *drammas* of Bhillamāla. These *pārupatha drammas* were the same as the *bhillamāla* or the *śrīmālīya drammas*. The commentary on *Lekhapaddhati* states that formerly goldsmiths of Śrīmāla caste, who appear to be most reliable, were in charge of mints. *Drammas* and *gadyāṇakas* are recorded as coins in the inscription of Karṇeśvara Mahādeva temple, (Dist. Ratnāgiri NPP. XII, p. 219). The inscription dated *VS* 1221 and 1236 of the reign of Mahārāja Kelhaṇadeva known from Sāṇderāva (Mārwār) refers to some coins of *drāelas* given as gifts to some deities. The word *drāela* is so written that it gives an idea of their being some particular type of *drammas*.[26]

SUB-DIVISIONS OF DRAMMA

There is specific reference to the half *drammas* (i.e.,

drammārdhika) issued by Vigrahapāla.[27] An epigraph from Jālor dated *VS* 1230 uses the phrase *drammārdha*. Specimens of the half-*drammas* belonging to various medieval *drammas* are well-known.

The Siyadoni epigraph[28] mentions a three-quarter of *dramma* as *dramma tribhāga*. The *vigrahapālīya drammas* are known to have this particular sub-division.

Quarter *drammas* are known. They were called *pāda*. The *pāda-drammas* are known as associated with several *drammas* such as *Ādivarāha*, the *pañcīyaka* and the *vigraha*. Actual specimens of quarter-*drammas* have been found at several places.

That a *pañcīyaka dramma* was a quarter *dramma* is clear from the Siyadoni inscription.[29] In the Bhilsa inscription[30] of *VS* 935, there is written *pa* in lines 4, 6, 7 and 11 standing for *pañcīyaka dramma*. The rent of the *vīthīs*, i.e., shops in the market was realised in the currency known as *pañcīyaka dramma* and paid by the donor to meet the expenses of the regular offering to God and Goddesses in the temple of Bhāilasvāmin.

In the *Upanitibhavaprapañcakathā* of Siddharṣi written at Bhillamāla in *VS* 962, *rūpaka* appears to have been the coin most used. The Ahar inscription[31] of *VS* 1010 belonging to the Guhila king of Allaṭa records the tax of one *dramma* on the sale of an elephant and two *rūpakas* on that of a horse. It is also mentioned in the Hathuṇḍi inscription[32] of *VS* 1053 and the Nadol Grant[33] of 1213. In the *Pṛthvīrājavijaya-Mahākāvya*,[34] the *drammas* struck by king Ajaya are called *rūpaka*. In the Prākṛt Grammar[35] of Hemacandra, it has been mentioned as *ruadau* which is the same as *ruo* of Rājapāladeva's inscription[36] dated *VS* 1202 found at Nadol. From a commentary on the *Gaṇitasāra* of Śrīdhara, it is clear that five *rūpakas* stand for one *dramma*. If this is true, some of the silver coins weighing about 13.5 grains were meant to be used as *rūpakas*. Half *rūpaka* was known as *bhāgaka*.

KĀRṢĀPANA

It is really interesting to find the term *kārṣa* in a tenth century epigraph[37] of Bījāpura. This *kārṣa* appears to have been associated with the well-known coin of *kārṣāpaṇa*. The *Karapadaraka Purāṇa* mentioned in the Sena records[38] of Bengal is to be understood as a silver coin. The *Purāṇa* of *Gaṇitasāra* and its commentary was a silver coin and equal in value to 16 copper coins. There is a reference to *dharaṇa* a silver coin in the *Gaṇita Sārasaṁgraha* of Mahāvīrācārya who appears to have lived in the court of a Rāṣṭrakūṭa monarch in the ninth century AD.[39]

COPPER COINS

Some terms found in literary works and inscriptions seem to have been associated with copper coins.

PAṆA

In the Kāmān inscription[40] of Bhojadeva, we find the mention of *paṇa* and *drammas* in connection with the charities to the temple of Kāmyakeśvara. Every potter was without any exception to pay one *paṇa* per wheel every month. Five *paṇas* make one *dramma*.

ṢOḌAŚIKAS

The Bilhari stone inscription mentions *śoḍaṣikas*.[41] V.V. Mirashi[42] thinks that they might be signifying some copper coins of the value of 1/16th *dramma*. The Jaunpur inscription[43] dated AD 1217 refers to this *dramma*.

VOḌRI

Voḍri is found mentioned in the Somanātha temple inscription[44] of Shargarh. In AD 1028, Ṭhākura Devasvāmin undertook to give a daily gift of a *voḍi*, i.e., *voḍri* for providing incense *parṇaśālā* which means huts for hermits. The *Gaṇitasāra* informs that *varāṭakas* were *cowries* (shells) and twenty such shells made one *kāgiṇi* or Sanskrit *kākiṇī* also called *boḍi*.

VIṀŚOPAKA

The *Gaṇitasāra* of Ṭhākkura Pheru equates *viṁśopakas*

with one *dramma*. As suggested by V.V. Mirashi[45] the coin was so named because it formed the twentieth part of a *dramma*. The *viṁśopakas* are referred to in an early epigraphic belonging to *VS* 943 (*c*. AD 886) and also in the Bījāpur inscription[46] of Dhavla dated *VS* 996 (AD 939). In the Rajor inscription[47] of Mathanadeva, it has been mentioned that three *viṁśopakas* on every sack brought for sale to the market and two *viṁśopakas* for mensem for every shop were charged to meet the expenses of the temple of Nīlakaṇṭha.

From the Nadlai stone inscription[48] of *VS* 1195 (AD 1138), it is known that Ṭhākura Rājadeva of Nadulai, a feudatory of Rāyapāladeva of Nadol, granted one *viṁśopaka* for the function of *rathayātrā* organised for the sake of his mother. The traders of Śākambharī assigned one *viṁśopaka* per heap of salt and one *dramma* on per horse sold by them for benefit of the temple of Harṣanātha in 973 AD.[49] The inscription[50] of 1200 AD found at Nana records a grant of thirtythree *drammas* and six *viṁśopakas* to the brāhmaṇas by a Gauḍa Kāyastha named Udayasīha for the maintenance of a *kapila* or a cow.

Viṁśopaka was associated with *vigraha drammas*, *varāha drammas*, *bhīmapriya drammas* and *vīsala drammas*. The *vṛṣa-viṁśopakas* are referred to in the Arthuna inscription[51] dated AD 1079 which may be identified either with the bull and horseman device or else those of bull and Śiva type. *Bhīmapriya viṁśopakas* named after Bhīma II of Gujarat are found mentioned in the Dāhedamera stone inscription[52] of Sāmantasiṁha of *VS* 1352.

LOHATIKA

A coin called *lohatika* is mentioned in Ālhaṇadeva's inscription[53] of *VS* 1205. The term *lo* of the Bhinmal inscription seems to be *lohatika*. According to a commentary on the *Gaṇitasāra*[54] of Śrīdhara, four *lohatikas* are equal to one *rūpaka*. D.R. Bhandarkar[55] takes the value of a *viṁśopaka* to be the same as that of a *lohatika*.

DRAMMĀRDHAVIṀŚAKA

1/40th part of *dramma* and worth 50 *cowries* is identified with the *drammārdha viṁśaka* coin as cited in the Sārṇeśvara temple inscription of *VS* 1010.

Bhāskarācārya in the *Līlāvatī* states that 1 *kākiṇī* was worth 20 *cowries* and *paṇa* equal to 4 *kākiṇīs* or 80 *cowries*; 16 *paṇas* equal to one *dramma* = 1280 *cowries*.

The *Gaṇitasāra* of Śrīdhara and its Gujarati commentary mention the contemporary denominations as follows :

4 *kādās* = 1 *gaṇḍā*

5 *gaṇḍās* = 1 *budi*

4 *budis* = 1 *paṇa*

16 *paṇa* = 1 *kahāvaṇa*

Kākiṇī denoted a *pāda-paṇa*, *kaparda* and *varātaka* are identical with *cowrie* shell :

5 *visā* = 1 *lohaḍiya* = 100 *cowries*

4 *lohaḍiyas* = 1 *rūā*, i.e., *rūpaka* = 400 *cowries*

5 *rūās* = 1 *dramma* = 2000 *cowries*

The *Gaṇitasāra* enumerates several sub-divisions of a *dramma* and their relevant value in *cowries* :

1 *dramma* = 2 *drammadhas* = 1000 *cowries*

1 *dramma* = 3 *vāmkudās*

1 *dramma* = 20 *lohāḍiyas*

1 *dramma* = 40 *adhosā* = 1/40th part *dramma* and 50 *cowries*

identified as *drammārdhaviṁśaka* coin in the Sārneśvara temple inscription of *VS* 1010.

1 *dramma* = 80 *savā* = *visās* = *savā* = *visā* *savāvisā* means 20 × 1 1/4 = 25.

1 *dramma* = 100 *visās* = *visā* valued at 20 *cowries* = *bodi* or *kākiṇī*.

1 *dramma* = 400 *pāvisās* = *pāvisā* = worth 5 *cowries*.

pāvisā = *pāda* = *visā*.

In Śrīdhara's *Pātigaṇita*, the general term for a coin is *rūpa* as we find in the numerical examples cited in the book.[56]

GOLD COINS

The record,[57] which refers to gold *drammas*, is dated in the Śaka year 799 = 877 AD. D.R. Bhandarkar[58] identifies the *kañcana drammas* with the gold coins issued by the Kalacurīs, the Candellas and the Gahaḍavālas. The *kañcana dramma* is identical with *survarṇa* and *niśka*. According to the *Līlāvatī* of Bhāskarācārya, 16 *drammas* were equal to one *niśka*. It is generally believed that gold coins, that were issued in northern India during the eleventh and twelfth centuries AD, are usually about 60 grains in weight and were known as *suvarṇa drammas*. Half and quarter *drammas* were also issued which have been found in good number.

There were some other gold *drammas* known as *raukma vīsalaprī* known after the name of king Vīsaladeva.[59]

There are some references to gold coins such as *dīnāra*, *heman*, *kanaka*, *kañcana* and *suvarṇa* in the *Gaṇitasāra Saṁgraha* of Mahāvīrācārya (ninth century AD). The gold coins known to Śrīdhara (tenth century) author of *Gaṇitasāra* were *niśka* and *Biṣṭa*.

A medieval Jaina work *Purātana Prabandha Saṁgraha* refers to some coins like *dāma-mūda* (p. 53 f.n.), *dramma-mūda* (p. 52) and *mūdaka* (p. 80) as current in those days. The commentary[60] of the *Purātana Prabandha Saṁgraha* furnishes some details about them when it says — i.e., 8000, 16,000 and 21,000 *mūdas* were given to kings Vīsaladeva, Hammīra and the Sultān respectively by the banker named Jagaḍu. This money was given on the occasion of the famine which took place in *VS* 1211-13.

Some inscriptions are important from the point of view of money economy, by informing the purchasing value of commodities of a *dramma*. The fact that a house could be purchased for sixteen *drammas* at Dhod in AD 1171 shows sufficiently the high purchasing power of *dramma*.[61] From the Bhinmal inscription[62] of *VS* 1306, it is known that from 1 *dramma*, accruing as interest, one could buy at Bhinmal either 8-1/3 *pāilis* of wheat, one *pāili* of *mūrig*, 2/3 *pāilis* of rice and 2/3 *kalaśas* of *ghī*. The Sānderāv stone inscription[63] *VS* 1221 of Kelhaṇa's reign indicates that one *dramma* could purchase one hael of *yugandheri*, i.e. the *jowār* (millet). Half a *dramma* from a custom house could suffice to celebrate an annual function festival of Śrī Mahāvīradeva.

Coins in South India

The inscriptions of south India give several names of coins, their denominations and sometimes mints. They supply stray information without giving details about the coinage of the times. The dynasties of south India ruling over different parts seem to have issued coins of the common name. *Gadyāṇa* was the most popular coin. Common names of coins in south India indicate mutual provincial trade with the help of coins. Though actual coins of the dynasties of south India are not found in large number, their mention in inscriptions indicates prosperity. Some medieval inscriptions of Orissa also mention the name of coins.

CĀLUKYAS AND KALACURĪS OF KALYĀṆA

There are references to coins, mints and denominations of coins in the contemporary inscriptions of the Cālukyas and Kalacurīs of Kalyāṇa. Among the coins mentioned in the inscriptions of the Cālukyas of Kalyāṇa, the following may be noted, *drammas*,[64] *gadyāṇa paṇa*,[65] *honu*,[66] *hāga*,[67] *kāgiṇī*,[68] *visā*,[69] *gulika*[70] and *bela*[71]. Some of these coins are frequently mentioned in the contemporary inscriptions. It becomes clear from the epigraphic references that there were many mints working in the Cālukya period. Considering the number or references to it, the mint at Lokkigundi seems to have been prosperous during the period. The existence of another mint at Sudi is evidenced by an inscription of the time of Tribhuvanamalla.[72] The inscription mentions gifts made by Uttavoga, the goldsmith and the mint-master of Tribhuvanamalla to God Kammaṭeśvara at Sudi. The gold coins were minted under the orders of Uttavoga who was the royal mint-master. He had the privilege of owning the die (*kammatada ani*) containing the royal seal (*undige*) for striking the coins.

Another inscription at Lakkuṇḍi of the time of Someśvara IV mentions such terms as *accu, āni, accina kāni* and *accina-mole* which are connected with the minting of coins.[73] The same inscription mentions the word *belliyagammata*, which shows that silver coins were also minted in addition to gold coins. In some cases, the coins are mentioned along with the name or the initial letter of the place of the mint. For example, *lokkiguṇḍi gadyāṇa* or *lokki gadyāṇa* are obviously Gadyāṇas minted in the mint at Lokkiguṇḍi.

Though it is difficult to know precisely the relative value of all the different coins mentioned in the inscriptions, some idea about them can be had from some inscriptions. An inscription from Nidugandi mentions the relationship between a *gadyāṇa* and a *paṇa*.[74] This inscription gives a list of donations in gold and specifies the total as six *gadyāṇas*. The details mentioned in are five and ten *paṇas*. The total of these two being six *gadyāṇas*, it becomes clear that one *gadyāṇa* consisted of ten *paṇas*. From references in other records of the period, the following table may be deduced :

1 *gadyāṇa* = 10 *paṇas*

1 *paṇa* = 4 *haga*

1 *paṇa* = 4 *kāgiṇī*

1 *haga* = 4 or 5 *visās*

1 *haga* = 2 *bek*

HOYSALAS

A large number of Hoyasala inscriptions mention various coins that were in circulation during the period. *Gadyāṇa, honnu, paṇa, haga, visā, bek, kani* and others are commonly met with the inscriptions of this period. From a study of contemporary inscriptions, the following table can be deduced.

1 *gadyāṇa* = 10 *paṇas*

1 *paṇa* = 4 *hegas*

1 *hega* = 4 *visās*

YĀDAVAS OR SEVUNAS OF DEVAGIRI

Inscriptions of the Yādavas or the Sevunas mention a large number of names of the coins which were in use. Minting of coins in gold and silver was in large number. *Ṭaṅke* was a tax levied during the period on those who had the privilege of minting coins under the orders of the government. Similarly the word *mudre* occurring in some inscriptions has been taken to mean the tax on the die containing the royal insignia for striking the coins payable by those who were permitted to use them.

The inscriptions of the period mention *niśka, dramma, gadyāṇa, suvarṇa, paṇa, cavula, hega, kākiṇī, bele* and *visā* as coins of this period. *Niśka, suvarṇa* and *gadyāṇa* seems to be synonymous. However, *gadyāṇa* was the most popular gold coin of the period as can be seen from the largest number of epigraphic references to it. An inscription mentions *raya gadyāṇa.* Another record refers to *ambili gadyāṇa.* It may be surmised that this *gadyāṇa* was minted at Ambili. *Lokki gadyāṇa* cotinued during this period. It is clear from the table that the Yādavas followed the Cālukyan system in different denominations of coinage.

1 *gadyāṇa* = 10 *paṇas*

1 *paṇa* = 4 *hegas*

1 *hega* = 5 *visās*

1 *visā* = 2 *belas*

Coins of Orissa

From several inscriptions,[75] it is, abundantly clear that silver *pala* or *śatamāna* weighing 320 *rattīs* was regarded as the standard of circulation in the monetary transactions in early medieval Orissa. Medieval Orissan inscriptions often speak of a coin called *māḍha* which was both of gold and silver. *Māḍha* in the sense of 40 *rattīs* was one-eighth of *śatamāṇa.*

The same word occurs in Telugu as *māḍha*, which not only means any coin or money but also an old gold coin weighing roughly about 25 grains.

The prevalence of the silver *śatamāna* or *pala* standard as the basis of calculation in monetary transactions as well as of the *māḍha* coins weighing half a *tolā* in the Kaliṅga area of southern India as late as the medieval period seems to be significant in this connection.

If an elaborate system of silver currency based on the weight standard of *śatamāna* was really prevalent in any part of ancient India, the weights of these pieces were as follows:

(1) 1 *Śatamāna* = 320 *rattīs* (585.6 grains)

(2) 1/2 *Śatamāna* = 160 *rattīs* (292.8 grains)

(3) 1/4 *Śatamāna* = 80 *rattīs* (146.4 grains)

(4) 1/8 *Śatamāna* (known to be called *śāṇa* also = 40 *rattīs* (73.2 grains) and

(5) 1/10 *Śatamāna* (said to be called 1/2 *śāna* also = 20 *rattīs* = 36.6 grains.

It will be seen that 1/4 *śatramāna* weighed 80 *rattīs* or one *kārṣa* (146.4 grains). It is clear that the silver *kārṣāpaṇa* 146.4 grains was known in some parts of the country, at least theoretically, although we have no silver punch-marked coins of this weight. The very name *kārṣāpaṇa* applied to the silver coin also suggests that its original weight, even if theoretically, was 80 *rattīs*. Thus the *śatamāna* would not appear to have been entirely unrelated to the *kārṣāpaṇa* as it was originally four times a *kārṣāpaṇa* while the later silver *purāṇa* was 1/10 of it in weight. The silver *māḍhas* (40 *rattīs*) of medieval Orissa prove the genuineness of the tradition regarding the silver *kārṣāpaṇa* weighing 80 *rattīs*.

Barter System

Even when coinage started, barter system played a considerable part in economy in ancient India. But its predominance was felt more in rural areas. We have the references of barter system in medieval literary works covering most transactions in the villages.[76] In the opinion of Medhātithi, (on Mnua, V.127) the merchants and traders also sometimes found it convenient to resort to barter. He explains that merchandise (*paṇya*) is the substance (*dravya*) that is sold for money or is exchanged for some other substance. In some other Sanskrit texts, we find that merchants visiting distant parts of the country are exchanging their own merchandise with wares of those regions.[77] Even in mathemetical texts like the *Līlāvatī*[78] and the *Gaṇitasārasaṁgraha*,[79] there are rules for determining the value in case of a barter. The medium of exchange in ealry medieval Kashmir was also paddy of *dhānya*. In the *Rājataraṅgiṇī*,[80] there are indications that in the ninth century AD, the land revenue of Kashmir was collected in the form of *dhānya*.[81] Even in the *Lokaprakāśa Khāris* of *dhānya* in fixed quantities are stated to be payments of rents, fines, wages, etc. and are said to have been equivalent to *dīnāras*. The evidence of Kalhaṇa coupled with the testimony of *Lokaprakāśa* leaves little doubt that *dhānya* was also the medium of exchange during the medieval period in Kashmir.

IMPACT OF MONEY ECONOMY

There was the revival of money economy on a wide scale during the medieval period as it is clear from the different names of coins and their denominations mentioned in inscriptions and literary works, as well as actual specimens. This revival of money economy is linked with trade and commerce which brought great prosperity. Though issued by different ruling dynasties, generally the uniformity of weight is noticed in gold and silver coins. They somehow must have served the purpose of mutual regional trade.

Growth of Trade and Industry

The literary works, such as, the *Upamitibhava Prapañcakahā*, *Kuvalayamālā*, *Śṛṅgāramañjarī* and *Tilakamañjarī* give an interesting account of trade. Sugarcane and cotton were commercial crops. The industries of textile, iron, jewellery, shipping, etc. developed. A number of new crafts and professions started. There was inter-provincial trade among the regions such as Maru, Mālwā, Dwarkā and Kośala, Ahar in Rajasthan became a great centre of trade, and it was frequently visited by the merchants of Karnataka, Lāṭa Madhyadeśa and Takka and they used to pay articles on sale. Merchants also carried on trade outside India with Siṁhala and Svarṇadvīpa and they might have got fabulous wealth in the form of silver and gold in exchange. They carried on their mercantile activities after defraying the state dues such as octroi duty, excise tax, ferry tolls, road cess and sales-tax.

Growth of Cities

The barter system was prevalent in rural areas, but the revival of money economy led to the growth of a large number of cities and towns in early medieval period. Traders from neighbouring villages brought their commodities for sale to Urban centres.

All Round Development

The great prosperity of this period led to the digging of wells, tanks, canạls and lakes for irrigation purpose. Roads, palaces, forts and temples were constructed in large number.

Emergence of Merchant Community

The emergence of new mercantile community is noticed from the ninth century AD because of the revival of money economy. Money lending business on interest also developed. Merchant guilds used to do banking business by depositing money on interest.

To conclude it may be summarily laid down that with the revival of trade and commerce, the money economy started showing signs of improvement during the early medieval period.

Gadahiyā or Indo-Sassānian Coins continued for long period. Mostly they are bullion pieces having different percentages of silver-copper alloy. The Śāhī rulers of Kābul issued the coins of their own devices known as horseman and Bull type in copper and silver. These coins influenced the coinage of the Tomaras, — Gahaḍavālas, Cauhāns in twelfth and thirteenth centuries — Gāṅgeyadeva of Kalacurī dynasty of Tripurī introduced the seated Goddess type in gold, silver and copper. Candella rulers of Tejaka Bhukti, Paramāra rulers of Mālwā and Kacchapaghāṭa rulers of Gwālior also issued coins of seated Goddess type. Kalacurīs of Ratnapur issued two types of coins namely Gajaśārdūla type on which figure of lion and elephant is prominent and the other is Hanumān type. The Karkoṭa dynasty of Kashmir, which was followed by Utpala dynasty, issued coins exclusively in copper of the standard Kuṣāṇa type. In south India, the ruling dynasties such as eastern Cālukyas, Hoysalas, Colas, Pāṇḍyas and Yādavas issued their own coins.

Notes

1. *Indian Feudalism*, p. 269, Second Edn., Delhi, 1980.
2. *The Early Rājpūt Dynasties*, New Delhi, 1980.
3. *Coinage of Medieval India*, pp. 68-72, London, 1893.
4. *NC*, 1958, pp. 157-65.
5. Murthy, A.V. Narasimha, *The Coins of Karnāṭaka*, Mysore, 1975.
6. Sircar, D.C., *Studies in Indian Coins*, pp. 17-18, Delhi, 1968.
7. *EI*, XIX, p. 58.
8. *Ibid.*, XXIV, p. 382.
9. *JNSI*, III, p. 37.
10. *EI*, XXII, pp. 121-24.
11. *Ibid.*, II, pp. 124-25.
12. *Ibid.*, XXV, p. 62.
13. *Ibid.*, XIII. p. 171-75.
14. *JASB*, XIX, pp. 45-46, EI. XXV, p. 3. fn. 1.
15. *EI*, I, p. 169.
16. *Ibid*, XXIII, pp. 133-34.
17. *ARRMA*, 1927-28, No. 3, p. 2.
18. *Ibid.*, 1922-23, No. 3, p. 2.
19. *ARRMA*, 1922-23, No. 3, p. 2.
20. *PRAS, WC*, 1908, p. 35.
21. *I. Ar.* 1955-56, p. 31.
22. *EI*, XXIII, p. 280.
23. pp. 33, 37, 39, 42, 55.

24. p. 33.
25. p. 13.
26. *PRAS, WC* 1909, p.52, EI, pp. 51-52.
27. *EI*, pp. 175-77.
28. *Ibid.*, I. pp. 175-77.
29. *Ibid.*, I., p. 169.
30. *Ibid.*, XXX, p. 213.
31. *IA*, LVIII, p. 162.
32. *EI*, X, p. 20.
33. *ARRMA*, 1937, No. 8.
34. V.88-89.
35. IV.33, *JNSI*, VIII, p. 134.
36. Jinavijaya, *Jaina Lekha Saṁgraha*, p. 333, Bhavanagar, 1921, Vol. 2.
37. *EI*, X. pp. 17.
38. *Ibid.*, XII.
39. Satya Prakash and Rajender Singh : *Coinage in Ancient India*, p. 311, New Delhi, 1968.
40. *EI*, XXIV, pp. 141 ff.
41. *EI*, I, p. 262.
42. *JNSI*, III, p. 38.
43. Bhandarkar, *List of Northern India*, No. 468.
44. *EI*, XXIII, p. 140.
45. *CII*, IV. p. clxxix, f.n. 7.
46. *EI*, X, p. 17 ff.
47. *Ibid.*, III, p. 263.
48. *Ibid.*, XI. p. 41.
49. *Ibid.*, II, p. 116, *IA*, XLII, p. 60.
50. *PRAS, WC*, 1908, p. 49.
51. *EI*, XIV, pp. 295 ff.
52. *ECD*, Appendix G. (III) line i.
53. *JNSI*, VIII, pp. 2, 138 ff.
54. p. 208.
55. *Ancient Indian Numismatics*, p. 208, Calcutta, 1921.
56. Satya Prakash and Rajender Singh : *Coinage in Ancient India*, p. 316, New Delhi, 1968.
57. *IA*, 1884, p. 136.
58. *Ancient Indian Numismatics*, p. 209, Calcutta, 1921.
59. *JNSI*, XVII, pp. 64-83.
60. p. 8.
61. *ARRMA*, 1922-23, No. 3.
62. *EI*, XI, p. 56 f.
63. *Ibid.*, XI, p. 47.

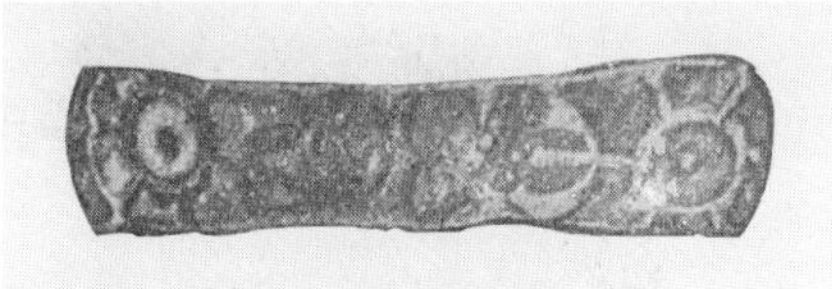

fig. 1

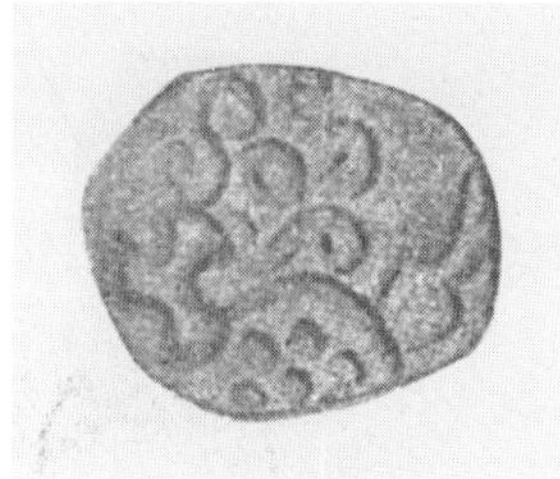

fig. 2

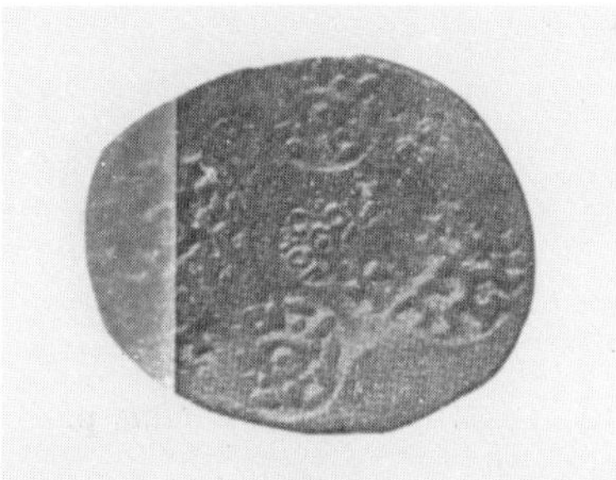

fig. 3

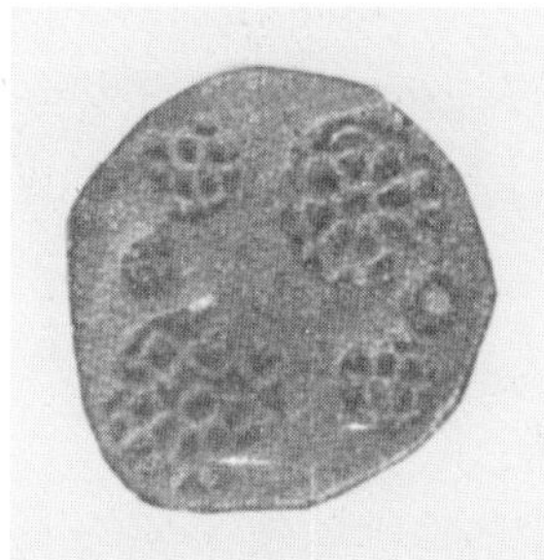

fig. 4

fig. 5

fig. 6

fig. 1. Gāndhāra; Janapada period; punch-marked silver coin

fig. 2. Kośala; Janapada period; punch-marked silver coin

fig. 3. Kāśī; Janapada period; punch-marked silver coin

fig. 4. Magadha; Janapada period; punch-marked silver coin

fig. 5. Magadha; Janapada period; punch-marked silver coin

fig. 6. Magadha; Janapada period; punch-marked silver coin

fig. 7

fig. 8

fig. 9

fig. 10

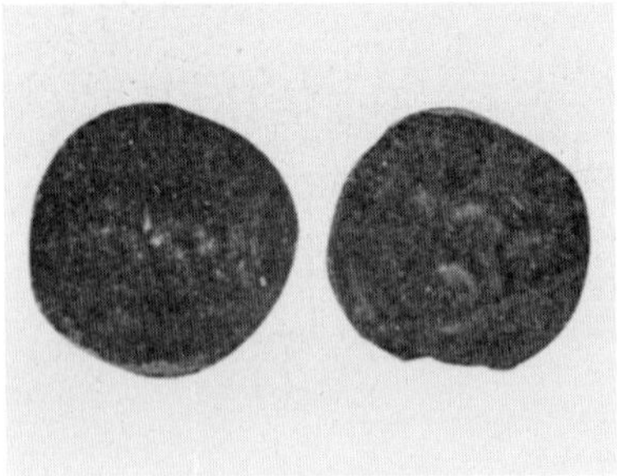

fig. 11

fig. 12

fig. 7. Magadha; Janapada period; punch-marked silver coin

fig. 8. Magadha; Mauryan period; punch-marked silver coin

fig. 9. Magadha; Mauryan period; punch-marked silver coin

fig. 10. Magadha; Mauryan period; punch-marked silver coin

fig. 11. Cast (all over northern India); Mauryan period; cast copper coin

fig. 12. Indo-Greeks (Demetrius II); Post-Mauryan period; die-striking silver coin

fig. 13

fig. 14

fig. 15

fig. 16

fig. 17

fig. 18

fig. 13. Indo-Greeks (Eucratides); Post-Mauryan period; die-striking silver coin

fig. 14. Indo-Greeks (Menander); Post-Mauryan period; die-striking silver coin

fig. 15. Śaka (Maues); Post-Mauryan period; die-striking copper coin

fig. 16. Śaka (Azes); Post-Mauryan period; die-striking silver coin

fig. 17. Śaka (Azilises); Post-Mauryan period; die-striking silver coin

fig. 18. Pārthian (Gondophares); Post-Mauryan period; die-striking silver coin

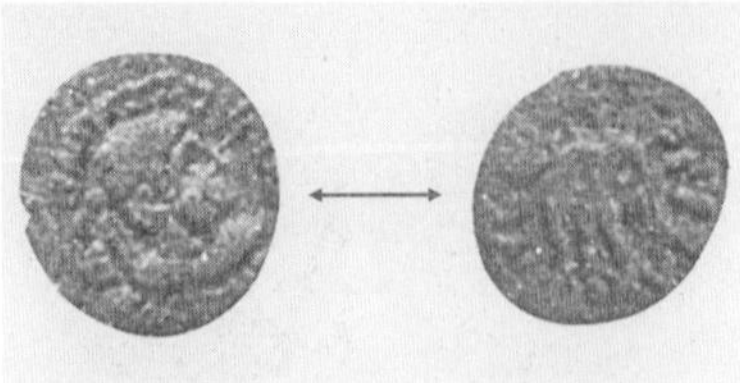

fig. 19

fig. 20

fig. 21

fig. 22

fig. 23

fig. 24

fig. 25

fig. 26

fig. 19. Kuṣāṇa (Kujula Kadphises); Post-Mauryan period; die-striking copper coin

fig. 20. Kuṣāṇa (Wima Kadphises); Post-Mauryan period; die-striking gold coin

fig. 21. Kuṣāṇa (Kaniṣka); Post-Mauryan period; die-striking gold coin

fig. 22. Kuṣāṇa (Huviṣka); Post-Mauryan period; die-striking copper coin

fig. 23. Kuṣāṇa (Vāsudeva); Post-Mauryan period; die-striking gold coin

fig. 24. Kuṣāṇa (Kidāra); Post-Mauryan period; die-striking gold coin

fig. 25. Roman; Post-Mauryan period; die-striking gold coin

fig. 26. Tribal (Auḍumbara king Dharaghoṣa); Post-Mauryan period; cast copper coin

fig. 27

fig. 28

fig. 29

fig. 30

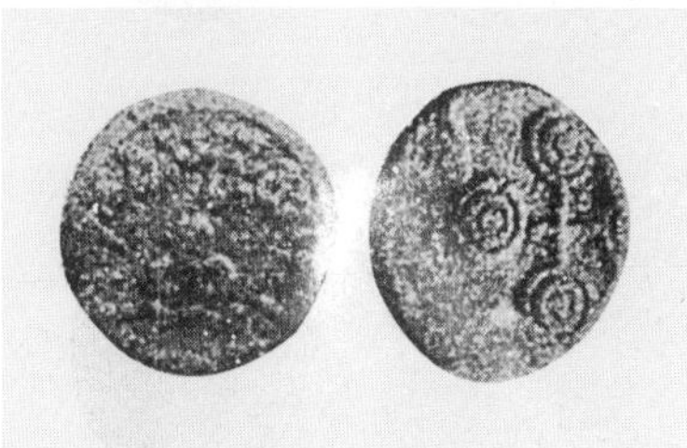

fig. 31

fig. 32

fig. 27. Tribal (Kuninda Amoghabhūti); Post-Mauryan period; die-striking silver coin

fig. 28. Tribal (Yaudheya); Post-Mauryan period; cast copper coin

fig. 29. Pāñcāla; Post-Mauryan period; cast copper coin

fig. 30. Ujjayinī; Post-Mauryan period; cast copper coin

fig. 31. Vāśiṣṭhiputra Śrī Pulumāvi; Post-Mauryan period; cast lead coin

fig. 32. Gautamīputra Śrī Yajña Sātakarṇi; Post-Mauryan period; die-striking silver coin

fig. 33

fig. 34

fig. 35

fig. 36

fig. 37

fig. 38

fig. 33. Western Kṣatrapa (Chasṭana); Post-Mauryan period; die-striking silver coin

fig. 34. Western Kṣatrapa (Nahapāna); Post-Mauryan period; die-striking silver coin

fig. 35. Western Kṣatrapa (Rudradāman); Post-Mauryan period; die-striking silver coin

fig. 36. Candragupta I; Gupta period; die-striking gold coin

fig. 37. Samudragupta; Gupta period; die-striking gold coin

fig. 38. Samudragupta; Gupta period; die-striking gold coin

fig. 39

fig. 40

fig. 41

fig. 42

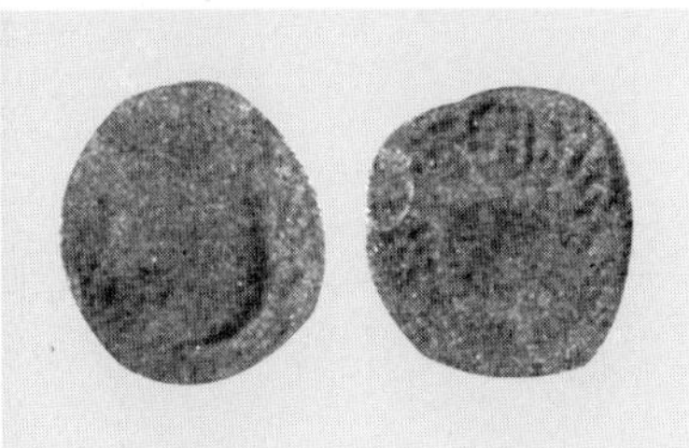

fig. 43

fig. 44

fig. 39. Candragupta II; Gupta period; die-striking gold coin

fig. 40. Candragupta II; Gupta period; die-striking silver coin

fig. 41. Candragupta II; Gupta period; die-striking copper coin

fig. 42. Kumāragupta II; Gupta period; die-striking gold coin

fig. 43. Hūṇa (Toramāna); Post-Gupta period; die-striking silver coin

fig. 44. Hūṇa (Mihirakula); Post-Gupta period; die-striking copper coin

fig. 45

fig. 46

fig. 47

fig. 48

fig. 49

fig. 50

fig. 45. Padmaṭaṅka; Post-Gupta period; punch-marked gold coin

fig. 46. Cālukyas of Bādāmī (Gadyāṇa); Post-Gupta period; punch-marked gold coin

fig. 47. Karkota dynasty of Kashmir Yaśovarman; Post-Gupta period; die-striking silver coin

fig. 48. Mihira Bhoja; early medieval period; die-striking bullion coin

fig. 49. Sāmantadeva; early medieval period; die-striking silver coin

fig. 50. Gāṅgeyadeva; early medieval period; die-striking gold coin

64. Hultzsch, E., *South Indian Inscriptions*, Madras, 1890-1929; Vol. XX, No. 47 and 77.
65. *Ibid.*, Nos. 39.60, 82 and 118.
66. *Ibid.*, Nos. 54, 68, 80 & 85.
67. *Ibid.*, No. 78, 129.
68. *Ibid.*
69. *Ibid.*, Nos. 54, 68, 80 and 85.
70. *Ibid.*, XV, No. 15.
71. *Ibid.*, Vol. XX. Nos. 47, 85, and 138.
72. *Ibid.*, Vol. XI, Pt. II, No. 153.
73. *Ibid.*, Vol. XI, pt. II, No. 67.
74. *Ibid.*, No. 189.
75. *JRAS*, 1952, pp. 4-10; *JASB*, 1909, p. 348; *JASB*, 1916, pp. 293-94; *EI*, XII, pp. 156-59; *JASB*, LXIV, pt. i, pp. 123 ff. *EI*, III, pp. 340-44; *JASB*, 1905, pp. 12-13; *EI*, XXVIII, pp. 44 ff.
76. Maity, S.K., *Early Indian Coins and Currency System*, p. 48, New Delhi, 1970.
77. *Samaraicakahā*, VI, p. 165, *Triśsastiśalākā*, Vol. I, pp. 7 ff.
78. p. 35, No. 85.
79. IV, 37-38.
80. V. 171.
81. Weber, *Indische Studies*, XVIII, pp. 346, 378.

9

Conclusion

In the preceding chapters, an attempt has been made to discuss the money economy in ancient India from about the sixth century BC to twelfth century AD.

Predominance of Metallic Coins

In the present anlysis, money economy has been divided into six periods namely (i) *Janapada*, (ii) Mauryan, (iii) Post-Mauryan, (iv) Gupta, (v) Post-Gupta and (vi) Early Medieval. It is evident from the present study that in ancient India, the total economy clustered around metallic coins in contrast to the situation prevailing in modern India where metallic currency has insignificant role to play in total economy because of the overwhelming predominance of paper and credit money. Therefore, the study of money economy in ancient India will mainly be the study of the system of coinage prevalent during the above-mentioned periods of ancient India.

Origin and Antiquity of Coinage

There is a controversy among scholars about the origin, antiquity and use of metal in coinage. Scholars advocate Greek, Persian, Babylonian and Indigenous theories for the origin of coinage. D.R. Bhandarkar believes that coinage was prevalent in Vedic Period, while, A.S. Altekar, D.D Kosambi and P.L. Gupta are of the opinion that it was current in eighth or seventh century BC. It appears that coinage originated in India during the second urban revolution which took place in the sixth century BC because of the inspiration from Persia but the mode of manufacturing was independent. Politically as well as economically, this period was important.

According to some scholars, copper came earlier into use for the manufacturing of coins than silver in India. But it seems that silver coins originated earlier as the earliest coins found at Kāśī and Kośala in the Gangetic Valley and Bent-bar coins of Gāndhāra region of sixth century BC are of silver.

Local and Standard Coins

During the *Janapada* period, money economy was initially local as different states issued their respective coinage. Later on, standard silver coins of definite size and of uniform weight were introduced throguhout the country by Magadha rulers. Scholars are of the opinion that standard silver coins started either during the time of Bimbisāra or Ajātśatru. It is more reasonable to say that standard coins started during the Nanda period. The Nandas are famous for their wealth as well as wide conquests. Foreign coins have also been discovered in north-west India which proves the existence of foreign trade during that period.

Introduction of Legal Tender Money

In the Mauryan period, it has been pointed out that money economy was highly developed with different denominations under state control. It was in the form of legal tender. It is difficult to agree with the view of D.D. Kosambi that financial stringency was one of the important factors for the downfall of Mauryan empire. No doubt, Mauryas introduced debased silver coins but it was essential for making payment on a large scale and efficient administration. It may be thus said that downfall of Mauryas was responsible for financial stringency.

Appearance of Gold Coins

From the monetary aspect, post-Mauryan period seems to be very sound. Gold coins were introduced in large number for the first time. Besides, coins of different metals and denominations, were issued. It served as medium of exchange for small transactions, and it penetrated in large parts of country. Besides a large number of states, city *nigamas*, and *śreṇis* or corporations also issued their coins generally in copper.

Decline of Money Economy

During the Gupta period, the money economy started becoming weaker. Though they issued coins in gold and of very high artistic quality but did not issue many copper coins. Comparative absence of issue of copper coins by central authority shows that there was hardly any easy medium through which masses could enter into exchange relations. People relied on barter or *cowries* for the payment of small transactions. Foreign trade was also not as extensive as in post-Mauryan times, and thus there was trend towards self-sufficient units of production in villages and towns. Hence, it would not be proper to consider Gupta as Golden period from the monetary aspect of the economy.

Money economy during the post-Gupta period declined considerably as a result of conquest of the Hūṇas, decline of silk trade and collapse of Sassānid empire. Because of the decline of foreign trade, there was shortage of the supply of gold and silver in India, and hence paucity of coins during this period has been confirmed by various scholars.

Revival of Money Economy

There was considerable revival of money economy during the early medieval period. This is associated with the revival of trade and commerce. R.S. Sharma has traced this revival from the eleventh century AD but it is more reasonable to place it from the ninth century onwards. It led to the growth of large number of cities and towns, construction of forts, temples, and emergence of new mercantile community. Money lending business on interest developed. Further, the different phases of the money economy in ancient India may be discussed under the following heads :

BARTER SYSTEM

As everywhere in the world, so also in India, barter had been the earliest stage of commercial transactions. It was the sole system of exchange before the money economy came into existence in ancient India. Even afterwards, it was current in rural and tribal areas, and whenever there was paucity of coins noticed specially in Gupta and post-Gupta period.

COWRIES

When metallic coins were not invented, *cowries* might have been the principal medium of exchange. A number of coin denominations associated with the *cowries* prove that they were widely used in various transactions by the people and businessmen in ancient India. *Kāparda* and *varāṭaka* were identical with *cowrie* shell.

METAL, RATIO AND SOURCE

The earliest coins known as the punch-marked coins are mostly found in silver and few in copper. Indo-Bactrian coins are generally of silver, copper, nickel and lead. Indo-Scythians and Indo-Parthians issued coins in silver and copper. Kuṣāṇa coins were issued in gold and copper. Most of the western Kṣatrapa coins are of silver. Lead remained the prime metal of south Indian coinage for a considerable period. Most of the indigenous coins such as city, tribal and monarchical coins are of copper. Gupta coins are found in gold but some are in silver and copper. Early medieval coins are in gold, silver and copper.

Ratio between gold and silver during second century BC was 1 : 10 and between silver and copper was 1 : 50. In Persia, the ratio between gold and silver was 1:13. It was thus profitable to exchange silver for gold in India as the author of *Periplus* has mentioned.

The ratio between gold and silver during Guptas was 1 : 7, and 1 : 9 during the Sātavāhanas. The ratio between silver and copper varied from 1 : 50 and 1:70.

In the Mauryan period, the source of silver had been Persia and Afghanistan. For Kuṣāṇas, the source of gold supply was Central Asia, Rome and local gold mines. For source of gold for Guptas had been China, South East Asia and some south Indian gold fields. There was complete absence of gold coins for four centuries in post-Gupta period. In early medieval period, gold came from Far East, Sumātrā, Jāvā and other places.

Technique of Manufacture

There were three main methods for the manufacturing of coins in ancient India. The earliest is the punch-marked. The punch-marked coins have a number of symbols punched upon them by different punches. Cast method was used for manufacturing the copper uninscribed coins. Lastly, the die-striking technique for manufacturing coins was borrowed from Greeks. On die-struck coins, symbols were carefully arranged and engraved on the die before, it was struck on the blank.

Minting was mostly the state monopoly. In many cases, the minting was entrusted to professional gold and silver smiths, Birbal Sahani published the material of ancient eleven mint localities in ancient India. They are Eran, Rohtak, Taxila, Mathurā, Atrañjikhera, Sāñcī, Kondapur, Sunet, Nālandā, Kāśī and Kadkal.

Different Names of the Coins

Names of the coins current in the ancient period are known from the literary works and inscriptions. Punch-marked silver coin was known as *kārṣāpaṇa.* The wheel-marked silver coin of Gāndhāra was known as *śatamāna. Prati* was also the name of *kārṣāpaṇa* as is known from the *Mahābhārata* and the *Kātyāyana Smṛti.* The name of the gold coin was *niśka, stater, suvarṇa* and *aureus*. Silver coin was known as *drachm* and *dīnārī*. During Kuṣāṇa period, ancient punch-marked coin was known by the name *purāṇa* and copper coin by name *nāṇaka*. Western silver Kṣatrapa coins were named *khattapaka* coins. *Rūpaka* was the name of silver coin during the Gupta period and *dramma* during the early medieval period. *Padmaṭarika* and *gadyāṇa* were the gold coins of south India. *Māḍha* was the name of both gold and silver coin in Orissa.

Debasement and Counterfeiting of Coins

The debasement and counterfeiting of coins was prevalent in ancient India. Debasement is noticed in the silver coins of Maurya period and gold coins of Gupta period issued after Skandagupta.

Standards and Denominations

Generally, coins in ancient India were issued of different standards and there were denominations. The punch-marked coins known as *kārṣāpaṇas* were issued to the standard of 56 grains. *Kārṣāpaṇa* became the standard medium of exchange from the time of Pāṇini who has mentioned its sub-multiples 1/2 as *ardha*, 1/4 as *pāda* and 1/16 as *māṣa*. The unit of old copper money known as *paṇa* was 80 *rattīs* or 146 grains. There were denominations copper money.

The Indo-Bactrians issued coins to the Attic standard of the Greeks. Gold coin known as *stater* was of 132 grains. Silver coin known as *drachm* was of 66 grains, *hemidrachm* was of 33 grains and *obol* was of 11 grains. *Tetradrachm* was of 4 *drachms*. During the reign of Eucratides, the weight of *drachm* was reduced to 36 grains and *tetradrachm* was reduced to 144 grains. This weight standard of silver coins was followed by western Kṣatrapas, the Sātavāhanas and the Guptas. The Kuṣāṇas adopted the Roman standard of 123 grains because it assumed international recognition for the purpose of trade. The same standard was adopted by Guptas for gold coins.

In early medieval period, *dramma* was the common name used for gold, silver and copper coins issued to the standard of 66 grains. Silver *pala* or *śatamāna* weighing 320 *rattis* was regarded as the standard of calculation in the monetary transactions in early medieval Orissa. *Gadyāṇa* was the standard unit of coinage in the South.

Conservatism

Conservatism was a very strong force in money economy in ancient time. The symbols of the punch-marked coins have regional characteristics. In Kashmir, the coin type king standing on the obverse and Ārdokṣo on the reverse was continued for one thousand years even after the change of dynasties and people. As the Kuṣāṇa money was well established and popular among the masses, the Gupta rulers continued the same type of coins for the convenience of the people.

IMPACT ON MODERN MONEY ECONOMY

The impact of money economy in ancient India on the monetary economy of the modern period is considerable. Ancient money was mainly in the form of metallic coins. The present money too is in the form of coins in addition to paper notes and bank money. Thus use of coins has been continuing and is of various denominations. It is popular all over the world and enjoys confidence of the people.

As early as the *Janapada* period, a coin of the value of a hundred units called *śatamāna* was known. The *Śrauta Sūtras* mention several terms, which indicate that the value was reckoned then in terms of multiples of ten. But this system probably did not find favour with the people and was soon abandoned. In current monetary economy, the **rupee** is reckoned equal to a hundred **paise**.

The modern name of **rupayā** is derived from the world *rūpa*. In the *Aṣṭādhyāyī* of Pāṇini, *rūpa* has been mentioned in the sense of figure. Kauṭilya in the *Arthaśāstra* has meant it in the sense of coins. Officers known as *rūpadarśaka* and *rūpatarka* were concerned with coins. There was the science of coins known as *rūpasutta*. Further, the modern term *dāma* seems to have been derived from the Greek silver coin *drachm* of Attic standard. In early medieval period, *dramma* was the common name for coinage.

In ancient period, there was die-striking method for preparing of coins. It was borrowed from the Greeks. On a die-struck coins, symbols are carefully arranged and engraved on a die before it is struck on the blank.

There were two sides of the coins — the obverse and the reverse in ancient India. On the obverse, we find the portrait of the king with the name and title of the king and on the reverse the deities and other symbols. Similarly on the coins of subsequent period, we find both obverse and reverse of the coin with the protrait and name of the issuing authority.

Buddhaghoṣa, the author of the fifth century AD, was great expert in the science of coins. He mentions the kinds of money current in diffierent parts of the country. Besides metallic money, he mentions the coins of bone or skin, fruits, seeds, wood, palmyra leaf, lac, etc. These have been perished but it served as medium of exchange.

Thus it seems that ancient money formed the basis of modern money economy.

List of Figures (Appendix)

Important Coins of Different Periods in Ancient India

Sl. No.	*Name of the Coin*	*Period*	*Technique of Manufacturing*	*Metal used*	*Weight (grains)*	*Obverse*	*Reverse*
1.	Gāndhāra (Bent-bar)	*Janapada*	Punch-marked	Silver	175	Six-armed symbol	Blank
2.	Kośala (Local)	*Janapada*	Punch-marked	Silver	42	Four symbols	Blank (Not illustrated)
3.	Kāśī (Local)	*Janapada*	Punch-marked	Silver	72	Five symbols	Blank (not illustrated)
4.	Magadha (Local)	*Janapada*	Punch-marked	Silver	—	Four symbols	Blank (not illustrated)
5.	Magadha (Standard type)	*Janapada*	Punch-marked	Silver	56	Five symbols : (i) The Sun, (ii) Six-armed, (iii) tree, (iv) Bull (v) Elephant	Some minute symbols (not illustrated)
6.	Magadha (Standard type)	*Janapada*	Punch-marked	Silver	56	Five symbols : (i) the Sun, (ii) Six-armed, (iii) three fishes around a circle	Some minute symbols (not illustrated)

(contd.)

Sl. No.	Name of the Coin	Period	Technique of Manufacturing	Metal used	Weight (grains)	Obverse	Reverse
						(iv) taurine within a semi-circle (v) five dots within a square.	
7.	Magadh (Standard type)	*Janapada*	Punch-marked	Silver	56	Five symbols : (i) the sun, (ii) six-armed, (iii) a hare on the hill, (iv) a bull, (v) a tree	Some minute symbols (not illustrated)
8.	Magadha (found all over the country)	Mauryan	Punch-marked	Silver	56	Five symbols : (i) the sun, (ii) six-armed, (iii) three-arched hill with crescent at the top (iv) tree in railing (v) Bull with a taurine in front	A big symbol (not illustrated)
9.	Magadha (found all over the country)	Mauryan	Punch-marked	Silver	56	Five symbols : Three human figures separately punched (iv) tree in railing (v) an elephant and a spider	A big symbol (not illustrated).

10.	Magadha (found all over the country)	Mauryan	Punch-marked	Silver	56	Five symbols : Three human figures placed into one punch (iv) a peacock on the hill (v) a steel yard	A big symbol (not illustrated)
11.	Cast (all over northern India)	Mauryan	Cast	Copper	Not known	An elephant to left	A three-arched hill with crescent at the top.
12.	Indo-Greeks (a) Demetrius II	Post-Mauryan	Die-striking	Silver	Indian Standard *Tetradrachm* 150 grains	Bust of king with name and title.	Zeus standing in front with Kharoṣṭhī legend
13.	(b) Eucratides	Post-Mauryan	Die-striking	Silver	Indian standard (37 grains *drachm*)	Bust of king with Greek legend, name and title	Dioskouroi standing, Kharoṣṭhī legend
14.	(c) Menander	Post-Mauryan	Die-striking	Silver	Indian standard *drachm* 37 grains	Bust of king with name and title in Greek	Winged Nike with Kharoṣṭhī legend
15.	Maues (Śaka)	Post-Mauryan	Die-striking	Copper	Not known	An elephant, head to right with trunk upraised and bell round the neck.	Caduceus, Greek legend.

(contd.)

Sl. No.	Name of the Coin	Period	Technique of Manufacturing	Metal used	Weight (grains)	Obverse	Reverse
16.	Azes (Śaka)	Post-Mauryan	Die-striking	Silver	37	King on horse-back holding a spear. Greek legend.	Zeus standing Kharoṣṭhī legend.
17.	Azilises (Śaka)	Post-Mauryan	Die-striking	Silver	37	King on horse-back holding an *aṅkuśa*. Greek legend.	Lakṣmī standing on a lotus, Kharoṣṭhī legend.
18.	Gondophares (Pārthian)	Post-Mauryan	Die-striking	Silver	37	King on horse-back, Greek legend.	Zeus standing, Kharoṣṭhī legend.
19.	*Kuṣāṇa Coins* (a) Kujula Kadphises	Post-Mauryan	Die-striking	Copper	Not known	Bust and name or Hermaius-Greek legend.	Herakles, Kharoṣṭhī legend.
20.	(b) Wima Kadphises	Post-Mauryan	Die-striking	Gold	121	King seated on a couch Greek legend.	Śiva standing in front of the bull holding trident in right hand Kharoṣṭhī legend.
21.	(c) Kaniṣka	Post-Mauryan	Die-striking	Gold	121	King standing holding a spear in the left hand	Buddha seated cross legged. Legend : Boddo

						offering altar. Iranian legend *śāo nāno śāo kaneṣki kusāṇo*	
22.	(d) Huviṣka	Post-Mauryan	Die-striking	Copper	Not known	King riding on an elephant. Iranian legend *śāo nāno śāo oeshki koṣāṇo*	Two-armed Śiva legend. Oesho.
23.	(e) Vāsudeva	Post-Mauryan	Die-striking	Gold	121	King standing with trident and offering altar. Iranian legend with Greek name.	Śiva standing with trident before the bull. Legend : Oesho.
24.	(f) Kidāra	Post-Mauryan	Die-striking	Gold	121	King standing with trident and offering altar. Legend Kedāra under kings arm.	Goddess seated on a high-backed throne. Legend Ārdokṣo
25.	Roman	Post-Mauryan	Die-striking	Gold	121	Head of Augustus with Roman legend.	Two bucklers and shield between the standing figures of Gaius and Lueius Caesar below legend.

(contd.)

Sl. No.	*Name of the Coin*	*Period*	*Technique of Manufacturing*	*Metal used*	*Weight (grains)*	*Obverse*	*Reverse*
26.	Auḍumbara king Dhara-ghoṣa (Tribal)	Post-Mauryan	Cast	Copper	37	Viśvāmitra standing.	Trident with axe, tree in railing Name of the King Dharaghoṣa.
27.	Kuninda Amog-habhūti (Tribal)	Post-Mauryan	Die-striking	Silver	34	Name Amogha-bhūti in Brāh-mī, 3 symbols.	Name of Amogha-bhūti inKharoṣ-ṭhi, 3 symbols.
28.	Yaudheya (Tribal)	Post-Mauryan	Cast	Copper	177	Kārttikeya stan-ding with Brāhmi legend meaning victory to the Yaudheyas	Female deity
29.	Pāñcāla	Post-Mauryan	Cast	Copper	267	Three symbols, tree in railing, trident with base and Mauryan 'r' mounted on with king's name in Brāhmī.	Female deity sta-nding on lotus.
30.	Ujjayinī (city)	Post-Mauryan	Cast	Copper	64	Ujjayinī symbol and an elephant	Eight-armed sym-bol and legend Ujjayinī in Brāhmī
31.	Vāśiṣṭhiputra Śrī Pulumāvi.	Post-Mauryan	Cast	Lead	Not known	Hill of three arches legend	Ujjain symbol

						in Brāhmī with the name of the king.	
32	Gautamīputra Śrī Yajña Sātakarṇi.	Post-Mauryan	Die-striking	Silver	37	Bust of the king with name in Brāhmī	Ujjain symbol surmounted by Crescent and six-arched hill with crescent. Legend same as on obverse but in Tamil language.
33.	*Western Kṣatrapa* (a) Chasṭana.	Post-Mauryan	Die-striking	Silver	37	Bust of King, inscription in Greek characters	Hill surrounded by crescent. Inscription in Brāhmī characters.
34.	(b) Nahapāna	Post-Mauryan	Die-striking	Silver	37	Bust of King, Inscription in Greek characters.	Arrow, thunderbolt. Inscription in Brāhmī characters.
35.	(c) Rudradāman	Post-Mauryan	Die-striking	Silver	37	Bust of king, inscription in Greek characters.	Three-arched hill sorrounded by crescent, and star inscription in Brāhmī characters.
36.	Candragupta I	Gupta	Die-striking	Gold	117.6	Kings and queen standing facing	Goddess seated on a lion with the

(*contd.*)

Sl. No.	Name of the Coin	Period	Technique of Manufacturing	Metal used	Weight (grains)	Obverse	Reverse
						each other with their names in Brāhmī	name of the tribe.
37.	Samudragupta	Gupta	Die-striking	Gold	115.1	*Aśvamedha* with legend.	Queen with legend.
38.	Samudragupta	Gupta	Die-striking	Gold	119	Tiger slayer with Brāhmī legend	Goddess with Brāhmī legend.
39.	Candragupta II	Gupta	Die-striking	Gold	134.3	King on horse-back with Brāhmī legend	Goddess with Brāhmī legend.
40.	Candragupta II	Gupta	Die-striking	Silver	31	Bust as on Kṣatrapa coins with traces of Greek letters.	Garuḍa with the name of the king in Brāhmī.
41.	Candragupta II	Gupta	Die-striking	Copper	44	Bust of the king with the title of the king, Vikramāditya in Brāhmī.	Garuḍa with the name of the king in Brāhmī.
42.	Kumāragupta II	Gupta	Die-striking	Gold	127	Three figures	Lakṣmī with Brāhmī legend. Apratigha.

43.	Toramāna (Hūṇa)	Post-Gupta	Die-striking	Silver	60	Head of the King	Peacock with out-spread tail with legend in Brāhmī
44.	Mihirakula (Hūṇa)	Post-Gupta	Die-striking	Copper	60	Bust of the King with the name in Brāhmī	Bull standing with Brāhmī legend Jayatu Vṛṣa.
45.	Padmaṭaṅka	Post-Gupta	Punch-marked	Gold	58	A large eight-petalled lotus flower.	Six small punches, four square punches contain a small flower each.
46.	Cālukyas of Bādāmī (Gad-yāṇa)	Post-Gupta	Punch-marked	Gold	117	Boar	Not known
47.	Karkota dynasty of Kashmir Yaśovarman.	Post-Gupta	Die-striking	Silver & Copper mixed	60	Standing king Gedava under the left arm.	Seated Goddess with the name of king.
48.	Mihira Bhoja	Early Medieval	Die-striking	Bullion	67	Boar in Carnation of Viṣṇu	Śrīmadādivarāha in Nāgarī letters.
49.	Sāmantadeva	Early Medieval	Die-striking	Silver	60	Horseman	Recumbant bull legend Śrī Spala-patideva
50.	Gāṅgeyadeva	Early Medieval	Die-striking	Gold	62	Goddess seated Cross-legged	Legend in three lines in bold Nāgarī letters *Śrīmad-Gāṅgeyadeva.*

Bibliography

ANCIENT LITERATURE

Amarakośa of Amarasiṁha, ed. by T. Ganapata Sastri, 4 parts, 1914-17.

Aṅgavijjā, ed. by Punyavijaya, Benaras, 1957.

Aṅguttara Nikāya, ed. by R. Morris and E. Hardy Pali Text Society, London, 1885-1900; Eng. Trans. (The Book of Gradual Sayings) Vol. I, II and V by F.L. Woodward and Vol. III and IV by E.M.Hare, Pali Text Society, London, 1932-36.

Arthaśāstra of Kauṭilya, ed. by R. Shamasastri, Mysore, 1919; Eng. trans. by R. Shamasastri, Third Ed., Mysore 1929; Ed. and Trans. by R. P. Kangle, 3 Vols. (2nd edition), 1970.

Aṣṭādhyāyī of Pāṇinī, Trans. by S. C. Vasu, Varanasi, 1891-98.

Atharvaveda, ed. by Roth and W.D. Whitney, Berlin, 1856; Ed. with Sāyaṇa's comm. by S.P. Pandit, Bombay, 1895-98; trans. by W.D. Whitney, Cambridge, Mass., U.S.A., 1955.

Bṛhadāraṇyaka Upaniṣad, ed. with trans. by D. Bohtlingk, Leipzig, 1889.

Bṛhatkalpabhāṣya of Saṅghadāsagaṇi, Com. Malayagiri and Kṣamakirti, Atmananda Jaina Sabha.

Bṛhat-Saṁhitā of Varāhamihira, ed. by H. Kern Bi. Calcutta, 1865; Ed. with Eng. trans. and notes by V. Subrahmanya Sastri and M. Ramakrishna Bhat, 2 Vols. Bangalore, 1947.

Chāndogya Upaniṣad, ed. with trans. by D. Bohtlingk, Leipzig, 1889.

Dīgha Nikāya, ed. by T.W. Rhys Davids and J.E. Carpenter, 3 Vols. Pali Text Society, London, 1890-1903, 1911; Eng. trans. (Dialogues of Buddha) by T.W. Rhys Davids, 3 Vols. SBB, London, 1899-1910, 1921 Trans. by Rahula.

Gautama Dharma Sūtra, Text ASS. Tr. SBE, II Ed. by A.A. Fuhrer, Bombay, 1916.

Gopatha Brāhmaṇa, ed. by Rajendra Mitra and H. Vidyabhushan, Calcutta, 1872.

Jātaka, ed. by V. Fausboll, 7 Vols. London, 1877-97; Eng. trans. under the Editorship of E.B. Cowell, 7 Vols. Cambridge, 1895-1913.

Kātyāyana Smṛti, ed. with reconstructed text, trans., notes and introduction by P.V. Kane, Bombay, 1933.

Kharataragaccha Bṛhadguruvāvali of Jinapal Upādhyāya, Ed. by Muni Jinavijaya, Bombay, 1956.

Kuvalayamālā of Uddyotana Sūri, ed. by A.N. Upadhye, 1969.

Lekhapaddhati, ed. by C.D. Dalal and G.K. Shri Gondekar, Baroda, 1925.

Mahābhārata, (Kumbhakonam) ed. by T.R. Krishnacharya and T.R. Vyasacharya, Bombay, 1905-10.

Mahābhāṣya of Patañjali, ed. by Kielhorn, BS. S. Poona, 1880-1909.

Mahāvagga, ed. by N.K. Bhagat, 2 Vols., Bombay, 1944-52.

Mānava Dharmaśāstra (or Manusmṛti), ed. by Jolly, London, 1887; Eng. trans. by W. Jones, Calcutta, 1794; Eng. trans. by G. Buhler, SBE, Oxford, 1886.

Mṛcchakaṭika of Śūdraka, trans. by Ryder, A.W. Cambridge, Mass., 1905.

Nārada Smṛti, ed. by J. Jolly, Calcutta, 1881; Eng. trans. by J. Jolly, SBE, VII, Oxford, 1880.

Pañcaviṁśa Brāhmaṇa, ed. by A. Vedantavagisa, Calcutta, 1869-74.

Pṛthvīrājavijaya of Jayānaka, ed. by G.H. Ojha and G.S. Guleri, Ajmer, 1941.

Purātanaprabandha Saṁgraha, ed. by Muni Jinavijaya, Calcutta, 1936.

Ṛgveda, ed. by A. Vedantavagisa, Calcutta, 1869-74; *Saṁhitā* and *Pāda* text with Sāyaṇa Comm. ed. by F. Max Muller (Second Ed.) 1890-2; *Saṁhitā* and *Pāda* text with Sāyaṇa's Comm. critically edited by Vaidika Saṁśodhan Maṇḍala, Poona. Four Vols, 1933, etc; Trans. by H. Grassmann, Leipzig, 1876-77. R.T.H. Griffith, Benaras, 1896-97; in part by Max Müller, SBE, Vol. XXXII, Oxford, 1891; and H. Oldenberg, SBE, Vol. XLVI, Oxford, 1897.

Samaraicchakata Śatapatha Brāhmaṇa, ed. by H. Jacobi, BI, Calcutta, 1923; ed. by A. Weber, London, 1885; Trans. J. Eggeling, SBE, XII, XXVI, XLI, XLIII, XLIV, Oxford, 1882-1900.

Sūtrakṛtāṅga, Niryukti, Bhadrabahu *Chūrṇi*, Jinadāsagaṇi, Ratlam, 1941. Bom. Śilāṅka Āgamodaya. Smriti, Bombay, 1917; Eng. trans. by H. Jacobi, SBE, XLV, Delhi, Reprint 1964.

Taittirīya Brāhmaṇa, ed. by A. Weber, Berlin, 1871-72; with Comm. of Madhva, Calcutta, 1884-99.

Tilakamañjarīkathā of Dhanapāla, Ns. p. Bombay, 1903.

Uttarādhyayana, Niryukti, Bhadrabāhu *chūrṇi* Jinadāsagaṇi, Ratlam, 1933; Eng. trans. by H. Jacobi, SBE, XLV. Delhi, Reprint 1964; Ed. J. Carpenter, Upsala, 1922.

Vinaya Piṭaka, Eng. trans. (*Vinaya* texts) by T.W. Rhys Davids and H. Oldenderg, SBE, Oxford, 1885; Trans. by Rahula Sankritayayana in Hindi, Mahabodhi Sabha, Sarnath, 1935.

Yājñavalkya Smṛti, ed. by A.F. Stenzler, Berlin, 1849; Eng. trans. by J.R. Gharpure, Bombay, 1936 ff.

MODERN LITERATURE

Agrawal, V.S., *India as known to Pāṇini*, Lucknow, 1953.

Aiyangar, Rangaswami, *Ancient Indian Polity*.

Allan, J., *Catalogue of the Coins of Ancient India* (in the British Museum), London, 1936.

———, *Catalogue of the Coins of Gupta Dynasty and of Śaśāṅka, King of Gauḍa* (in the British Museum) London, 1914.

Altekar, A.S., *Bayana Hoard*, Bombay, 1954.

———, *The Coinage of the Gupta Empire*, Varanasi, 1957.

Bajpai, K.D., *Indian Numismatic Studies*, Delhi, 1976.

Bhandarkar, D.R., *Ancient Indian Numismatics*, Calcutta, 1921.

———, *List of Inscriptions of Northern India*, Appendix to LI, XIX-XXIII.

Brown, C.J., *The Coins of Indian*, Calcutta, 1922.

Campbell Colin, *An Introduction to Money and Banking*, Illinois (U.S.A.), 1978.

Chakrabortty, S.K., *A Study of Ancient Indian Numismatics*, Delhi, 1973 (Second Edn.).

Chandler, Lester, V., *The Economics of Money and Banking*, Delhi, Fourth Edn. 1967.

Chattopadhyay, B., *The Age of Kuṣāṇas — A Numismatic Study*, Calcutta, 1967.

Crowther Geoffery, *An Outline of Money*, London, 1955.

Cunningham, A., *Coins of Alexander's Successors in the East, the Greeks and Indo-Scythians*, Pt. I, London, 1869.

———, *Coins of Ancient India from the Earliest times down to the Seventh Century* AD., London, 1891.

———, *Coinage of Medieval India*, London, 1893.

———, *Later Indo-Scythian*, Varanasi, 1962.

Dadachangi, B.E., *Monetary System of India*, Bombay.

Dikshitar, V.R.R., *Mauryan Polity*, Madras, 1932.

Elliot, *Coins of Southern India*, 1886.

Fleet, J.R., *Inscriptions of the Early Gupta kings and their Successors*, CII, III, Calcutta, 1888.

Gardener, Percy, *A Catalogue of Indian Coins in the British Museum. The Greek and Scythic Kings of Bactria and India*, London, 1886.

Gopal Lallanji, *Early Medieval Coin types of Northern India*, Varanasi-5, 1966.

Gupta, P.L., *The Amaravati Hoard of Silver Punch-marked Coins*, Hyderabad, 1963.

———, *Roman Coins from Andhra Pradesh*, Hyderabad, 1965.

———, *Coins*, New Delhi, 1969.

Gupta P.L., and Hardaker T.R., *Silver Punch-marked Coins of the Magadha-Maurya Kārṣāpaṇa, Series*, Bombay, 1985.

Hari, A.G., *Money, Debt and Economic Activity*, New York, Second Edn., 1958.

Hultzsch, E., *South Indian Inscriptions*, 3 Vols. (ASI, NIS, Vols 9, 10 and 29), Madras, 1890-1929.

Jayaswal, K.P., *Hindu Polity*, Bangalore, Third Edn. 1955.

Jinavijaya, *Jain Lekha Saṁgraha*, Bhavnagar, 1921.

Johnson, H.G., *Money, Trade and Economic Growth*, London, 1962.

Kane, P.V., *History of Dharmaśāstra*, 5 Vols., Poona, 1930-53.

Keynes, John Maynard, *Treatise on Money*, London, 1965.

Kosambi, D.D., *Indian Numismatics*, New Delhi, 1981.

Lahiri, A.N., *Corpus of Indo-Greek Coins*, Calcutta, 1965.

Lüders, *Lüder's List of Brahmi Inscriptions up to 400 AD*, EI.X.

Maity, S. K., *Early Indian Coins and Currency System*, New Delhi, 1970.

Majumdar, R.C., *The Age of Imperial Unity*, Bombay, 1951.

Majumdar, R.C. & Altekar, A.S., *The Vākāṭaka Gupta Age*, Benaras, 1954.

Marshal, John & Alfred Foucher, *The Monuments of Sanchi*, 3 Vols.

Mukherjee, B.N., *Kuṣāṇa Genealogy*.

Murthy, A.V. Narasimha, *The Coins of Karnataka*, Mysore, 1975.

Narain, A.K. & Gopal Lallanji, *The Chronology of Punch-marked Coins*.

Nigam S.S., *Economic Organisation in Ancient India (200 BC-AD 200)*, Delhi, 1975.

Ojha, G.H., *OJHA Nibandha Saṁgraha*, Udaipur.

Puri, K.N., *Excavations at Rairh during Sam. 1995-96 (AD 1938-39)*, Jaipur.

Rapson, E.J., *Cambridge History of India*, Vol. I., *Ancient India*, Cambridge, 1922.

———, *Catalogue of the Coins of the Andhra dynasty, the Western Kṣatrapas, the Traikutaka dynasty and the Bodhi dynasty*, London, 1908. (Cat. of Indian Coins in the British Museum, Vol. IV).

———, *Indian Coins*, Strassburg, 1897.

Ray, S.C., *Stratigraphic Evidence of Coins in the Indian Excavations and some allied Issues*, Varanasi, 1959.

Robertson, D.H., *Money*, London, 1956.

Roy, P.C., *The Early Rajput Dynasties*, New Delhi, 1980.

Sahani, Birbal, *The technique of casting coins in Ancient India*, New Delhi, 1973.

Sahani, Dayaram, *Report of Archaeological Remains and Excavations at Bairat*, Jaipur.

Sarma, S.P., *Coinage of the Sātavāhana Empire*, New Delhi, 1980.

Sastri, K.A. Nilakanta, *Comprehensive History of India*, Bombay, 1957.

Satya Prakash & Rajender Singh, *Coinage in Ancient India*, New Delhi, 1968.

Scoff, W.H., *Periplus of the Erythrean Sea.*

Sharan, Mahesh Kumar, *Tribal Coins — A study*, New Delhi, 1972.

Seth, M.L., *Monetary Economics*, Agra, 1978.

Sharma Dasharath, *Early Chauhan Dynasties*, Delhi, 1959.

Sharma, R.S., *Indian Feudalism (c. 300-1200* AD), Delhi, Second Edn. 1980.

———, *Perspectives in Social and Economic History of Early India*, Delhi, 1983.

———, *Urban Decay in India* (c. *300-1000*), Delhi, 1987.

Shastri, Ajaymitra, *India as seen in the Bṛhat Saṁhitā of Varāhamihira*, Delhi, 1969.

Shastri, Ajaymitra, *India as seen in the Kuṭṭanimata of Dāmodaragupta*, Delhi, 1975.

Sinha, B.P., *The Decline of the Kingdom of Magadha, c. 455-1000* AD, Patna, 1954.

Sircar, D.C., *Select Inscriptions bearing on Indian History and Civilization*, Vol. I, Calcutta, 1965.

———, *Studies in Indian Coins*, New Delhi, 1968.

Simth, V.A., *Catalogue of the Coins in the Indian Museum*, Calcutta, Oxford, 1906.

———, *Early History of India*, Oxford, 1924.

Taran, W.W., *The Greeks in Bactria and India*, Cambridge, Second Edn., 1951.

Thakur Upendra, *The Hūṇas in India*, Varanasi, 1967.

Thomas Edward, *Prinsep's Essays.*

Tiwari, J.N. & Gupta, P.L, *Numismatography*, Varanasi, 1964.

Trivedi, H.V., *Catalogue of the Coins of the Naga Kings of Padmavati*, Gwalior, 1957.

Weber, A., *History of Indian Literature*, (Eng. trans. by J. Mann and Th. Zechariae) Varanasi, Sixth Edn. 1961.

Whitehead, R.S., *Catalogue of Coins in the Punjab Museum*, Lahore, Vol. I, Oxford, 1914.

Wilson, H.H., *Ariana Antigua*, London, 1841.

Winternitz, M., *History of Indian Literature*, (Eng. trans. by Mrs. S. Ketkar) Vol. I, Calcutta, 1927.

JOURNALS, REPORTS, PROCEEDINGS ETC.

Annals of the Bhandarkar Research Institute, Poona.

Annual Reports of the Archaeological Survey of India.

Annual Reports, Rajputana Museum, Ajmer.

Epigraphia Indica, Mysore.

Imperial Gazetteer, II.

Indian Antiquary, Bombay.

Indian Archaeology — A Review, New Delhi.

Indian Historical Quarterly, Calcutta.

Journal Asiatique, Paris.

Journal of the Asiatic Society of Bengal, Calcutta.

Journal of the Bihar and Orissa Research Society, Patna.

Journal of the Economic and Social History of Orient, Leiden.

Journal of the Numismatic Society of India, Varanasi.

Journal of the U.P. Historical Society, Lucknow.

Memoirs of the Archaeological Survey of India.

Numismatic Chronicle.

Numismatic Supplement.

Prācya Pratibhā, Bhopal.

Transactions of International Congress in Prehistoric Archaeology.

Index